China across the Divide: The Domestic and Global in Politics and Society

D1609813

China across The Divide

The Domestic and Global in Politics and Society

Edited by Rosemary Foot

OXFORD
UNIVERSITY PRESS

OXFORD
UNIVERSITY PRESS

Oxford University Press is a department of the University of Oxford.
It furthers the University's objective of excellence in research, scholarship,
and education by publishing worldwide.

Oxford   New York

Auckland   Cape Town   Dar es Salaam   Hong Kong   Karachi
Kuala Lumpur   Madrid   Melbourne   Mexico City   Nairobi
New Delhi   Shanghai   Taipei   Toronto

With offices in

Argentina   Austria   Brazil   Chile   Czech Republic   France   Greece
Guatemala   Hungary   Italy   Japan   Poland   Portugal   Singapore
South Korea   Switzerland   Thailand   Turkey   Ukraine   Vietnam

Oxford is a registered trademark of Oxford University Press
in the UK and certain other countries.

Published in the United States of America by
Oxford University Press
198 Madison Avenue, New York, NY 10016

© Oxford University Press 2013

Library of Congress Cataloging-in-Publication Data
China across the divide : the domestic and global in politics and society /
edited by Rosemary Foot.
pages; cm
Includes index.
ISBN 978-0-19-991986-4 (hardback : alk. paper) — ISBN 978-0-19-991988-8
(pbk. : alk. paper)
1. China—Foreign relations.   2. China—Foreign economic relations.
I. Foot, Rosemary, 1948–
JZ1730.C543 2013
320.951—dc23
2013000207

CONTENTS

LIST OF FIGURES

ACKNOWLEDGMENTS

This edited collection originated from a seminar series held at St. Antony's College, the University of Oxford, in the autumn and winter of 2010. Subsequently, additional chapters were commissioned to fill in some important gaps in our coverage of the issues deemed vital to deepening understanding of the interaction of the global and domestic levels in the study of China's external relations. I am grateful to the participation of an informed audience in helping us to sharpen our arguments, and especially to Amy King and Tiang Boon Hoo who provided expert commentary on two of the chapters submitted here. The Asian Studies Centre administrator based at St. Antony's College, Oxford, ensured that the series ran smoothly and I pass on my thanks to her.

Oxford University Press in New York under the editorial guidance of David McBride has provided much valuable support, including commissioning reviews of the manuscript to which individual authors have worked to respond. I would also like to acknowledge the financial help given by the University of Oxford's Centre for International Studies, the University's Leverhulme Programme for the Study of Contemporary China, and the Asian Studies Centre, St. Antony's College. Without their support it would not have been possible to draw in scholars of the quality that are represented here. Finally, I thank Dr. Tim Kennedy for his editorial and technical assistance at the final stages of this project. Stacey Victor proved to be an attentive and constructive copy-editor. Ken Kopp and Elisa Oreglia were generous hosts at the final stages of this book project.

ABOUT THE CONTRIBUTORS

Rosemary Foot is Professor of International Relations and John Swire Senior Research Fellow in the International Relations of East Asia, St Antony's College, University of Oxford. Her research interests cover U.S.-China relations, international security in the Asia-Pacific, and human rights in International Relations. Her most recent publications include (with Andrew Walter) *China, the United States, and Global Order* (Cambridge University Press, 2011).

William A. Callahan is Chair of International Politics and China Studies at the University of Manchester, and Co-Director of the British Inter-University China Centre, Oxford University. From September 2013, he will be Professor of International Relations at the London School of Economics and Political Science. His recent books, *China Dreams: 20 Visions of the Future* (Oxford University Press, 2013), *China: The Pessoptimist Nation* (Oxford, 2010), and *China Orders the World: Normative Soft Power and Foreign Policy* (co-edited with E. Barabantseva, Johns Hopkins, 2012), examine the relation of identity and security in Chinese politics.

Feng Zhang is a Lecturer in the School of Management and Governance, Murdoch University, Australia. He will be a Fellow in the Department of International Relations, the Australian National University, from January 2014. He completed his Ph.D. in International Relations at the London School of Economics and Political Science in 2009; subsequently he took a position as Assistant Professor at Tsinghua University in Beijing, before moving to Australia. His publications have appeared in such journals as *European Journal of International Relations* and *Survival*, and he is now completing the preparation of his Ph.D. thesis for publication.

Robert S. Ross is Professor of Political Science at Boston College, and Associate, John King Fairbank Center for East Asian Research, Harvard University. His current research focuses on the rise of China and East Asian security, nationalism and Chinese defense policy, and U.S.-China relations.

Among his recent publications are *New Directions in the Study of Chinese Foreign Policy* (Stanford University Press, 2006) and *China's Ascent: Power, Security, and the Future of International Politics* (Cornell University Press, 2008).

Frank N. Pieke is Chair Professor of Modern China Studies at Leiden University. He has research interests in international migration, transnationalism, and cultural diversity, including a long-term interest in Chinese migration and ethnicity in Europe and, more recently, the emergence of international immigrant groups in China. His most recent book is entitled *The Good Communist* (Cambridge University Press, 2009). Earlier books include *Transnational Chinese: Fujianese Migrants in Europe* (Stanford University Press, 2004, with Pál Nyíri, Mette Thunø, and Antonella Ceccagno).

Karl Gerth is University Lecturer in modern Chinese history at Oxford University. His latest book is *As China Goes, So Goes the World: How Chinese Consumers are Transforming Everything* (Hill & Wang, 2010), which explores the wide-ranging ramifications of China's shift toward a market economy over the past thirty years. He is also the author of *China Made: Consumer Culture and the Creation of the Nation* (Harvard University Press, 2004).

Andrew Walter is Professor in International Relations at the University of Melbourne and formerly Reader in International Political Economy at the London School of Economics and Political Science. His current main areas of research concern the diffusion of financial regulation in the global economy, the political aftermaths of economic crises, and East Asia in the global political economy. His recent books include *Governing Finance: East Asia's Adoption of International Standards* (Cornell University Press, 2008), *Analyzing the Global Political Economy* (Princeton University Press, 2009), *China, the United States, and Global Order* (Cambridge University Press, 2011, with Rosemary Foot), and *East Asian Capitalism: Continuity, Diversity and Change* (Oxford University Press, 2012).

Gudrun Wacker is Senior Fellow in the Research Division Asia at the German Institute for International and Security Affairs (Stiftung Wissenschaft und Politik, SWP) in Berlin. She studied Sinology in Berlin, Tuebingen and Taipeh. Her research and many publications focus on Chinese foreign and security policy, especially EU-China relations, Sino-Russian and Sino-Central Asian relations; China and the Asia-Pacific region; China's domestic development and minority policy (with special reference to Xinjiang); and the internet in China.

Joanna I. Lewis is an Assistant Professor of Science, Technology and International Affairs (STIA) at Georgetown University's Edmund A. Walsh School of Foreign Service. Her research focuses on energy and environmental issues in China, including renewable energy industry development and climate change policy. Her most recent book is *Green Innovation in China: China's Wind Power Industry and the Global Transition to a Low-Carbon Economy* (Columbia University Press, 2012). Dr. Lewis serves as an international advisor to the Energy Foundation China Sustainable Energy Program in Beijing, and is a Lead Author of the Intergovernmental Panel on Climate Change's Fifth Assessment Report. She holds a Ph.D. in Energy and Resources from the University of California, Berkeley.

ACRONYMS

BASIC	Brazil, South Africa, India, China grouping
BECon	Beijing Energy Efficiency Center
BRICS	Brazil, Russia, India, China, South Africa grouping
CASS	Chinese Academy of Social Sciences
CCAA	China Center of Adoption Affairs
CCP	Chinese Communist Party
CDM	Clean Development Mechanism
CIA	Central Intelligence Agency (U.S.)
COP	Conference of the Parties
ERI	Energy Research Institute
EU	European Union
FAR	First Assessment Report
FDI	Foreign Direct Investment
FYP	Five-Year Plan
GDP	Gross Domestic Product
GEF	Global Environmental Facility
GHG	Greenhouse Gases
GW	Gigawatt
G-20	Group of 20
G-77	Group of 77
HIV	Human Immunodeficiency Virus
IMF	International Monetary Fund
IEA	International Energy Agency
IOC	International Olympic Committee
IPCC	Intergovernmental Panel on Climate Change
KP	Kyoto Protocol
MAP	Mutual Assessment Process
MFA	Ministry of Foreign Affairs
MOP	Meeting of the Parties
MOST	Ministry of Science and Technology
NCCC	National Coordination Committee on Climate Change

NDRC	National Development and Reform Commission
NGO	Non-Governmental Organization
OECD	Organization for Economic Cooperation and Development
PBOC	People's Bank of China
PLA	People's Liberation Army (China)
PRC	People's Republic of China
RMB	renminbi
R2P	The Responsibility to Protect
SARS	Severe Acute Respiratory Syndrome
SEPA	State Environmental Protection Agency
UN	United Nations
UNCHR	UN Commission on Human Rights
UNCED	United Nations Conference on Environment and Development
UNEP	UN Environment Program
UNFCCC	United Nations Framework Convention on Climate Change
UNHRC	UN Human Rights Council
UNSC	UN Security Council
WTO	World Trade Organization
WWF	World Wildlife Fund

Introduction

China across the Divide

ROSEMARY FOOT

Understanding China's world role has become one of the crucial intellectual exercises of the twenty-first century. This book sets out to show that a full and sophisticated understanding of that topic requires us to capture some of the key complex and simultaneous interactions between the global and domestic levels in the study of China's external relations. Our approach is receptive to work in international relations (IR) that questions the notion that the domestic and international represent two different levels of analysis subject to their own internal logics.[1] It also contributes to a further breaching of the divide between those in the field of China studies who predominantly study China's domestic society and politics and those who focus mainly on its relations with the outside world.[2] While the interpenetration of the domestic and international spheres has long been recognized in the IR field, less often have various forms of that interaction been specified or applied overtly to the study of China. Unusual too is the multidisciplinary approach adopted here: security and political economy specialists in the field of IR are joined by historians, environmental scientists, and social anthropologists to examine, across three main sections of the book, Chinese conceptions of the country's status and role in global politics; some of the transnational processes that are transforming China and that provoke transformation in other parts of the world; and the impact of globalization on China and the domestic responses—from resistance to embrace—that it generates.

Three conceptual developments in the field of IR have proven helpful to this examination of China across the domestic and external divide in the current era. The first relates to the greater prominence given in IR

since the early 1990s to the role of ideas in shaping state identity, affecting perceptions of global status, and influencing the formulation of policy.
In Judith Goldstein and Robert Keohane's formulation, ideas play a role
in making policy by providing actors with maps that help them navigate
from a principled belief to a particular outcome.[3] But ideas can perform
other important functions: they can help state and other actors to frame
political action as well as to interpret the global order of which they are
a part—functions shown most directly in the first two chapters in this
volume. Arguments about the sources of state behavior and identity, for
example, where persuasive, can shape common understandings about the
nature of the activities that seem appropriate for the state to take. These
understandings provide us with clues about the range of behavior a state
is likely to undertake, a vital source of information in an era of uncertainty
and change. Where these understandings harden or narrow—a process
that can be observed by others – they are likely to translate into policies
that attract a reasonable degree of domestic consensus and to which those
outside the state will have to react and respond. This latter point suggests,
then, that ideas are especially important to chart when states rise in influence. Resurgent states, or emerging powers (to adopt the more frequently
used terminology), raise the expectation of external actors that they will
be better placed to contribute to a world order that they themselves are
playing a major role in shaping. Increases in relative power can also change
domestic expectations and fuel domestic nationalist sentiment, as chapter
3 attests. In these circumstances, domestic groups may well demand better levels of protection for domestic societal interests as well as tangible
evidence of the benefits to be derived from increased status vis-à-vis significant others in the global system.

Second, the concept of transnationalism has raised our awareness of
the importance of the non-state sector and has highlighted the pathways
and consequences of intersocietal enmeshment. Transnational linkages
between like-minded groups in other societies may challenge loyalty to the
home state, or form the basis for movements powerful enough to shape
the behavior of individual states, as has sometimes been the case among
the human rights and environmental groups that have a role in the policy
areas discussed in chapters 7 and 8. In these cases, much of the transnational activity is purposive in form, designed to reach objectives valued by
professional non-state groupings.[4] Indeed, much of the writing on transnationalism is directed toward determining the influence of transnational
actors on a country's foreign policy.[5] However, we give significant attention
here to another form of transnationalism—that which takes the attention
away from purposive action to focus more on the unintended consequences

arising from transnational processes. Decisions made in one policy area that might at first appear to be discrete and unconnected can have multiple and unintended effects in others, crucial examples of which can be found in chapters 4 and 5 of this edited collection. Both of these chapters cast new light on some of the less-remarked-upon global consequences of China's rise, as well as on the relationship between the Chinese state and its citizens, and the transformation of some of the major cities in which they live. These chapters also highlight that even governments recognized as having powerful central institutions can find it challenging to align means and ends, as well as policy decision and policy outcome.

The third factor relates to the phenomenon we have come to label "globalization." Globalization refers to a growing degree of interconnectedness, noticeable predominantly over the last three decades as a result of the technical and communications revolutions. Societal borders have diminished in salience as events in one corner of the globe come to have an impact on others in another corner underlining the sense that we live in a shared space rather than in discrete, territorially bounded, units. Technological advances in communication have provided opportunities to develop a global discourse on values and experience, some aspects of which may generate a sense of community beyond membership of a state. We are reminded of this shared existence whenever we are affected by the operations of global financial markets, or disrupted and disturbed by the effects of climate change, migratory flows, or large-scale human rights abuse—all topics that are covered in this edited collection.

Globalization thus differs from the idea of interdependence which underlines, in the formulation made famous by Robert Keohane and Joseph Nye,[6] the vulnerabilities and sensitivities experienced between separate but interconnected state units. When states are described as mutually sensitive, this implies recognition that the actions and policy decisions of one state will affect other states in the system. Vulnerability interdependence, however, suggests that interstate relationships may be more costly for one political unit than for another, an imbalance in costs that is experienced particularly acutely in instances in which an interstate relationship comes to be disrupted. As China's relative power has grown, many more states, and especially those with which it has become economically more closely linked, have come to assess the relative costs and benefits of sustaining or injuring those ties with China.

For this reason, the concept of interdependence is certainly pertinent to several of the chapters in this volume. However, in its focus on individual governmental assessments of a state-to-state relationship it is less helpful to our project—one that is designed predominantly to show diverse forms of interstate and intersocietal enmeshment and to uncover the intersection between the domestic and external spheres in state decision making. The experience of globalization and the levels of domestic resistance or acceptance that it generates are more central to our analytical purposes. We are interested in the ways in which the domestic and external realms complement each other but also at times pull in different directions. When these two levels are in tension, they pose fundamental challenges to those tasked with taking decisions—a situation illustrated well in chapter 6.

One result of the growing porousness of the borders separating the domestic and global is the threat that this poses to the individual state's ability to control events and to the core values of domestic society. This, in turn, has often led domestic populations to expect or demand that the state try hard to protect the domestic interests and values that appear to be under challenge. In addition, cross-border forces have also made us attentive to a range of political actors beyond the nation-state that are capable of constraining or enabling the state and societal action, sometimes playing a role in influencing the balance of social power inside societies and reconstituting the individual state.

Nevertheless, while these phenomena have captured most states in the global system, study of this weakening of the domestic–external divide is particularly interesting with respect to China—a state that has been presumed to have a close association with Westphalian definitions of state sovereignty, and one that has an authoritarian political system undergoing dramatic evolution as new forces and interests expecting representation come to the fore.[7] Moreover, China has emerged as a major global actor at a time when there is a dense network of formal and informal global institutions that make demands on our domestic ways of life. We live in an era replete with instances of global public and private rule making designed to assist us with the management or resolution of global collective action problems. Many of these rules, norms, and associated regulatory standards reach deeply inside the state and affect our ways of governing and living.[8] While it remains valuable to study the role of domestic processes and domestic interests in shaping policies toward the outside world, as liberal theorists have long argued,[9] it also has become essential to examine the reverse as well as circular flows of influence.

Unlike the conditions facing previous rising powers—such as Japan, Germany, or the United States from the close of the nineteenth century— China has risen (or more accurately, re-emerged) into what Andrew Hurrell has usefully described as a hybrid global society that is both Westphalian and post-Westphalian in its central characteristics, a world where "cosmopolitan conceptions of governance coexist, often rather unhappily, with many aspects of the old pluralist order."[10] On the one hand, global governance challenges have required China to engage in domestic reform in order to respond to external challenges that no single state can satisfactorily deal with on its own. However, on the other hand, it is also the case that China's position as a relatively powerful and centralized state participating in these interactive processes is now one of signal importance, especially as a result of the material successes that have come from the reform and opening policies adopted after the late 1970s. Beijing's influence in global markets, its impact on the global environment, its presence in all major international organizations, and its active diplomacy in all major regions of the world are reconstituting this hybrid global society.

However, the consequences of greater global institutional presence and involvement are not straightforward to determine. While we agree that the international realm provides the social structural context for policy development and policy change, it is also understood that this social environment does not dictate in an exact manner the actual domestic policy outcomes. This leeway at the domestic level is especially evident in the case of strong states that enjoy the benefits of an international system built on forms of global hierarchy and that, at the domestic level, are capable of organizing various degrees of domestic resistance or acceptance. States are not simply passive, sponge-like, bodies floating downstream in the currents agitated by the forces of globalization but can often mediate those international forces leading to "diverse national responses to common international trends."[11] China, for example, is one of the five permanent members of the UN Security Council that enjoys veto power. It is a nuclear weapons state and is recognized as such in the Nuclear Non-Proliferation Treaty of 1968. It also has a sizable overseas aid budget and is a leading trading state. Thus, it can be and has been shaped by global society, but its relatively privileged position in the global hierarchy provides some capacity for it to shape the global system. Moreover, the greater pluralism in China's domestic society that has come in tandem with the reform process has generated the space for the articulation of views that may favor resisting global institutional demands, especially those requirements that are perceived to have potentially negative consequences for the key goals of promoting development, stability, and national unity. In these instances, there may be outright rejection of global governance requirements, or more passively failure to implement international agreements arrived at.

Added to the direct and contemporary evidence of increases in China's status in the global system, the country also has a sense of being beholden to an exceptionalist tradition, as our chapter 2 argues, based on its long civilization, the concept of honor embedded in the idea of tribute, and its strong Han cultural identity. Imperial tradition dictated the prime goals of the emperor to be "to preside over a stable and harmonious order" and to overawe all others when they beheld the fruits of this enviable order—in the economy, the arts, and philosophy.[12] This sense of uniqueness and a capacity to awe others with the glories of Sinic culture make forced compliance with the requirements of external bodies difficult to contemplate and reinforce a desire for external respect of its own traditions and ways of life. In the perceived absence of that respect, nationalist sentiment can grow in strength, resulting sometimes in various protectionist policies or in unilateral assertiveness as chapter 3 demonstrates.[13]

Domestic resistance is, too, bound up in paradoxical ways with China's twin identity as great power and also as developing country. China may have the second largest economy in the world, but its gross domestic product (GDP) per capita places it, at best, as a middle-income country—a position from which it might find it difficult to advance. It has the world's second largest military budget, but limited power projection capability and, as yet, no overseas bases. In 2011, it stands at number 101 out of 187 countries with comparable data on the Human Development Index—an index that is a composite measure of three basic elements of human development: namely, health, education, and income.[14] These paradoxes generate contrary expectations at the global and domestic levels. As China's global presence has grown, so have the demands made of China. Many overseas political actors argue that Beijing should enhance its levels of contribution to global public goods. In response to these demands, Chinese officials often begin their explanations of their government's international role by referring to the domestic challenges that their country faces and the contributions their growth rates and reductions in poverty levels have made to global growth and stability. These reactions imply a reluctance to take on broader international responsibilities not related to these goals. For many Chinese commentators, these calls for Beijing to contribute more to global governance are perceived as traps of Western origin, and are in fact new forms of containment, designed primarily to distract it from its domestic development agenda and prevent the continuation of its rise.[15]

Beyond the raised expectations of other governments are those of Chinese citizens. They have assumed a different relationship with a government materially more powerful than at any point in Chinese history, yet one that has not yet managed to provide an adequate degree of welfare protection for the bulk of its citizenry. The opening of borders has allowed many Chinese to work in foreign territories in search of the goods and resources essential to the powering of the Chinese domestic economy, or to offer services to those overseas societies for official state and personal enrichment. But, as chapter 4 demonstrates, the relaxation of China's own immigration policy has also meant that Chinese workers can find themselves in new, sometimes competitive, relationships with overseas migrants who themselves are searching for better economic opportunities in a part of the global economy that is actually thriving. For those Chinese who travel abroad, they require government intervention and protection when things go wrong, as with the outbreak of civil war in Libya in 2011 that required the transportation home of some 30,000 Chinese laborers. For those Chinese residing in China's major cities and in competition with or fearful of the new migrant, they expect government regulatory frameworks to control the flow and for the leadership to prioritize the economic opportunities and personal security of its own people. Others in China, including those expressing the nationalist sentiments that are discussed in chapter 3, seek nothing less than evidence that the success of China's growth model is being translated into tangible gains in relationships with outsiders—whether that relates to success for China in sovereignty disputes, in diplomatic economic negotiations, or in other more diffuse areas where its increases in relative power are believed able to make a positive difference.

Since the Chinese Communist Party (CCP) perceives its right to rule as resting on the understanding that only it can offer Chinese future prosperity in a domestic political system marked by reasonable levels of social stability and opportunity this new relationship between rulers and ruled has taken on particular salience. Demands emanating from both private and public global actors and that are seen as potentially threatening or conducive to the development of these domestic goals are interpreted in this light, as chapters 6 to 8 are designed to highlight. When global actors call for currency revaluation, improved protections for human rights, greater control over China's CO_2 emissions, or better market access, the leadership's response will largely be determined by what these demands might mean for China's economic development, national unity, and social stability.[16] At a time of global economic recession and domestic leadership transition, these determinations have taken on a greater edge with the prospect that levels of resistance inside China to globalizing forces that threaten desired domestic outcomes may increase.

The national and international levels, thus, interact in several different and complex ways, as the three main sections to this volume show. The first section, comprising three chapters, reflects on new ideas and debates that have emerged in China about the country's global status and relationships with external actors in an era marked by its increased wealth and influence. How do Chinese citizens, whether intellectuals, officials, or the general public, see themselves in relation to the dominant rules and norms of global society? What can we learn about the bases of resistance to or acceptance of those global forces inside China? What do Chinese expect of their government in light of its new-found strength in relation to its global status and the policies that it promotes? In the first chapter, William A. Callahan examines dominant conceptions of a post-Western world order currently being debated in China by some officials and intellectuals. These conceptions range from idealistic visions of world harmony to realist power political models. These voices seek to provide a "grand strategy" for China, to give content to the poorly specified Hu-Wen formulation of "harmonious world" and "harmonious society," first introduced in 2005, and to use various media to promote this vision to the wider, interested, Chinese public.[17] In chapter 2, Feng Zhang expands the focus to look at the role of different schools of thought in constructing an idea of Chinese exceptionalism that is capable of and may already be shaping the way in which China negotiates its interactions with global society and which, in some formulations, represents a form of resistance to the requirements of a Western liberal order. Robert S. Ross, in chapter 3, broadens the source of new ideas still further and investigates more directly mass opinion. He examines the role of nationalist sentiment in constraining and shaping the leadership's diplomacy and in turn influencing how China's neighbors and other states view China as a re-emergent regional and global actor.

The second section, made up of two chapters, emphasizes transnational relations and some of their unintended consequences—consequences that are of signal importance because these unintentional elements are simultaneously remolding the Chinese state and citizen as well as peoples overseas. These chapters explore the fate of actors that exist in two or more worlds, cognitively or corporally, yet who retain both positive and negative connections with those worlds. Frank N. Pieke in chapter 4 explores this interaction through an examination of new migrant groups inside China and the rather novel Chinese experience of being a destination for international migrants. Chapter 5 by Karl Gerth examines the way that Chinese consumerism is transforming global supply chains and Chinese society itself, generating demands for new regulation or cultural renegotiation in order to constrain particular forms of consumer desire.

The third and final section focuses on three global issues that have high levels of domestic social and political salience for China. In this part, Andrew Walter in chapter 6, deals with imbalances in the global economy and the debate over revaluing the renminbi, an issue that has prompted both other governments and the International Monetary Fund (IMF) to put pressure on China to abjure its narrow focus on its own domestic economic concerns

INTRODUCTION (9)

and to develop a broader concern for the needs of the global economy. Chapter 7 by Gudrun Wacker concerns China's interactions with the global human rights norm, a clear case where international expectations of China emanating from state and non-state actors have met domestic resistance, predominantly but not solely at the level of the Chinese state. Finally, Joanna I. Lewis in chapter 8 focuses on China's environmental diplomacy and the Chinese government's struggle to align its domestic interests in growth, development, and energy security with the expectations of significant global actors concerned about climate change at a time when China has emerged as the leading emitter of greenhouse gases. In all these cases, the domestic consequences of close alignment with global demands are seen as difficult to negotiate in the absence of powerful interests and values at the domestic level that agree to those forms of alignment.

Each of these eight chapters is outlined in more detail in the next section. However, before detailing the core arguments of the chapters that follow, three main points derive from this analysis and are worth underscoring. The first and most important is that deeper understandings of Chinese behavior and Chinese thought about its world role will only come from recognizing the interpenetration of the global and domestic levels. It is no longer sufficient to explore many areas of the Chinese state and society without investigation of the broader context in which policies and actions are undertaken. Similarly, we cannot fully understand aspects of China's international behavior without exploring dominant values and interests held at the domestic level. The second is that China's decisions and behavior have major intended but, crucially, many unintended consequences at both the global and domestic levels. China's actions at the individual or group level often have a hugely decisive impact, but many of these outcomes may not have been envisioned when a decision has first been taken. However, given China's demographic weight and growing centrality in regional and global society across all policy areas, it is incumbent on the Chinese government, society, and those most affected by its policies to anticipate and expect such decisive outcomes and if necessary to adjust policies accordingly. The third point is that the growing domestic and global pluralism that these chapters illustrate makes it both more unrealistic to discuss China as though it is a unitary state and a more complex undertaking to assess the ways in which the demands of global society are going to be mediated at the domestic level. There are many more political actors who play a role in shaping Chinese decision making and behavior, but they themselves must operate in a global system that is multilayered, that involves a range of private and public interests that are difficult to navigate. This edited collection pushes the boundaries of understanding on these three aspects of modernity in a globalized world. While the topics chosen are central to current debates about China's world role, the volume is also intended to prompt further work of this kind and to suggest pathways for moving the scholarly agenda forward.

Finally, this volume does not explicitly set out to explain what China's re-emergence implies for twenty-first-century global order. Nevertheless, we do see strong hints of that throughout the text.[18] For example, the first three chapters of this book suggest both how China's leaders might deploy the country's increase in relative power or might feel compelled by domestic sentiment to represent those changing power realities abroad. While the most pessimistic of the scenarios outlined in that first section may not come to pass, they all suggest more sustained Chinese attempts to adapt global norms to a set of principles deriving from China's historical and other domestic experiences—mythical or factual—or to decide its foreign policies on the basis of nationalist rather than globalist ideas. The second section of the book shows how China's economic and demographic weight is transforming patterns of production and consumption as well as the flows of migration that have become familiar to us over the course of earlier centuries. Chinese leaders are not consequential to world order solely because of the decisions they take; they are consequential because China's footprint, now that it is integrated into the global system, is so large. The final three chapters, in their focus on the domestic–global nexus, suggest a cooperative China where domestic and international requirements meet, but one that will put its domestic concerns first where these requirements do not. This implies an erosion of more solidarist conceptions of global order and a weakened ability to manage and resolve the collective challenges of the twenty-first century.

CHAPTER OUTLINES

Chapter One. China's Harmonious World and Post-Western World Orders: Official and Citizen Intellectual Perspectives by William A. Callahan

To explain China's recent turn from a modest foreign policy to a more assertive global stance, the chapter argues that we need to pay closer attention to how citizen intellectuals are challenging the foreign policy establishment's monopoly on discussion of China's place in the world. These new voices emerged as an unintended consequence of President Hu Jintao's "harmonious world" policy, which created space for citizen intellectuals to talk about new post-Western world orders. Their views of China's strategic futures can be found in official, academic, and populist writings about China's new role in the world. This chapter explores these views by comparing President Hu Jintao's official "harmonious world" foreign policy with Pan Wei's *The China Model* (2009) and Liu Mingfu's *The China Dream* (2010). These official and unofficial sources chart a set of futures ranging from China fitting into the current international system to China gradually changing international norms to Beijing asserting a completely different model of politics, economics, and society. The chapter concludes that tensions between China and the West are likely to increase in the next few years; populist voices demanding a post-Western world order are growing louder with Beijing's transition to the fifth-generation leadership that has assumed power as Hu Jintao and Premier Wen Jiabao retire in 2012–13.

Chapter Two. Chinese Exceptionalism in the Intellectual World of China's Foreign Policy by Feng Zhang

Although exceptionalism is an important dimension of China's foreign policy, it has not been a subject of serious scholarly research. This chapter examines the manifestations and sources of contemporary Chinese exceptionalism and explain its implications for foreign policy. Chinese exceptionalism is defined by great power reformism, benevolent pacifism, and harmonious inclusionism. While resting on an important factual basis, it is constructed by mixing facts with myths through selective use of China's vast historical and cultural experiences. Exceptionalism does not determine policy, but by being an essential part of the worldview of the Chinese government and many intellectuals, it can become an important source for policy ideas and can shape and constrain policy choice. It can further be seen as a normative theory for China's foreign policy, as one among six major schools competing for ideational influence in China's foreign policy formation.

Chapter Three. The Domestic Sources of China's "Assertive Diplomacy," 2009–10: Nationalism and Chinese Foreign Policy by Robert S. Ross

From 2009 to 2010, China adopted a more contentious foreign policy. On a range of issues, China engaged in seemingly disproportionately assertive diplomacy toward relatively minor issues in East Asia, eliciting hostile diplomacy from nearly all of its neighbors. China's contentious diplomacy did not reflect realist assumptions about the sources of foreign policy, such as a major challenge to China's security or improved military capabilities. Rather, China's policy change reflected the emergence in China of significant domestic economic and political instability and the corresponding increased pressures on the Chinese leadership to adopt a nationalist foreign policy. An examination of two case studies, Chinese policy toward United States–South Korean naval cooperation and the Japanese arrest of a Chinese fisherman, reveals the domestic sources of China's contentious diplomacy and how nationalist ideas among the public influenced the leadership's responses.

Chapter Four. *Immigrant China* by Frank N. Pieke

International migration to the People's Republic of China is a new phenomenon that will have profound consequences for the future of the international migration order. For decades, China has received large numbers of foreign students, expatriates, returned overseas Chinese, and ethnic Chinese refugees. However, in the past few years immigration to China has become much more diverse and numerous. Chinese students and scholars abroad returned to China in ever greater numbers. Traders and labor migrants from all over the world are attracted by China's trading opportunities, political stability, and prosperity. Middle-class Koreans, Taiwanese, and Southeast Asians are looking for cheaper living costs and better jobs. European, North American, and Australian university graduates travel to China for employment or to start businesses. This chapter investigates the extent to which government policy making and the formation of immigrant groups and ethnic relations are informed by unique features of China's late socialist society and government or, alternatively, follow patterns similar to established developed immigrant countries in Asia, Europe, and North America.

Chapter Five. *Transnational Consumers: The Unintended Consequences of Extreme Markets in Contemporary China* by Karl Gerth

What are the transnational political, societal, and cultural consequences created by the reintegration of China into transnational markets? While world political and business leaders celebrate the advent of mass consumption in China, reconnecting Chinese with global markets also creates complex problems not easily solved. This chapter examines the negative and largely unintentional transnational consequences of China's emergence as a consumer culture by examining four "extreme markets" for babies and wives, sexual services, organs, and endangered species. As this chapter shows, these extreme markets confirm that transnational consumption has had unintended consequences for the Chinese state and society, prompting regulatory and cultural adjustments that have only just begun.

Chapter Six. Addressing Global Imbalances: Domestic and Global Dynamics by Andrew Walter

China's contribution to global payments imbalances poses a significant challenge to claims by the Chinese leadership that its policies are consistent with global economic and political stability, as well as to arguments that China's foreign policy stance has been broadly convergent with global norms, rules, and standards. Since this inconsistency has become increasingly costly for China, it requires explanation. This chapter argues that standard accounts of China's foreign economic policy choices do not explain this well and that, instead, its choices have been shaped by a complex and evolving dynamic between the leadership and two different audiences, domestic and external. Both these audiences have influenced Chinese policy making to a greater degree over time, increasing the difficulty of responding effectively to the imbalances problem.

Chapter Seven. Norms Without Borders? Human Rights in China by Gudrun Wacker

Human rights have been one of the focal issues in China's foreign relations for the past two decades. Since the Tian'anmen crackdown in 1989, China finds itself closely monitored and faces serious international criticism for its treatment of human rights. But how has the human rights situation in China developed since the Tian'anmen caesura and what dynamics drive this development? This chapter seeks to respond to these questions by arguing that a complex web of factors and relations at the domestic as well as the international level influences China's behavior in this policy area. China's new role in world politics and its society's ongoing integration into world affairs have led it to become more deeply involved with the human rights idea, internationally as well as domestically. While China has learned how to withstand international pressures, growing demands and expectations from within Chinese society have led to gradual if incomplete improvements in the human rights situation in the People's Republic. Despite this progress, the chapter emphasizes that China's willingness to accept the validity of human rights still has its limitations, especially when challenges arise to national sovereignty and stability, as well as to the Communist Party's hold on power.

Chapter Eight. China's Environmental Diplomacy: Climate Change, Domestic Politics, and International Engagement by Joanna I. Lewis

China has historically been a reluctant player in global environmental forums. However, as China's role in contributing to global climate change—one of the great global environmental challenges of our time—has increased, so has its role in international environmental diplomacy. China's contributions to climate change, namely, greenhouse gas emissions from fossil fuel combustion and industrial activity, are inherently linked to China's economic development strategy. Beijing's approach toward climate change therefore must be understood in the context of its overall energy development strategy, which is driven by its overall economic development goals. Even as international pressure and attention shift to China as the largest global emitter, China's actions internationally are still predominantly shaped by domestic, rather than international, factors. This chapter demonstrates how China's energy challenges are shaping the way its leadership is approaching climate mitigation at the domestic level, which in turn is shaping its positioning in international climate negotiations. An increase in the scientific and technical understanding of its own energy and emissions situation—an understanding promoted in part by increased international engagement—has permitted China's policy makers to legislate with more confidence domestically. Low carbon development is now positioned at the core of China's overarching national five-year economic plans; the 12th Five-Year Plan has established a domestic policy framework to implement carbon management programs alongside a low carbon development strategy. These significant domestic changes have permitted an equally striking shift in China's approach to global environmental diplomacy, particularly in the context of the international climate change negotiations.

NOTES

1. For work that makes this case, see, for example, Peter Gourevitch, "Domestic Politics and International Relations," in *Handbook of International Relations,* edited by Walter Carlsnaes, Thomas Risse, and Beth A. Simmons (London: Sage

Publications, 2002), pp. 309–28; Andrew Moravcsik, "Integrating International and Domestic Theories of International Bargaining," in *Double Edged Diplomacy: International Bargaining and Domestic Politics*, edited by Peter Evans, Harold Jacobson, and Robert Putnam (Berkeley: University of California Press, 1993); James N. Rosenau, *Along the Domestic-Foreign Frontier* (Cambridge: Cambridge University Press, 1997); Jeffrey Checkel, "International norms and domestic politics: Bridging the rationalist constructivist divide," *European Journal of International Relations*, Vol. 3, No. 4 (1997), pp. 473–95. Neoclassical realism has also become prominent in recent years and it too emphasizes interactions between domestic and international levels. See, in particular, Gideon Rose, "Neoclassical realism and theories of foreign policy," *World Politics*, Vol. 51, No. 3 (1999), pp. 144–72.

2. Those in the China field that have recognized the linkage between the domestic and international levels include Miranda A. Schreurs and Elizabeth Economy, eds., *The Internationalization of Environmental Protection* (Cambridge: Cambridge University Press, 1997); Hongyi Lai *The Domestic Sources of China's Foreign Policy: Regimes, Leadership, Priorities, and Process* (London: Routledge, 2010); Wang Gungwu and Zheng Yongnian, eds., *China and the New International Order* (Abingdon: Routledge, 2008); David Zweig, *Internationalizing China: Domestic Interests and Global Linkages* (Ithaca, NY: Cornell University Press, 2002).

3. Judith Goldstein and Robert O. Keohane, eds., *Ideas and Foreign Policy: Beliefs, Institutions and Political Change* (Ithaca, NY: Cornell University Press, 1993).

4. See Peter M. Haas, "Do regimes matter? Epistemic communities and Mediterranean pollution control," *International Organization*, Vol. 43, No. 3 (1989), pp. 377–403; Anne-Marie Slaughter, *A New World Order* (Princeton, NJ: Princeton University Press, 2004); Alec Stone Sweet, "Islands of Transnational Governance," in *Restructuring Territoriality: Europe and the United States Compared*, edited by Christopher K. Ansell and Giuseppe di Palma (Cambridge: Cambridge University Press, 2004), pp. 122–44.

5. See, for example, Matthew Evangelista, *Unarmed Forces: The Transnational Movement to End the Cold War* (Ithaca, NY: Cornell University Press, 1999); Margaret Keck and Kathryn Sikkink, *Activists Beyond Borders: Advocacy Networks in International Politics* (Ithaca, NY: Cornell University Press, 1998).

6. Robert O. Keohane and Joseph S. Nye, *Power and Interdependence: World Politics in Transition* (Boston: Little Brown and Company, 1977).

7. On the latter point see, for example, Bonnie Glaser and Phil Saunders, "Chinese civilian foreign policy research institutes: Evolving roles and increasing influence," *The China Quarterly*, No. 171 (2002), pp. 597–616; Quansheng Zhao, "Policy-making Processes of Chinese Foreign Policy: The Role of Policy Communities and Think Tanks," in *Handbook of China's International Relations*, edited by Shaun Breslin (London: Routledge, 2010), pp. 22–34; Linda Jakobson and Dean Knox, *New Foreign Policy Actors in China*, SIPRI Policy Paper No. 26 (September 2010).

8. Relevant examples include the voluntary Basel Banking rules, global anti-doping legislation, and targets set in international climate change negotiations under the UN's Framework Convention on Climate Change.

9. For an approach that looks at the role of societal actors and their influence on a state's foreign policy preferences, see Andrew Moravcsik, "Taking preferences seriously: A liberal theory of international politics," *International Organization*, Vol. 51, No. 4 (1997), pp. 513–53. Domestic influences are also treated in models that emphasize cognitive processes and bureaucratic politics. For a fuller discussion of such approaches, see Steve Smith, Amelia Hadfield, and Tim Dunne, eds.,

Foreign Policy: Theories, Actors, Cases (Oxford: Oxford University Press, 2008), especially section 2.

10. Andrew Hurrell, *On Global Order* (Oxford: Oxford University Press, 2007), p. 9.

11. Keohane and Milner have argued this in their study of the linkages between the national and world economies. See Robert Keohane and Helen V. Milner, eds., *Internationalization and Domestic Politics* (New York: Cambridge University Press, 1996), p. 14.

12. Vivienne Shue, "Legitimacy Crisis in China?" in *State and Society in 21st-Century China: Crisis, Contention, and Legitimation,* edited by Peter Hays Gries and Stanley Rosen (New York: RoutledgeCurzon, 2004), p. 31.

13. For a powerful reference to the importance of respect in China's external relations, see Wang Gungwu, "US and China: Respect and Equality," lecture given at the Lowy Institute, Sydney, March 17, 2011. Available: http://lowyinstitute.org/Publication.asp?pid=1535.

14. China, Country Profile: Human Development Indicators. Available: http://hdrstats.undp.org/en/countries/profiles/CHN.html.

15. David Shambaugh, "Coping with a conflicted China," *The Washington Quarterly,* Vol. 34, No. 1 (2011), pp. 17–9. Shi Yinhong has written: "Among the primary enduring concerns determining China's external posture and foreign policy, there has been what could be described as an overwhelming concern: the Chinese government often feels that the west's demands, in terms of shouldering international responsibility, will surpass what China can do and thereby hurt its economic and other interests." See "China, 'global challenges' and the complexities of international cooperation," *Global Policy,* Vol. 2, No. 1 (2011), p. 90.

16. Dai Bingguo, China's State Councilor in charge of external relations, stated in "Adhere to the Path of Peaceful Development," December 6, 2010, that China's core interests are: "first, China's form of government and political system and stability, namely the leadership of the Communist Party of China, the socialist system and socialism with Chinese characteristics. Second, China's sovereignty, territorial integrity and national unity. Third, the basic guarantee for sustainable economic and social development of China." Available: http://china.usc.edu/ShowArticle.aspx?articleID=2325.

17. See, for example, "Hu Makes 4-point Proposal for Building Harmonious World," September 16, 2005. Available: http://www.china.org.cn/english/features/UN/142408.htm.

18. For more extensive discussion of this topic, see Rosemary Foot and Andrew Walter, *China, the United States, and Global Order* (New York: Cambridge University Press, 2011).

PART ONE

Ideational Debates

CHAPTER 1

༺❀༻

China's Harmonious World and Post-Western World Orders

Official and Citizen Intellectual Perspectives

WILLIAM A. CALLAHAN

Although we did not recognize it at the time, Beijing's current assertive foreign policy started in September 2005 when Chinese President Hu Jintao delivered a major speech to a global audience at the United Nations. From the podium of the General Assembly Hu introduced "Harmonious World" as a new concept of global politics, explaining that his goal was to "build a harmonious world of lasting peace and common prosperity." In this new world order, different civilizations would coexist in the global community, making "humanity more harmonious and our world more colorful."[1]

To show how proclamations of building a harmonious world may have contributed to China's current tensions with its Asian neighbors and Western powers, it is necessary to trace how Hu's foreign policy encourages China's officials and its citizen intellectuals to talk about new post-Western world orders. These ideas, while difficult to show are causally linked to new foreign policies, frame political action in ways that can contribute to policy outcomes. To explore these ideas and the debates that have ensued, this chapter compares Beijing's official view of "building a harmonious world" with the views of China's future—and the world's future—of two influential citizen intellectuals: Professor Pan Wei, in *The China Model: Reading 60 Years of the People's Republic* (2009), and Senior Colonel Liu Mingfu in *The China Dream: The Great Power Thinking and Strategic Positioning of China in* the *Post-American Era* (2010).[2] I leave it to the next two chapters in this edited collection to explore more widely the kinds of ideas about China's place in the world that are emerging from officials, academics, and the mass public, though I argue below that the two perspectives studied in this chapter have been particularly critical to shaping such wider views.

The China Model uses traditional Chinese ideas to craft an alternative to Western world order; *The China Dream* argues that the People's Republic of China (PRC) needs to have a military rise to guard its economic rise. These two books are of particular importance because they exemplify how popular voices increasingly influence debates among foreign policy experts. They each became social phenomena and media events, provoking debates that spread their influence far beyond their core audiences of philosophers and military officers into China's broader civil society.[3] In this way, the work of citizen intellectuals can give us a sense of the parameters—ranging from idealist world order to realist power politics—of the discussions of China's proper role in the world that are increasingly popular in Beijing.

While many assert that China will be a different kind of world leader that appeals to non-Western norms,[4] these debates about future world orders show how China's officials and citizen intellectuals are reproducing familiar themes: liberalism, idealism, and realism. Indeed, in many ways it is best to understand them in terms of Deng Xiaoping's slogan from the early reform era: "socialism with Chinese characteristics." Many argue that China's ideology has shifted from "socialism" to "Chinese characteristics." However, this chapter shows how alternative world orders each entail a productive tension between "socialism" and "Chinese characteristics."

Socialism is not dead in China; although its power as a revolutionary ideology is weak, it is thriving as a lifestyle and a way of thinking that continues to inform broad discussions of the "Chinese experience," the "China model," and the "China dream."[5] Even with its many problems, the Chinese Communist Party (CCP) is not about to collapse: it is the wealthiest political party in the world, has 80 million members, and is still growing in size. While Chinese nationalism is strong, as chapter 3 attests, and Confucianism is a growing force (see chapter 2), Chinese tradition does not dominate the discussion of "Chinese characteristics" as much as people in the West might think.

It is necessary, then, to pay attention to the nuance of foreign policy discussions in China to see how realism, idealism, and liberalism are combined in a range of different ways. Indeed, rather than building a harmonious world, it is important to understand how these texts are harmonizing "socialism" with "Chinese characteristics." Ideas thus are very important as Beijing faces what Chinese strategist Shi Yinhong calls its "era of many troubles" as the PRC's fifth generation takes control in 2012–13.[6]

As shown below, all three proposed world orders—harmonious world, the China model, and the China dream—are not only vague but are unlikely to be actualized in the medium term. In other words, although predictions of American decline are popular, the United States is still likely to dominate global affairs for the next few decades. China's strategic futures are important, however, because they show how Chinese officials and citizen intellectuals are starting to think beyond the current world system to craft post-Western world orders. Their impact thus may be destructive of the status quo: even if such alternative world orders are not realized, they still can serve to delegitimize European- and American-influenced global norms.[7]

The chapter argues two points: (1) Hu's harmonious world foreign policy has had unintended consequences by creating opportunities for citizens to talk about a wide range of possibilities for China's future, including a range of post-Western world orders that produce different combinations of socialism with Chinese characteristics; (2) although these strategic dreams often come from unexpected quarters, citizen intellectuals are growing in influence, due in part to the commercialization of old media and the spread of new media. While the Central Party apparatus is still very strong, such citizen intellectuals can no longer be written off because they have become a significant source of ideas about China's future—and the world's future.

CITIZEN INTELLECTUALS

Reflecting on their country's recent economic success, China's policy makers and public intellectuals are now asking "what comes next?" How can China convert its growing economic power into enduring political and cultural influence around the globe? People in China thus are experiencing a heady mix of ambition and anxiety about the possibilities for the twenty-first century, which they feel is "The Chinese Century."[8]

To see where China is going, most scholars outside China look to the PRC's international relations literature and conduct elite interviews with scholars and officials in Beijing.[9] This chapter takes a different approach to highlight what Chinese people are saying to each other in public space and popular culture. A broad view of Chinese politics enables us to better explore the grand aspirations and deep anxieties of a wide variety of public intellectuals when they think about China's future.

They are "citizen intellectuals"[10] not because they are in opposition to state power as dissidents but because they take advantage of China's new social and economic freedoms to choose when to work with the state and when to work outside state institutions. While China's scholar-officials have labored to frame and give content to official foreign policy positions over the past few decades, this new group of citizen intellectuals is pushing beyond the existing policy narrative, often in ways that challenge it. Citizen intellectuals are able to do this because they are both outsiders and insiders; relative outsiders who often cultivate connections with elite insiders. For example, the preface of *The China Dream* is written by Lieutenant General Liu Yazhou, the political commissar of China's National Defense University who is the son-in-law of former president Li Xiannian. While many dismiss citizen intellectuals as irrelevant because they are not "part of the foreign policy establishment,"[11] their status as relative outsiders actually gives them more leeway to think about China's alternative futures.[12]

The chapter is not arguing that there is a direct link between citizen intellectuals and official foreign policy making. Since the opaque nature of Zhongnanhai (China's Kremlin) obscures the dynamics of foreign policy making, it argues instead that citizen intellectuals can give us a strong sense of the parameters within which foreign policy discussions take place. Rather than framing public opinion as a negative force that constrains Chinese foreign policy (toward Japan or America, for example), analysis that focuses on citizen intellectuals' ambitious ideas can demonstrate how these ideas might operate to push Chinese foreign policy in new directions. Indeed, this recognition of the role of public voices in policy discussions is growing among China's scholarly community as well as overseas.[13] Careful scholars, such as Renmin University's Shi Yinhong, for example, now frame their analysis of Chinese foreign policy in terms of both the leadership and public attitudes, which include citizen intellectuals.[14]

Analysis of China begins then to resemble analysis of other countries, which thus treats China as a normal nation. While much has been written about the impact of neoconservative ideology on U.S. foreign policy, little work has been done on the impact of ideas on the foreign policy of the world's most important rising power, China.

HU JINTAO'S HARMONIOUS WORLD

Before looking at China's alternative world orders, it is helpful to get a better idea of how Hu Jintao's harmonious world works. After Hu announced it at the United Nations (UN) in September 2005, harmonious world was explained in two official documents: "China's Peaceful Development Road," (2005), and Hu Jintao's "Report to the 17th Party Congress" (2007).[15]

A harmonious world will be built, according to *China's Peaceful Development Road*, through "mutual dialogues, exchanges and cooperation" that lead to "mutual benefit and common development." The White Paper explains that "upholding tolerance and opening to achieve dialogue among civilizations" is necessary because the "diversity of civilizations is a basic feature of human society, and an important driving force for the progress of mankind." China will lead this dialogue because "opening, tolerance and all-embracing are important features of Chinese civilization." The goal is to build a harmonious world that is more "democratic, harmonious, just and tolerant." Hu's harmonious world will be peaceful because "The Chinese nation has always been a peace-loving one. Chinese culture is a pacific culture. The spirit of the Chinese people has always featured their longing for peace and pursuit of harmony."

Thus, China's foreign policy, according to the White Paper, is more than simply policy. It presents a new way of thinking about the world—and about the future: "Peace, opening-up, cooperation, harmony and win-win are our policy, our idea, our principle and our pursuit." The text is reflective of what Feng Zhang refers to as the official version of Chinese exceptionalism in chapter 2 in this volume.

Hu Jintao confirmed "harmonious world" as China's official foreign policy when he invoked it at the CCP's 17th Party Congress in October 2007. Whereas Hu spoke to world leaders at the UN General Assembly, here Hu was reporting the country's recent progress and future plans to a domestic audience of 2,217 party delegates assembled at Tiananmen Square's Great Hall of the People.

As at the UN, Hu stressed that building a harmonious world was necessary because of the "ever closer interconnection between China's future and destiny and those of the world.... The Chinese people will continue to work tirelessly with the people of other countries to bring about a better future for humanity." Hu stressed that China's goal was to build a more democratic and egalitarian harmonious world because "We maintain that all countries, big and small, strong and weak, rich and poor, are equal."

The high status of harmonious world was proclaimed in a characteristically Chinese way: at the end of the congress the assembled party members adopted an amendment enshrining "the building of a harmonious world characterized by sustained peace and common prosperity" in the CCP constitution. Joining the pithy slogans of Mao Zedong, Deng Xiaoping, and Jiang Zemin, this honor established harmonious world as Hu Jintao's strategic legacy.

Yet harmonious world's laudable goals are hardly earth-shattering—who would argue against global peace, prosperity, and harmony? Hu's methods for building a harmonious world are not very innovative either. In both his UN speech and his "Report to the 17th Party Congress," Hu stressed that

China would use multilateralism, the UN Charter, international law, and universally recognized norms of international relations to build a harmonious world. Yet China is hardly alone in pursuing liberalism's mainstream diplomacy; actually the European Union's robust multilateralism is much more effective than China's rather limited multilateralism.

To fully appreciate the impact of Hu's harmonious world policy it is necessary to examine it in the context of China's domestic politics and its international affairs. When we remember what was going on in 2005—the United States–United Kingdom war in Iraq was spiraling into insurgency and civil war—it is easy to see why global opinion may well have welcomed Hu's new concept. To a world largely weary of American unilateralism and incensed at the Bush doctrine of regime change, Hu's policy of world harmony may well have been compelling. In outlining this strategy, Hu Jintao did not even need to mention George W. Bush, the United States, or Iraq; it was enough to simply criticize "hegemonism" and "power politics," while supporting multilateralism, international law, and the United Nations. Beijing had been trying to change China's global image for years; Hu was reasonably successful in this endeavor at that time by drawing a clear distinction between a bellicose America and a peace-loving China.

The PRC thus was able to take advantage of U.S. overcommitment in Iraq and Afghanistan to assert itself as an alternative center of power in Asia. Hence, we should not be surprised at Beijing's lack of enthusiasm for the Obama administration's "pivot" back to Asia in 2011.

However, the domestic context for China's harmonious world foreign policy is more complex. As in many rapidly developing countries, China's dramatic transition to a market economy has created a new set of winners and losers. Urban areas on the east coast have benefited much more than rural areas and the interior; and the educated much more than the less educated. While Deng Xiaoping's economic reform policies have lifted more than 300 million people out of absolute poverty since 1979, China has become increasingly polarized between wealthy urban elites and impoverished people in rural areas.[16] One of the enduring concerns of the CCP is national unity, and these economic reforms have risked tearing the country apart at the seams.

"Harmonious society" appeared as a policy narrative in 2004 to address the negative fallout from China's spectacular economic growth. It describes a set of government policies that seek to "rebalance" China's economic and social polarization. There are new funds, for example, to provide free public education and subsidized health care to disadvantaged people, especially those in rural areas. Harmonious society is a very detailed set of policies that looks to the party-state to solve China's economic and social problems. Harmonious society's state-centric intervention into society thus appeals to a particular blend of socialist modernity and Chinese tradition. While English-language descriptions of the policy stress its Confucian roots,[17] in Chinese it is called "harmonious socialist society."

What can Beijing's experience of building a harmonious society in the PRC tell us about China's goal to build harmony on a global scale? A strong state is necessary to build China's harmonious society at home. Although it is common for Chinese writers to proclaim "Harmonious society to be [a] model for the world,"[18] Hu is not clear about whether a strong state is necessary to build a harmonious world abroad. Just before the 17th Party Congress in 2007, the PRC-owned Hong Kong newspaper *Wen Wei Po* certainly thought so; it enjoined Hu Jintao to take the lead as the "'formulator, participant and defender of world order', in order push the entire world toward harmony."[19]

OPENING THE DEBATE ON HARMONIOUS WORLD

Since 2005, harmonious world has come to define Beijing's foreign policy narrative; whenever President Hu or Prime Minister Wen Jiabao talks to foreign leaders or foreign audiences, he repeats the "harmonious world of lasting peace and common prosperity" mantra.[20] Unfortunately, neither leader has discussed the details of how China will build a harmonious world. Even the three main documents describing harmonious world spend most of their time discussing other things: harmonious world is only one of four points discussed in Hu's UN speech, one of five points raised in the "China's Peaceful Development Road" White Paper, and briefly mentioned in one of the twelve sections of Hu's "Report to the 17th Party Congress." The most that we can say is that Hu's harmonious world follows harmonious society policy in appealing to the mix of (1) a state-centric top-down notion of "socialism" and (2) "Chinese characteristics" that point to the traditional ideal of harmony. It is deliberately ambiguous because the more Beijing clarifies its vision of a harmonious world, the more this policy concept will necessarily exclude nation-states and peoples who have different ideals of world order.

While official descriptions of harmonious world lack substance, the concept has generated huge interest among China's official intellectuals and citizen intellectuals. Before 2005 only one discussion of China's international politics used the phrase "harmonious world"; the phrase was more often used to describe events like a Buddhist world conference. "Light

and Shadow in a Harmonious World" (2003) is not a sophisticated theoretical discussion of world order; rather, this essay in *Beijing Real Estate*
offers advice about lamps and lampshades to the capital's elite interior
designers.[21]

After Hu introduced harmonious world at the United Nations, however,
thousands of commentators and academics began to use it to describe not
just Beijing's foreign policy but a new world order.[22] Rather than focusing
on how China would use the UN and international law to build a harmonious world, these citizen intellectuals are more interested in how Chinese
ideals—both traditional and socialist—can help shape the post-Western
world order.

Soon after Hu's UN speech, the CCP's official newspaper *The People's
Daily* asked three well-known public intellectuals—the Chinese Academy
of Social Sciences's Wang Yizhou,[23] Renmin University's Jin Canrong, and
the Central Party School's Men Honghua—to explain this new diplomatic
concept to the masses. They largely repeated Hu's formula of "building a
harmonious world of lasting peace and common prosperity" through the
UN and international law. But they also stressed how Beijing would use
ideals from traditional Chinese culture to "restructure the world." In this
formulation, China would not be just the "initiator of a harmonious world"
but also "a major practitioner of it."[24]

This is a good example of how citizen intellectuals can help the state while
still maintaining a measure of scholarly independence and integrity. Over
the next few years, citizen intellectuals also invoked harmonious world to
develop new ideas of world order, especially post-Western orders that look
to a combination of socialist and indigenous Chinese ideals. China's inter-
linked domestic and foreign policies of harmonious society and harmonious world, which appeal to Chinese values like harmony over "Western"
values like freedom, thus have opened up space for a wide debate about
China's future.

Certainly, it is easy to dismiss "harmonious world" as simply propaganda.
Indeed, since Beijing now vigorously employs "harmony" to explain domestic and foreign policy, China's "netizens" now use it ironically to criticize the
party-state: "*bei hexie le*—been harmonized"—means that you have been
censored on the web or otherwise harassed for expressing your views. But
harmonious world should be taken seriously simply because many Chinese
intellectuals do—both to support official policy and to suggest policy alternatives. In this way, the deliberate ambiguity of official harmonious world
pronouncements has created a strategic vacuum that is being filled by a
range of official, unofficial, and quasi-official theories, concepts, and grand
strategies for the Chinese century.

IDEALISTIC ORGANIC ORDER: PAN WEI'S *THE CHINA MODEL*

"The China model" is one of the hottest topics in the PRC, provoking debate among top scholars from the humanities and social sciences as well as among opinion makers in the popular press.[25] Yet it is not part of official discourse: neither Hu Jintao nor Wen Jiabao has ever mentioned the China model in his official statements—except to deny its existence.[26] Other party leaders have actually warned their compatriots about the "dangers" of discussing this topic, since foreigners might see it as a threat. This mix of vociferous debate in the public domain and deafening silence from official quarters makes the China model a good example of citizen intellectual work.

As with harmonious society/harmonious world, the China model discourse is part of a broad discussion about China's future direction. The China model discourse is characteristically triumphalist, showing Beijing's supreme confidence; but its combative style also suggests there are serious doubts about China's future. Citizen intellectual discourse typically intertwines aspirations and anxieties, and the China model discourse is no exception. According to Zhang Wei-wei, one of the concept's key advocates, the debate reveals the "enormous challenges and endless opportunities that China now faces."[27]

Initially the China model referred to the PRC's economic development model; but with the rise of confidence in 2008–09 after the successful Beijing Olympics and the PRC's sixtieth-birthday celebration, it took on new life to describe a whole "Chinese system" of politics, economics, and society that is seen as *unique*. Two citizen intellectuals, Peking University's Pan Wei and Zhang Wei-wei from the Geneva School of Diplomacy and International Relations, are actively promoting this new China model through their books: *The China Model* (2009) and *China Shock* (2011).[28] Although the China model appears only to concern the PRC's domestic issues, it is actually discussed in terms of what citizen intellectuals see as a grand Cold War-type battle between rival social systems: the Chinese model versus the Western model.

One paradox associated with this nativist view of China's dream is that both Pan and Zhang have extensive international experience. Pan received his Ph.D. from the University of California, Berkeley, on a scholarship provided by an American foundation; Zhang received his Ph.D. from the University of Geneva, and he has worked in Switzerland for decades. As Deng Xiaoping's official English-language interpreter in the mid-1980s, Zhang traveled to more than 100 countries. Yet in the 2000s both began to change. Initially, Pan's Ph.D. dissertation, and then his first book, analyzed "the politics of marketization in rural China," explaining the problems that peasants faced in the new system. Pan then became well-known for his advocacy of political reform in terms of promoting the rule of law and a neutral judiciary, although as an alternative to liberal democracy. Zhang's first books analyzed the relationship between economic and political reform in China.[29] Thus both looked primarily to (Western) social science to understand economic and political reform in the PRC.

However, in the mid-2000s, as part of a broader trend among Chinese intellectuals, Pan and Zhang started to draw on cultural arguments and China's imperial tradition to explain Beijing's new power. Like many of China's other New Left intellectuals who now argue for neoconservative values, Pan comes from an elite academic family, and spent his youth in the countryside during the Cultural Revolution.[30] Rather than pursuing transnationally shared social goals—like equality—Pan and Zhang both now proclaim that to achieve its full potential China needs to jettison the "Western model," and find its own way. In recent years, they have gone one step further to preach the China model in Europe's halls of power: Zhang lectured the Dutch Senate, and Pan the British Parliament.[31] Although Deng Xiaoping condemned Chinese culture as "feudal superstition," Zhang and Pan look to traditional values to chart the world's future. In their discussion of the China model they have discarded methods and concepts associated with universal social science and have turned more narrowly to the peculiarities of unique Chinese civilization.

To see this transformation from universal (social) science to Chinese uniqueness—and its implications for China's strategy—it is helpful to examine Pan Wei's arguments in more detail. To many, the China model is simply shorthand for "authoritarian state + free market capitalism."[32] However, Pan is not satisfied with this description. In "The Modern Chinese System: Analysis of the China Model of Economics, Politics and Society," the long introduction to Pan's popular edited volume *The China Model*, he argues that social science concepts like "authoritarianism" and "the free market" cannot explain China's unique experience. China's experience, in his view, "challenges the 'market/state planning dichotomy' of western economics, the 'democracy/autocracy dichotomy' of western political science, and the 'state/society dichotomy' of western sociology."[33]

These concepts are not "universal," he argues, because they grow out of Europe's (and then America's) particular historical and cultural experience. Since China has a radically different, unique, and independent historical experience, Pan states that it can only be judged by its own set of concepts. However, Pan is doing more than describing the Chinese experience. Through his books and speeches in China and abroad, Pan is building his unique China model to challenge the very idea of "universal values" such as democracy and human rights.[34]

Pan explains the China model in terms of three "indigenous" Chinese submodels—*guomin* economics, *minben* politics, and *sheji* society—that are contrasted with "Western" approaches to order and governance. Western philosophy generally starts from the assumption that society is divided and sees order in terms of balancing competing interests through "checks and balances." Chinese philosophy, Pan tells us, starts from the assumption of unity and sees order as a process of integrating divisions into an organic whole, ultimately into the "World of Great Harmony" (*Datong shijie*). While Western economics sees a struggle between free markets and state intervention, China's *guomin* economic model harmonizes the public (*guo*) and private (*min*) sectors. While Western politics looks to legalistic concepts of competing "rights," China's people-centered *minben* political order is based on "mutual responsibility." While Western sociology sees a battle between the state and civil society, China's economic development and political stability are based on *sheji* society's organic integration of officials and the people.

Guomin economics, *minben* politics, and *sheji* society are all new concepts; but Pan looks to China's two traditions—ancient Chinese culture and modern socialist ideology—to argue that they are an integral part of Chinese civilization. He quotes many passages from classical Chinese philosophy to show how his "China model is the 21st century's new edition of the Chinese system." Pan also looks to socialism to describe his public/private *guomin* economy, which he concludes is the same as what CCP "officials call the 'socialist market economy with Chinese characteristics.'"[35] While most economists date China's economic success to the start of Deng Xiaoping's reforms in 1978,[36] Pan reclaims the Maoist period (1949–78) as part of the China model's "60 years of achievement" because "our country's state-owned sector was built in [the PRC's] first 30 years." The economic, political and social submodels all rely on a strong CCP, which Pan describes as "an advanced, neutral, united ruling group."[37]

The China model is famous for building China's ultramodern cities—Shanghai, Shenzhen, and Beijing—and China's official 12th Five Year Plan (2011–15) seeks to speed up China's urbanization process. Pan, on the other hand, appeals more to traditional Chinese village life to explain the *sheji* social model. *Sheji* is an interesting term because it refers both to a whole society and to the local village shrine where officials and common people pray for "prosperity and harmony" by making offerings to ancestors. Pan tells us that Chinese society is based on a "family theory" (*jiating lunli*) that values responsibility—unlike Western society, which is based on individual rights. *Sheji* society, according to Pan, is the bedrock of the success of China's political and economic models: the PRC's state-owned enterprises and private companies are both run like small family businesses; the party loves the people like a caring father; while the masses are loyal, grateful, and respectful, like good children.

Although Pan's description of *guomin* economics seems to balance the public and private sectors, he is very clear that the state is in control in China. As he puts it: "The West and China have taken two different roads: in one, capital, [i.e. the private sector] has captured the state, in the other the state surrounds capital." Leaders are selected from among "sages" (*xianneng*) instead of through competitive multiparty elections. In Pan's view, China is neither a democracy nor an autocracy because the PRC is a "meritocracy." It has the rule of law and an independent judiciary, he claims, but little room for open debate in "civil society," which Pan sees as a battleground of special interests that divides the organic whole.[38]

One of the main goals of the China model discourse thus is to affirm and support Beijing's current system of governance, which is dominated by the CCP. The China model involves tight state control of politics, economy, and society to promote the key values of stability, unity, and statism. It sees Chinese political–economic–cultural trends diverging from Western hegemony, and pits the China model against the "Western" model to promote Chinese exceptionalism against so-called universal values.[39]

In this formulation, Chinese society is figured as a conflict-free organic whole that must be defended from Western corruption. According to Pan, Chinese critics who advocate deeper political reform actually want "to demolish the Forbidden City in order to build the White House" in China so "foreign forces can control China's military, politics, economy and society." China thus is at a "crossroads": "In the next 30 years; what direction will the Chinese nation take? Will it preserve China's rejuvenation? Or will it have superstitious faith in the western 'liberal democracy' system, and go down the road of decline and enslavement?"[40]

Many of Pan's colleagues, however, initially were not convinced, asking: "Since today's West is China's future. Why strain yourself making a China model?"[41] But as the enthusiastic reaction to Pan's edited volume *The China Model* shows, rather than looking to the West for models, now many influential Chinese intellectuals find the correct path to "wealth and power" (*fuqiang*) in their own country.[42] To guarantee China's continued success, Pan tells us that Chinese scholars need "to be confident about their own native civilization to promote the formation of 'Chinese discursive power' and the rise of the 'Chinese school'."[43] The PRC here changes from student to teacher, whose China model can contribute to global prosperity and create global harmony.

Pan's invocation of the "Chinese school" shows that he is concerned with more than China's domestic politics. As the director of Peking University's Center for China and Global Affairs, it should not be surprising that Pan's China model dovetails nicely with the growing demand among the PRC's international relations scholars for a "Chinese school of IR theory." This group of scholars expands from the China model's focus on domestic politics to apply Chinese concepts of order and harmony on a global scale— Great Harmony (*datong*), All-Under-Heaven (*tianxia*), and the Kingly Way (*wangdao*).[44] Indeed, in "The Modern Chinese System" Pan likewise discusses these concepts at length; his goal, after all, is the "World of Great Harmony."

Although not directly supported by the party leadership, the China model discourse infuses debates about wealth and power in China. Pan's explanation shows the productive tension between "socialism" and "Chinese characteristics" I referred to earlier: he appeals to the traditional ideals of Chinese civilization to support the socialist party-state. Still, Pan's plan for the future—although very detailed—is quite vague; he sees the China model less in terms of a set of policy prescriptions than as the sign of China's "cultural renaissance." The description of his ideal Chinese society tells us more about how China (and the world) *should* be, rather than how we might get to this utopian future.

STRATEGIC COMPETITOR: LIU MINGFU'S *THE CHINA DREAM*

Liu Mingfu's *The China Dream: The Great Power Thinking and Strategic Positioning of China in the Post-American Era* generated huge local and global interest when it was published in 2010.[45] In contrast to Beijing's policies of peaceful rise and harmonious world, Liu tells us that to guard its economic rise, China needs to have a "military rise" to contest American hegemony. He warns that China should not strive to become an economic superpower like Japan, which would make China a "plump lamb" that other military powers might gobble up. To be a strong nation, a wealthy country needs to convert its economic success into military power. Rather than follow Deng Xiaoping's peace and development policy of beating swords into ploughshares, Liu tells us that China needs to "Turn some 'money bags' into 'ammunition belts.'"[46]

Yet *The China Dream* does not see conflict with the United States as inevitable: "China's military rise is not to attack America, but to make sure that

China is not attacked by America." Liu is using the logic of deterrence to stress that China must seek peace through strength: its peaceful rise to great power status must include a "military rise with Chinese characteristics that is defensive, peaceful, limited, necessary, important and urgent." If the United States chooses to accommodate China's rise rather than challenge it, then "China's dream need not be America's nightmare," he tells us. The goal of this peaceful military rise is "to grasp the strategic opportunity for strengthening the military" in order to surpass America to become the world's number one military power.[47]

Why should we care about *The China Dream*? Liu is a senior colonel in the People's Liberation Army (PLA), who teaches at China's National Defense University (NDU), so it is reasonable to infer that he reflects some part of the military's views. Yet since Liu is a political officer who deals with ideology rather than a field officer who leads the troops, it is necessary to question whether *The China Dream* is actually that important. Liu himself stresses that his book is not a reflection of official policy: it was written for a mass-market audience and published by a commercial press. Yet even Liu admits that his book "reflects a tide of thought."[48]

Although some commentators warn us not to exaggerate Liu's "extreme" views,[49] *The China Dream* is an important part of the conversation about China's strategic future taking place in the barracks, on the web, and among citizen intellectuals. In response to the book, over 80 percent of the netizens polled by *Huanqiu shibao* [*Global Times*] agreed that China should pursue global military supremacy.[50] The Maoist website "Utopia" reported, with glee, both this popular support and—more important— how foreigners were feeling threatened by *The China Dream*.[51] Indeed, in *On China* Henry Kissinger has analyzed Liu's book as a key example of China's "Triumphalist View."[52]

The book also has been the source of debate among China's military intellectuals. Some have depicted Liu's China dream as a "fantasy," while others like the widely quoted PLA strategist Colonel Dai Xu are even more pessimistic about the likelihood of inevitable conflict between China and the United States.[53] Indeed, compared with the conspiracy theories that characterize much of China's strategic thought,[54] *The China Dream* is quite "reasonable." This debate about China's future is likely to continue, and for this reason we should value *The China Dream* in the same way as *The China Model*: it is important because people are talking about it—and influenced by it.[55]

The China Dream stands, then, as a key example of Chinese citizen intellectuals' plans for the future, where Beijing successfully converts economic resources into enduring global political power. Liu builds on the line of argument first broached in the celebrated Chinese television documentary *The Rise of Great Powers* (2006). This popular series was path-breaking because it challenged China's official historiography; rather than taking the Maoist line of seeing world politics as a contest between Western imperialism and China's anti-imperialist nationalism, *The Rise of Great Powers* studied how Western countries conquered the world to define the modern age. *The China Dream* quotes liberally from Western futurologists: John and Dora Naisbitt's *Megatrends China* (2010), Martin Jacques's *When China Rules the World* (2009), and Goldman Sachs's Jim O'Neill as well as other forecasters of Chinese boom and Western bust. Liu's core message is that Beijing needs to take advantage of the current "period of strategic opportunity" to become the global "champion" that is "world number one."

Although it draws on China's dynastic history and contains dashes of exotic Chinese culture—including discussions of Du Fu's medieval poetry, the kingly way (*wangdao*), and Sunzi's *Art of War*—*The China Dream* is not really interested in classical Chinese thought. Liu's book primarily employs familiar geopolitical concepts to craft China's grand strategy: deterrence, balance of power, and peace through strength. Moreover, Liu also uses socialist history and concepts to argue that "building socialism" in China is a part of "building a harmonious world." In particular, he is fascinated by the Great Leap Forward (1958–61), seeing the outrageous ambition of this Maoist mass movement as the key to China's success in the twenty-first century.[56]

Mao here is described as a top ideologist of "world number one-ism" because he dared to craft a grand plan to surpass America, stating that beating the United States would be China's greatest contribution to humanity. As recent studies have documented, the Great Leap Forward led to the world's worst famine with a death toll of over 30 million people.[57] Liu admits that the Great Leap Forward "suffered defeat" and that "a large population met an irregular death."[58] But Mao's key mistake, Liu tells us, was that he got the timetable wrong: rather than fifteen years, China would need ninety years to become the world's number-one power. Liu thus understands Deng Xiaoping's post-Maoist reform and opening policy as a continuation of Mao's Great Leap Forward plan. China's current (and future) success, in this telling, is the product of Mao's ambitious aspirations. (The World Bank's Chief Economist Justin Yifu Lin, on the other hand, persuasively argues that Mao's political campaigns to develop heavy industry retarded China's economic development.[59])

What are Liu's goals once his China dream comes true? In the book's conclusion he tells us that Beijing will make three major innovations to guarantee China's long-term peace and security:

- Create the miracle of a hierarchical Chinese-style democracy that is bet-ter than the more egalitarian American-style democracy.
- Create the miracle of "wealth distribution" that is fairer than the "welfare state."
- Create the miracle of "long-term honest and clean governance" in a single-party state that is more effective than "multiparty competition."[60]

Liu's three major innovations are ideological and bureaucratic rather than technological. Like Pan, he narrows world politics to a battle between the China model and the American model. *The China Dream* thus is intertwined with the American dream of democracy and prosperity. Liu celebrates a cer-tain type of competition: competition between great powers is natural and good, while competition between political parties is a problem. His China model looks to the CCP as the source of ideas for a better, stronger, and more creative country that would be a model for the world.

Despite all his optimism, Liu still nurses various national anxieties. Like many strategists, he is convinced that Washington is actively conspir-ing to contain the rejuvenation of the Chinese nation. He sees competi-tion with the United States as a zero-sum game of total victory—or total defeat: "If China in the 21st century cannot become world number one, cannot become the top power, then inevitably it will become a straggler that is cast aside."[61] In this respect, Liu's book shows the uneasy combina-tion of ambition and anxiety that is common among China's citizen intel-lectuals. He frames China's ambition in simple terms: to be the world's number-one superpower. Like many other speeches, books, articles, blogs, and films, *The China Dream*'s optimism about China's future is infectious; it oozes confidence by presenting China's rise almost as inevitable, a matter of when—not if. But an important undercurrent of pessimism remains in Liu's combative formulation of global politics.

How do these ideas relate to Hu Jintao's concept of "harmonious world?" Rather than follow Hu Jintao's advice to build a world that tolerates different social systems and civilizations, Liu explains that "in order to build a har-monious world, [China's] competitive spirit must be strengthened." China's competitive spirit is not just economic, but militaristic: "To rejuvenate the Chinese nation, we need to rejuvenate China's martial spirit."[62] Rather than talk about China's strategic industries as "national champions," Liu stresses how China needs to become the "champion nation." In this way, Liu refocuses China's ambitions from economic growth back to political–military power.

However, Liu looks to ideas associated with harmonious society as the ultimate challenge to a bold Chinese strategic future. In his view, China's own internal problems present the greatest challenge to his vision. Rather than being a crisis of governance or institutions, Liu sees China's problems as a "leadership crisis" of civilian cadres who are corrupt, mediocre, and inflexible. After a detailed discussion of how civilian corruption brought down the Communist Party of the Soviet Union, Liu proposes that Beijing solve its leadership crisis through better "knowledge planning" and better cadre training. The main goal of Liu's ambition is not to build a harmonious world or promote the China model for the benefit of humanity but simply to strengthen China's party-state. He thus appeals much more to the "socialism" element in "socialism with Chinese characteristics." It is necessary to note, however, that Liu also employs China's dynastic history and civilization in his arguments for a strong leadership.[63]

TENSIONS AMONG COMPETING WORLD ORDERS

As argued earlier, Deng Xiaoping's 1982 slogan "socialism with Chinese characteristics" can help us understand how alternative world orders are conceptualized in China. Hu's harmonious world contains a balance between socialist construction and harmonious culture. Pan's China model is based on China's traditional concepts of harmony and order; but it actualizes its normative view of society through China's party-state. Liu's goal in the *China Dream* is to complete Mao Zedong's Great Leap Forward to surpass the United States to become world number one—an argument that he, like Pan, frames in terms of Chinese history and civilization.

These three views of the world's future show the range of commentary produced by the opportunities opened by harmonious world discourse. All are very optimistic about China's future: they believe that China's success will continue, and that the rejuvenation of the Chinese nation largely is inevitable. They all agree that China needs its own worldview, which is by definition different from European and American world orders. In different ways, they all feel that China has a moral mission to improve the world, either as a peace-loving nation or through its martial spirit. Otherwise, all three are quite vague about the details of their world orders; Pan and Liu, in particular, are much clearer about what they do not like—America and the West—than they are about what they do like. Their impact thus may be more negative—to delegitimize the current world order—than positive in the sense of promoting a coherent post-Western world order.

Alongside these shared themes, there are tensions between Hu's, Pan's, and Liu's visions of the future, which offer different concepts and different methods for ordering the world. Hu's harmonious world employs mainstream liberal views of international politics: equal nation-states engaging in multilateral diplomacy toward positive sum win-win solutions of mutual security and prosperity. But he quickly switches to see world harmony as the tolerant interaction of discrete, but still equal, civilizations. Pan's China model likewise focuses on civilization. However, his world harmony is holistic and hierarchical; the ultimate goal is to integrate all "divisions" into the natural organic whole—the "World of Great Harmony" (*Datong shijie*). Rather than a positive-sum win-win strategy, the China model does not allow for much diversity in China or abroad. Liu's China dream, on the other hand, is not about diplomacy or harmony—it is a zero-sum great power competition that produces clear winners and losers. But as with the other two worldviews, Liu's nations quickly become civilizations, and then races: he ultimately sees world politics as a competition between the "yellow race" and the "white race."[64]

There are unexpected crossovers: although Hu presented harmonious world as a diplomatic strategy, citizen intellectuals also try to recruit the military into their harmonious world. In October 2010, for example, the UN Undersecretary-General Sha Zukang gave General Chi Haotian the "World Harmony Award" for his contributions to world peace. Chi was an odd choice for a harmony prize: this former Defense Minister is most famous for ordering the military assault on protesters in Beijing on the night of June 3, 1989, which killed approximately one thousand citizens. Although the Chinese press announcement suggested that this was a UN award, it actually came from the World Harmony Foundation, which is organized by a Chinese businessman.[65] The "World Harmony Award," which was a response to Chinese dissident Liu Xiaobo's Nobel Peace Prize, highlights how citizens and officials think that world harmony, diplomacy and the military are intertwined in China. It also suggests that world harmony is not necessarily peaceful.

This was confirmed when China's new Confucius Peace Prize was given to Russian Prime Minister Vladimir Putin in 2011 primarily for his decision to go to war in Chechnya in 1999. As the award committee explained, Putin's "iron hand and toughness revealed in this war impressed the Russians a lot, and he was regarded to be capable of bringing safety and stability to Russia."[66] While Confucianism talks about peace coming from harmony, here peace is the result of violence.

Hence, in all three scenarios there is a tension between the more modest goal of fostering world harmony and the more aggressive project of harmonizing the world—by force, if necessary.

CONCLUSION

How can we explain Beijing's recent turn from a modest foreign policy to a more assertive global stance? While there are material sources of this change, this chapter, in ways that the Introduction to this volume has suggested, shows that we also need to pay close attention to how ideas shape opinion makers' views of the world. Alongside China's current "era of many troubles" in East Asia, Europe, and America there is a growing unrest among China's citizen intellectuals; new voices are challenging the foreign policy establishment's monopoly on discussion of China's place in the world. Indeed, prominent strategist Yan Xuetong recently lamented the declining status of professional strategists in the face of popular (and populist) views from outside the security studies fraternity.

However, this chapter has shown that it is necessary to recognize that China has multiple strategies and multiple futures—for many Chinas. Citizen intellectuals like Pan Wei and Liu Mingfu are important because they take advantage of the openings provided by vague government policy to develop China's geostrategy in new directions. Such citizen intellectuals are interesting and influential because as relative outsiders they can give us a sense of the parameters within which official policies (like harmonious world) are formulated, implemented, defended—and rejected. Together with Hu's harmonious world, they provide a range of views—from idealist to realist—that help us to understand better the range of possibilities for China's post-Western world order.

What they do not provide is clear answers about China's future foreign policy. But such arguments beg the question of whether Beijing actually has a clear foreign policy that could be discovered through Kremlinological methods. My argument is that rather than search for a clear unified foreign policy, it is more productive to analyze a range of views and catalogue the possibilities that are being discussed in China, while noting both their negative and their positive influences.

It is common for Chinese theorists to assert that China will be a different kind of superpower which offers more peaceful, moral, and harmonious norms as its contribution to world civilization—a point that is illustrated in chapter 2 in this volume. This should not be surprising; rising powers typically promote their unique values as the moral model for a better world order—Europe's *Mission civilisatrice*, America's free world, Japan's economic miracle, and so on. But rather than promote a "Chinese exceptionalism" the chapter's examples suggest that Chinese international relations (IR) theory is better understood as a response to mainstream IR theory; instead of being a unique alternative, it is *intertwined* with the dominant schools of realism, liberalism, and idealism. Although they are not exactly the same as theories in Europe and America, the difference is a matter of degree rather than of kind: a Chinese-inflected realism, for example.

Citizen intellectuals also remind us that analysis of Chinese foreign policy still needs to take socialism seriously. While its power as a revolutionary ideology has declined, socialism as a way of thinking (especially in its Leninist–modernist form) still informs the way that problems and solutions are formulated in China. This helps to explain the enduring influence of top-down centralized planning in China's various dreams of the future.

Finally, although official and unofficial Chinese texts tend to write as if China's victory is imminent, in fact the PRC is unlikely to catch up to the United States economically, politically, culturally, or militarily in the next few decades. This disjuncture between grand ambitions and middling capabilities could lead to conflict because Beijing is promising its citizens much more than it can deliver in terms of global power and influence. A "propaganda gap" of this kind could well increase tensions between China and the West in the next few years, especially as populist voices demanding a post-Western world order are growing louder with Beijing's transition to the fifth-generation leadership that assumes power as Hu Jintao and Wen Jiabao retire in 2012–13.

NOTES

1. Hu Jintao, "Nuli jianshe tejiu heping, gongtong fanrong de hexie shijie—zai Lianheguo chenglie 60 zhounian shounaohuiyi shang de jianghua" ["Making an effort to build a sustainable, peaceful, and united prosperous harmonious world"], [speech at the Summit for the 60th anniversary of the United Nations], *Renmin ribao* [*People's Daily*], September 16, 2005, p. 1. For a discussion of China's new assertive foreign policy since 2009, see David Shambaugh, "Coping with a conflicted China," *The Washington Quarterly*, Vol. 34, No. 1 (Winter 2011), pp. 7–27; Shi Yinhong, *Quanqiuxing de tiaozhan yu Zhongguo: Duoshi zhi qiu yu Zhongguo de zhanlüe xuyao* [*China and Global Challenges: China's Strategic Needs in an Era of Many Troubles*] (Changsha: Hunan renmin chubanshe, 2010).
2. Pan Wei, ed., *Zhongguo Moshi—Jiedu Renmin Gongheguo de 60 Nian* [*The China Model: Reading 60 Years of the People's Republic*] (Beijing: Zhongyang bianshi chubanshe, 2009); Liu Mingfu, *Zhongguo meng: Hou Meiguo shidai de gaguo siwei zhanlüe dingwei* [*The China Dream: The Great Power Thinking and Strategic Positioning of China in the post-American Era*] (Beijing: Zhongguo youyi chuban gongsi, 2010).
3. See, for example, Pan Wei, "Zhongguo moshi shi chuse de liyi pingheng xingshi" ["The China model provides excellent balance of interests"], *Caijing wang*, April 12, 2010. Available: http://www.caijing.com.cn/2010-04-12/110414851.html; "Chen Zhiwu, Pan Wei tan Zhongguo moshi" ["Chen Zhiwu and Pan Wei discuss the China model"] *Renwu zhoukan*, August 28, 2011. Available: http://www.21ccom.net/articles/zgyj/gqmq/2011/0829/44209.html; E'hu Shusheng, "Caifang Hugong

Pinglun zhi Liu: Guanyu Liu Mingfu de *Zhongguo meng*" ["Six critical comments on Liu Mingfu's *The China Dream*"], *Qiangguo Luntan* [Strong Nation Forum] bulletin board, *People's Daily* (Beijing), February 23, 2010. Available: http://bbs1.people.com.cn/postDetail.do?boardId=2&treeView=1&view=2&id=978544 20 [September 7, 2011].

4. See Yan Xuetong, "Xun Zi's thoughts on international politics and their implications," *Chinese Journal of International Politics*, Vol. 2, No. 1 (Summer 2008), pp. 135–65; Qin Yaqing, "Guoji Guanxi Lilun Zhongguo Pai Shengcheng de Keneng he Biran" ["The Chinese school of international relations theory: Possibility and necessity"], *Shijie jingji yu zhengzhi*, No. 3 (March 2006), pp. 7–13.

5. See Frank N. Pieke, *The Good Communist: Elite Training and State Building in Today's China* (Cambridge: Cambridge University Press, 2009), pp. 180–95.

6. "An era of many troubles" is the subtitle of Shi, *Quanqiuxing de tiaozhan*.

7. See Randall L. Schweller and Xiaoyu Pu, "After unipolarity: China's visions of international order in an era of U.S. decline," *International Security*, Vol. 36, No. 1 (Summer 2011), pp. 57–62.

8. I explore the cultural politics of China's mix of ambitions and anxieties in William A. Callahan, *China: The Pessoptimist Nation* (Oxford: Oxford University Press, 2010).

9. Daniel Lynch, "Chinese thinking on the future of international relations: Realism as the *Ti*, rationalism as the *Yong*?" *China Quarterly*, Vol. 197 (March 2009), pp. 87–107; Shambaugh, "Coping with a conflicted China."

10. For a more detailed analysis of the category "citizen intellectual," see William A. Callahan, "Shanghai's alternative futures: The World Expo, citizen intellectuals and China's new civil society," *China Information*, Vol. 26 (July 2012), p. 2.

11. Allen Carlson, "Moving beyond sovereignty? A brief consideration of recent changes in China's approach to international order and the emergence of the Tianxia concept," *Journal of Contemporary China*, Vol. 20, No. 68 (January 2011), p. 98; also see Phillip C. Saunders, "Will China's dream turn into America's nightmare?" *China Brief*, Vol. 10, No. 7 (April 1, 2010).

12. For another analysis that appeals to unofficial texts, see Christopher R. Hughes, "Reclassifying Chinese nationalism: The geopolitik turn," *Journal of Contemporary China*, Vol. 20, No. 71 (September 2011), pp. 601–20.

13. Linda Jakobson and Dean Knox, *New Foreign Policy Actors in China*, SIPRI Policy Paper No. 26 (Stockholm: Stockholm International Peace Research Institute, 2010).

14. Shi, *China and the Challenges of Globalization*, pp. 2–39.

15. PRC State Council, "China's Peaceful Development Road," White Paper (Beijing: Xinhua, December 22, 2005); Hu Jintao, "Hold High the Great Banner of Socialism with Chinese Characteristics and Strive for New Victories in Building a Moderately Prosperous Society in All Respects: Report to the Seventeenth National Congress of the Communist Party of China on Oct 15, 2007." Available: http://www.china.org.cn/english/congress/229611.htm.

16. For a critical analysis of China's economic success, see Yasheng Huang, *Capitalism with Chinese Characteristics: Entrepreneurship and the State* (New York: Cambridge University Press, 2008).

17. "Harmonious world: China's ancient philosophy for new international order," *People's Daily*, October 2, 2007. This article also discusses harmonious society.

18. Qin Xiaoying, "Harmonious society to be model for the world," *China Daily*, October 13, 2006.

19. "Wen Wei Po reports 17th Party Congress report to include 'harmonious world' concept," *Wen Wei Po* (Hong Kong), October 15, 2010, translated in OSC: 20071015710009.

20. Beijing's latest White Paper continues this trend (State Council, "China's Peaceful Development" (Beijing: Xinhua, September 6, 2011).

21. Jin Shu, "Guang yu ying hexie shijie" ["Light and shadow in a harmonious world"], *Beijing fangdi chan*, No. 7 (July 2003), pp. 108–09.

22. According to a search of the China Academic Journals Full-Text Database of articles published between 2005 and 2010, 1,194 use "*hexie shijie*-harmonious world" in their title, and 3,355 use it as a keyword. This does not include books, chapters, and newspaper articles.

23. Wang has since moved to Peking University.

24. "PRC academics advocate building more harmonious world, society," *Renmin wang* [People's Net], November 9, 2005, translated in OSC: 200511091477.

25. See Zhang Wei-wei, "Yige qijo de pouxi: Zhongguo moshi jiqi yiyi" ["The analysis of a miracle: the China model and its significance"] *Qiushi*, No. 6 (2011). Available: http://www.qstheory.cn/hqwg/2011/201106/201103/t20110325_74156.htm; Yang Jisheng, "Wo kan 'Zhongguo moshi'" ["How I see the 'China model'"], *Yanhuang Chunqiu*, No. 1 (January 2011). Available: http://www.yhcqw.com/html/yjy/2011/111/11111154637F25138183GEIIK85G9CDD4JB.html.For a partial translation of these two articles, see David Bandurski, "Zhang vs. Yang on the China model," *China Media Project*, March 29, 2011. Available: http://cmp.hku.hk/2011/03/29/11205/.

26. "China's development 'not a model': Premier Wen," *Xinhua*, March 14, 2011.

27. Zhang, "Yige qijo de pouxi."

28. Pan Wei, "Dangdai Zhonghua tizhi: Zhongguo moshi ed jingji, zhengzhi, she-hui jiexi" ["Modern Chinese System: Analysis of the China Model of Economics, Politics and Society"], in *Zhongguo moshi: jiedu renmin gongheguo de 60 nian [The China Model: Reading 60 Years of the People's Republic]*, edited by Pan Wei (Beijing: Zhongyang bianshi chubanshe, 2009), pp. 3–85; Zhang Wei-wei, *Zhongguo zhen-han: Yige "wenming xing guojia" de jueqi [China Shock: The Rise of a "Civilization-State"]* (Shanghai: Renmin chubanshe, 2011). In 2012, Zhang's book was revised and translated into English as *The China Wave* (Zhang Wei-wei, *The China Wave: Rise of a Civilizational State* (Singapore: World Scientific, 2012)).

29. Zhang Wei-wei, *Ideology and Economic Reform Under Deng Xiaoping* (London: Kegan Paul, 1996); Zhang Wei-wei, *Transforming China: Economic Reform and Its Political Implications* (London: Macmillan, and New York: St. Martin's Press, 2000).

30. Other examples of New Left/neoconservative intellectuals are Hu Angang, Cui Zhiyuan, and Yan Xuetong. See Peter Martin and David Cohen, "Your Questions for Pan Wei," in *The Interpreter* (Sydney: The Lowy Institute for International Policy, July 13, 2011). Available: http://www.lowyinterpreter.org/post/2011/07/13/Your-questions-for-Pan-Wei.aspx.

31. Zhang, "Yige qijo de pouxi"; Pan Wei, *The Chinese Model of Development* (London: Foreign Policy Centre, October 11, 2007); Pan Wei, *Western System versus Chinese System*, China Policy Institute Briefing Series—Issue 61, University of Nottingham, July 2010.

32. Yasheng Huang, "Rethinking the Beijing consensus," *Asia Policy*, No. 11 (January 2011), pp. 1–26.

33. Pan, "Dangdai Zhonghua tizhi," p. 6.

34. Also see Pan's contribution to "Explaining the Rise of China: A Challenge to Western Social Science Theories?," Panel sponsored by the Harvard-Yenching Institute and the Fairbank Center for Chinese Studies, Harvard University, April 5, 2010. Available: http://www.harvard-yenching.org/sites/harvard-yenching.org/files/featurefiles/Rise%20of%20China%20 Transcript_final.pdf.
35. Pan, "Dangdai Zhonghua tizhi," pp. 5, 12.
36. Justin Yifu Lin, Fang Cai, and Zhou Li, *The China Miracle: Development Strategy and Economic Reform*, rev. ed. (Hong Kong: Chinese University Press, 2003).
37. Pan, "Dangdai Zhonghua tizhi," pp. 29, 30.
38. Ibid., pp. 18, 29
39. Other voices in the exceptionalist tradition are discussed in Chapter 2 in this volume.
40. Pan, "Dangdai Zhonghua tizhi," pp. 58, 83, 82, 22, 56.
41. Ibid, p. 6.
42. See Bandurski, "Zhang vs. Yang on the China model."
43. Pan, "Dangdai Zhonghua tizhi," p. 6.
44. See Yan, "Xun Zi's Thoughts"; Qin, "Guoji Guanxi Lilun Zhongguo Pai"; Zhao Tingyang, *Tianxia Tixi: Shijie Zhidu Zhexue Daolun* [*The Tianxia System: The Philosophy for the World Institution*] (Nanjing: Jiangsu jiaoyu chubanshe, 2005). For a discussion of the China school, see William A. Callahan and Elena Barabantseva, eds., *China Orders the World: Normative Soft Power and Foreign Policy* (Baltimore: Johns Hopkins University Press, 2012).
45. See Li Yue, "Liu Mingfu: Zhong-Mei Jingzheng Shi Yi Chang Tianjingsai" ["Liu Mingfu: Sino-US competition is a track and field competition"], *Jingbao* (Shenzhen, China), January 23, 2010. Available: http://jb.sznews.com/html/2010-01/23/content_941864.htm; Cheng Gang, "Liu Mingfu Dui Benbao Shuo: Zhongguo Zheng Dang Shijie Guanjun he 'Taoguang Yanghui' Bu Maodun" ["Liu Mingfu tells this paper: China struggling to be the world's number one power does not contradict the 'lay low' policy," *Huanqiu shibao*, March 2, 2010. Available: http://world.huanqiu.com/roll/2010-03/730751.html; Chris Buckley, "China PLA officer urges challenging U.S. dominance," Reuters, March 1, 2010; Saunders, "Will China's dream turn into America's nightmare?"
46. Liu, *Zhongguo meng*, pp. 255, 244.
47. Ibid., pp. 263, 25.
48. Cited in Buckley, "China PLA officer urges challenging U.S. dominance."
49. Saunders, "Will China's Dream turn into America's nightmare."
50. "Benqi Huati: Zhongguo Ying Zhuaqiu Diyi Junshi Qiangguo Diwei Ma?" ["Current topic: Should China pursue the status of top military power?"], Huanqiu Debate website. Available: http://debate.huanqiu.com/2010-03/730727.html [September 9, 2011].
51. Cheng Gang, "Jiefang jun daxiao Liu Mingfu zhuzhang Zhongguo zhengzuo shijie di yi junshi qiangguo" ["Liu Mingfu of the PLA emphasizes that China will become the world's number one superpower"], in *Wuyouzhixiang* [Utopia], March 3, 2010. Available: http://www.wyzxsx.com/Article/Class22/201003/134608.html [July 14, 2011].
52. Henry Kissinger, *On China* (New York: Allen Lane, 2011), pp. 504–07, 521.
53. "China's aim of being top military superpower may be a dream," *Global Times*, March 3, 2010. Also see Zhang Wenmu, *Lun Zhongguo Haiquan*, 2nd ed. [*China's Maritime Power*] (Beijing: Haiyang chubanshe, 2010); Major General Luo Yuan, "Zhongguo Yao

Cheng Yiliu Qiangguo Buxu You Shangwu Jingshen" ["To become first class power China must have martial spirit"], *Huanqiu shibao,* December 12, 2010.

54. See Gilbert Rozman, *Chinese Strategic Thought toward Asia* (New York: Palgrave, 2010).

55. See "Zhengdang Shijie 'Guanjun Guojia,' Zhongguo Meng?" ["Is striving to become the world's 'champion country' the China dream?"], *Huanqiu wang* [Global Web], March 3, 2010. Available: http://opinion.huanqiu.com/roll/2010-03/732792. html; E'hu Shusheng, "Caifang Hugong Pinglun zhi Liu," *Qiangguo Luntan* [Strong Nation Forum] bulletin board.

56. Liu, *Zhongguo meng,* pp. 9–13.

57. Yang Jisheng, *Mubei: Zhongguo Liushi Niandai Da Jihuang Jishi* [*Tombstone: An Account of Chinese Famine in the 1960s*] (Hong Kong: Cosmos Books, 2008).

58. Liu, *Zhongguo meng,* p. 11.

59. See Justin Yifu Lin, Fang Cai, and Zhou Li, *The China Miracle: Development Strategy and Economic Reform,* rev. ed. (Hong Kong: Chinese University Press, 2003).

60. Liu, *Zhongguo meng,* pp. 298–302.

61. Ibid., p. 9.

62. Ibid., pp. 184, 245.

63. Ibid., p. 245.

64. Ibid., p. 22.

65. "Chi Haotian huo lianheguo shijie hexie renwu jiang" ["Chi Haotian wins U.N.'s world peace prize"], *Xinhua* (Beijing), October 28, 2010; also see http://www.whf-foundation.org.

66. Quoted in Edward Wong, "For Putin, a peace prize for a decision to go to war," *New York Times,* November 15, 2011.

CHAPTER 2

ᕫᕫᕫ

Chinese Exceptionalism in the Intellectual World of China's Foreign Policy

FENG ZHANG*

Studies of Chinese foreign policy have long recognized that China possesses a distinctive set of foreign policy principles derived from the country's historical experience and its complex political and cultural traditions. Few analyses, however, have deployed the idea of "Chinese exceptionalism." Occasionally, a particular form of China's exceptionalism is suggested, such as when Barry Buzan notes "an inward-looking type of national exceptionalism"[1] and when Samuel Kim distinguishes between American exceptionalism in terms of Manifest Destiny and Chinese "exemptionalism" in terms of the so-called Middle Kingdom complex.[2] Chris Alden and Daniel Large, in the special case of China–Africa relations, posit a form of exceptionalism characterized by the rhetorical claims of mutual respect and political equality.[3] However, such investigations, generally, are insufficiently detailed for understanding the nature of China's claim to uniqueness in international relations.

If by exceptionalism we mean the unique qualities—from the particular set of political and social values to the special historical trajectory and foreign relations experience—that differentiate one country from another,

*. Thanks are due to Rosemary Foot for her helpful guidance on this chapter. Some materials used in this chapter will also appear in Feng Zhang, "The rise of Chinese exceptionalism in international relations," *European Journal of International Relations*, Vol. 19, No. 3 (2013).

then China certainly has its own version. Many other countries, from the United States to Singapore, can also be described as exceptionalist. But because China is a rising great power, the specific character and quality of its exceptionalism matter more than those of most other countries, just as American exceptionalism has long been a prominent topic in the foreign policy literature. This literature, however, has long been written as though exceptionalism were all of the American type or a variant of it.[4] This chapter attempts to show a Chinese version of foreign policy exceptionalism that is distinct from the American brand. Its main purpose is to identify and explain the exceptionalist assertions that can be found in China's copious historical literature, official documents, and intellectual writings.

These exceptionalist ideals have been in place for a long time, from imperial China through the revolutionary People's Republic of China (PRC) and on to the present day. However, only recently have Chinese views of international relations, in the official, semi-official, and intellectual circles been gathering pace and showing some originality of thought. The five years between 2005 and 2010, for example, have marked the appearance of three distinctive sets of literature whose academic and policy influence is likely to grow: neo-Tianxiaism (*tianxia* is a Chinese term usually translated as "all under heaven") symbolized by the philosopher Zhao Tingyang,[5] the project on China's pre-Qin thoughts of international relations led by Yan Xuetong at Tsinghua University,[6] and the "China model" literature with notable inputs from Pan Wei at Peking University whose work is discussed in detail in chapter 1 in this volume.[7] The Chinese government, meanwhile, has also produced new concepts such as "peaceful development" and "harmonious world," both of which have been consolidated in the official discourse since 2005. Future historians might look back and identify 2005 as the start of post-reform-China's cultural and ideological rise. Although a coherent Chinese vision is still in the making, we can no longer ignore Chinese ideas about international relations and their policy impact. As the Introduction to this volume points out, arguments about the sources of state behavior and identity, for example, where persuasive, can shape common understandings about the nature of the activities that seem appropriate for the state to take. Exceptionalism does not determine policy, but by being an essential part of the worldview of the Chinese government and many intellectuals, it can become an important source for policy ideas. Indeed, it could be interpreted as a normative theory for China's foreign policy, as one, and a hitherto neglected, intellectual school among six major schools competing for ideational influence in China's foreign policy formation.

Identifying China's exceptionalism is important for another purpose. Scholars are increasingly asking the question of what China thinks and wants in international politics: "The great strategic issue of our times is not just China's rising power but whether its worldview and applied theory will reproduce, converge with, or take a separate path from the world order and ideas produced in the era of trans-Atlantic dominance."[8] However, most international relations (IR) theories offer little guidance as to what China will want, other than a few very general predictions such as the realist one that a rising China will expand its interests abroad.[9] Constructivists, on the other hand, are interested in ideas but many focus on policy content, neglecting detailed examination of China's foreign policy discourse and behavior.[10] One aim of this chapter is to provide that detailed examination from the angle of exceptionalism—an important perspective on the emerging Chinese visions of international relations. It also challenges the widespread perception that China has never had a foreign relations ideology.[11] One trouble with Chinese foreign policy today is not that it does not have a vision or ideology but that this vision, still in its inception, is vague, self-centered, and largely defensive. A further implication is that the sources for the ideational construction of China's foreign policy will come largely from its own historical and cultural traditions rather than from the West. As traditions are being revived in China, analysts must also come to grips with the role of history and culture in contemporary Chinese policy thinking.

The chapter begins with a brief discussion of the role of intellectuals in China's foreign policy, suggesting the importance of intellectual debates for understanding policy evolution. Two main sections follow to examine the features and sources of contemporary Chinese exceptionalism. The final section draws out the implications by comparing Chinese exceptionalism with American exceptionalism and by placing it within the larger intellectual world of China's foreign policy.

INTELLECTUALS AND CHINA'S FOREIGN POLICY

What roles have China's intellectuals played in the formulation of its foreign policy, and how has that changed over time? In imperial China, especially after the year 622 when a formal examination system was introduced to select talents for government service, the *shi* (scholar) occupied a central position in state power and was an integral part of the ruling apparatus. After the end of the nineteenth century, however, this class became increasingly marginalized in Chinese society and politics and was transformed into what we now call *zhishi fenzi* (intellectual). As a result, intellectuals were removed from the center to the periphery of state power.[12] This did not mean the complete loss of their influence, however, as the May Fourth Movement of the late 1910s and 1920s, whose intellectual ideas shaped China's momentous twentieth century, demonstrated.[13]

The fate of intellectuals in the PRC has endured some remarkable vicissitudes. Their abuse by the Maoist totalitarian regime left little room for policy influence.[14] They gained some freedom in the Deng era but were far from an independent political influence. Although this is still generally the case, intellectuals have been playing a more important role in China's public policy debates in the post-Deng era. Both the Jiang Zemin and Hu Jintao regimes allowed greater freedom of expression and at times encouraged those from the "think tank" and the university communities to participate in policy discussion and consultation.[15] Since the early twenty-first century, observers have increasingly noted "China's intellectual awakening," contending that China's intellectuals are more influential than their counterparts in many Western countries paradoxically because China's repressive political system makes intellectual debates a surrogate form of politics.[16]

Intellectual debates are important because they provide a window into the thinking and making of China's foreign policy. Chinese intellectuals are currently engaged in a number of intensive, extensive, and animated debates.[17] The most consequential is perhaps the debate on whether or not to revise or even abandon Deng Xiaoping's strategic injunction of *Tao Guang Yang Hui* (commonly if somewhat misleadingly translated as "hide our capabilities and bide our time"),[18] almost universally seen to have been the fundamental principle underpinning Chinese foreign policy since the early 1990s. This is really a debate about the future direction of China's grand strategy. Other important and consequential debates include whether China needs alliances,[19] the relationship between its U.S. policy and its neighborhood policy in the Asian region, and the causes of the deterioration of its security environment after 2008. I examine exceptionalism as one and a hitherto neglected intellectual and political agenda while placing it within the overall intellectual world of China's foreign policy. Importantly, Chinese exceptionalism is the product of a number of groups and individuals, including the government as well as intellectuals, but intellectuals and their ideas are a significant contributor to the formation of this school, and since they discuss this topic in far greater detail than government officials, they are the more helpful guide for understanding the foundation and evolution of China's exceptionalism.

CONTEMPORARY CHINA'S EXCEPTIONALISM

Chinese exceptionalism is a historical phenomenon with distinctive yet related manifestations in different eras of China's long history. Imperial China's (221 B.C.–A.D. 1911) exceptionalism, for example, may be characterized as a mixture of imperial sinocentrism, benevolent pacifism, and magnanimous inclusionism, compared with Maoist China's (1949–76) exceptionalism made up of revolutionary sinocentrism, great power entitlement, and moralism.[20] A new triumvirate of ideas characterizes China's exceptionalism since the reform period, particularly from the late 1990s: great power reformism, benevolent pacifism, and harmonious inclusionism.

Great power reformism

The PRC government and many intellectuals have inherited the historical understanding of China as a great power, and they take it for granted that, though it may be long and hard to realize, being a great power is China's historical destiny, especially in economic terms. One commentator attributes China's inveterate "great power dream" to an implicit sinocentric mentality influenced by the myth of imperial China as the "heavenly dynasty."[21] But, importantly, the emerging discourse is more than just a normal claim to China's great power status; it increasingly stresses the unique qualities of the *Chinese-ness* attached to this great power status. As Zhao Tingyang, an influential philosopher at the Chinese Academy of Social Sciences (CASS), declares, China can become a new kind of great power—one that is responsible for the whole world, but in a different way from earlier empires.[22]

This attempt to define China as a new great power is part of the larger political and intellectual project to construct China's national identity, create China's worldview, and develop a Chinese diplomatic philosophy for its foreign relations. A necessary task of developing such a philosophy is held to be the need to surpass Western theory and practice, that is, to show that China will not repeat the violent and disastrous paths of rising powers in Western history, that a rising China will strive to build a peaceful and harmonious world rather than playing the zero-sum game of power politics, and that China will provide a new ideal for the common development of all countries in the world.[23] An implicit assumption is that for China—an ancient, proud, and in many ways superior civilizational state—to follow the Western precepts of great power politics is at best inappropriate and at worst humiliating. A rising China cannot just be a great power of material strength, which would make it no different from other great powers in history; instead, it must also become a "knowledge producer"[24] by digging deep into China's traditional historical and cultural resources,[25] to be able to develop unique qualities for playing its role in the new era.

In short, China's great power reformism is the exceptionalist claim that China as a great power will challenge the typical historical trajectory of rising powers, redefine the meaning of being a great power, and reform world politics through the development and practice of its unique international relations principles and ideals. Such a claim is commonplace in the official and semi-official discourse, particularly in the assertion that China has always conducted a peaceful foreign policy and will not threaten or challenge anyone, and it is intimately connected with the two other components of contemporary China's exceptionalism.

Benevolent pacifism

The claim to pacifism has a distinguished pedigree in Chinese history. Imperial China, at least for certain dynasties such as the Ming (1368–1644), professed to offer peace and benevolence in its foreign relations and thus to confer order and stability in its periphery. Many Chinese scholars argue that the basic international purpose of the Ming and of the Chinese empires in general was to "share the fortune of peace" with other polities by conducting a peaceful foreign policy.[26]

The essential claim of contemporary pacifism is no different from that of its imperial predecessor. However, imperial Chinese foreign policy, having now been mythologized and presented as an alternative to Western models, is utilized as the most important evidential support for pacifism today. It is frequently asserted that the culture of imperial China gave rise to a peaceful and defensive empire with war viewed only as a last resort. According to Li Shaojun, a prominent IR scholar in CASS, traditional culture stabilized China's internal and external relations through assimilation and integration of different peoples and cultures. Contrasting Chinese with Western culture, he claims that the former has contributed to ethnic integration inside China while the latter has given rise to numerous wars and conflicts in the global expansion of capitalism.[27]

Having established imperial China's pacifist tradition, emphasized China's agonizing experience in the modern world, and professed China's intention to never inflict similar sufferings on other countries, the PRC claims that it will always adopt a peaceful foreign policy, will never threaten anyone, and will help to maintain world peace through its own development. This discourse pervades official and semi-official statements. A particularly famous example is China's "peaceful rise" thesis propagated by the influential "scholar-official" Zheng Bijian.[28] The best official articulations are the government's 2005 and 2011 White Papers on "China's peaceful development"[29] and State Councilor Dai Bingguo's essay on "Persisting with Taking the Path of Peaceful Development" released in December 2010.[30]

Harmonious inclusionism

The third component of the emerging exceptionalism is "harmonious inclusionism." The idea consists of a set of interrelated propositions. First, rejecting the legitimacy of the domination of one country, ideology, or approach in world politics, it advocates international cooperation and accommodation by adopting an open, tolerant, and inclusive attitude toward the multiplicity and diversity of political and cultural traditions in the world. China itself will seek further integration with the international system. Second, inclusionism refers not just to the acknowledgment of the legitimacy of different political and cultural traditions and the need to incorporate them into global governance but also the position that all countries need to be included in a process of achieving common security, development, and prosperity based on open multilateralism and mutually beneficial cooperation. The objective is to realize common and universal security and development for all countries, not just for one or a few great powers. For its part, China offers to share the benefits of its development with other countries, accommodate political and cultural differences, and strive to create a "harmonious world."

On the face of it, this seems a rather lackluster—if not a vague and vacuous—position, and this may be the reason we have commonly missed it. But, in fact, this perspective is already making an impact even at this early stage, not only occupying a central place in the official policy discourse but also inspiring a wave of research on its implications for future policy change, and it might become the most profound among China's special claims about international relations once the associated ideas are fully developed. At this point, effective examination of it requires the tracing of three recent discourses in China's intellectual circles: the application of the ancient idea of "harmony with difference" (he er butong), the ongoing official discourse on the "harmonious world" (hexie shijie), and the popular "neo-Tianxiaism" (xin tianxia zhuyi).

The term "harmony with difference" is often traced back to a famous passage in the Confucian *Analects*: *junzi he er butong*. In Confucian thought, *he* means harmony (acknowledging differences while harmonizing their relationships) whereas *tong* means sameness. Thus the foregoing passage can be rendered as "the exemplary person harmonizes with others, but does not necessarily agree with them." Chinese scholars frequently argue that China's holistic mode of thinking suppresses the assertion of individualism and promotes the harmonious coexistence of differences and is thus tolerant of other cultures and open to the inclusion of other traditions in a process of harmonizing differences. According to the distinguished sociologist Fei Xiaotong, the "harmony with difference" idea reflects Chinese respect for mutual understanding, mutual tolerance, and symbiosis of cultural diversity.[31] Another scholar asserts that it is a philosophical pathway to perpetual peace, or in the indigenous Chinese locution, to "great harmony" (*datong*).[32] Among Western scholars, William A. Callahan, whose work is also represented in chapter 1 of this volume, contends that "harmony with difference" describes an imminent logic and flexible methodology by an appeal to difference and ambiguity in order to achieve the utopia of "great harmony."[33] This can certainly be seen as China's exceptionalist problem-solving approach.

The current Chinese leadership has effectively exploited this idea in statements and official documents. According to an official in the Ministry of Foreign Affairs, Chinese officials have creatively extended the meaning of "harmony with difference" in applying it to the field of international relations. Now *he* refers to a state of harmonious and nonconfrontational relationships and *tong* refers to the sameness in viewpoints. Thus *he er butong* can be presented as the principle that countries should conduct harmonious relations with one another while maintaining differences in views. At the same time, these differences should not compromise their harmonious relationship, friendly interaction, or mutually beneficial cooperation.[34] Thus, while acknowledging the diversity of the world, countries should actively seek the convergence of their interests, enlarge consensus, promote multilateralism, and strive for harmony and progress in international society.

Starting with President Jiang Zemin's 2002 speech,[35] "harmony with difference" has found its way into major speeches Chinese leaders have made abroad, and it has apparently been developed into the more wide-ranging concept of the "harmonious world" since 2005, heralding, as some observers call it, a new era in Chinese diplomacy.[36] President Hu Jintao's September 2005 speech to the United Nations (UN) world summit is widely seen by Chinese analysts as the occasion when China articulated "harmonious world" as a unique Chinese concept and theory of international relations. His April 2006 speech to Yale University continued this theme and embodied elements of both pacifism and inclusionism.[37] Scholars have quickly followed suit and begun to argue that "harmonious world" represents a new Chinese paradigm for world order.[38] Indeed, it is the clearest example yet of China's harmonious inclusionism. Hu's UN speech, for example, explains the virtue of diversity and difference, emphasizes the importance of dialogue and mutual learning, and promotes common development and the construction of a harmonious world that tolerates and includes different civilizations.[39]

Almost concomitantly, at the unofficial level a neo-Tianxiaism has emerged with a similar though far more sophisticated proposal for the future world order. I call it "neo-Tianxiaism" because although its proponents deploy the ancient concept of *tianxia* for theory construction, they have deprived it of the old meaning and tried to applied it to present reality.[40] Here harmonious inclusionism is even more prominently asserted. Zhao contends that the *tianxia* ideal has created the most peaceful and inclusive principle by seeking the maximization of cooperation and the minimization of conflict on the basis of acknowledging the world's diversity. The *tianxia* is inclusive of every cultural or spiritual system, acknowledges the independent role of every culture, rejects seeing any other culture as the enemy, and creates universal values on the basis of cultural inclusion.[41]

THE SOURCES OF CHINESE EXCEPTIONALISM

Why has this exceptionalism in contemporary China arisen? What are its historical, cultural, and intellectual sources? Why has it taken the current form? How has it been constructed? Why are so many Chinese intellectuals apparently enthralled by the idea of an exceptionalist China? To answer these questions requires attention to the political role that the concept performs in contemporary China at a particular juncture in global politics.

The political project of Chinese exceptionalism

China's exceptionalism is historically and culturally bounded: a historical understanding of China as *a*, if not always *the*, great power, and an allegedly culturally derived holistic mode of thinking which privileges peace and harmony. But history and culture, while exerting profound and subtle influences, do not by themselves determine the peculiarities of China's exceptionalism. That depends also on the international structural context in which China finds itself and hence the causal interactions between material structure, history, and culture in producing particular kinds of exceptionalism at different times. Structure establishes permissible and constraining conditions under which particular ideas of exceptionalism emerge.[42] The central theoretical question is how history and culture have been interpreted and used by later generations for their own purposes within the limits established by international structure. In other words, we shall examine how material conditions have worked with perceptions of Chinese history and culture to produce particular kinds of exceptionalism.

The most consequential material condition for contemporary China's foreign relations is a changing international structure where China's position has rapidly been elevated to the center of world politics, now approaching a point where it can rival the United States—the world's lone superpower—in certain areas. Although since the mid- to late 1990s Chinese analysts have characterized the world power configuration as "one superpower (the United States), many great powers (Europe, Japan, China, and Russia),"[43] they expect the rise of China and other countries to transform U.S. unipolarity into some sort of multipolarity in which China would play a greater role. Maoist China's quest for great power entitlement is now seen as being fulfilled. During this structural readjustment, an important question as seen by Chinese analysts is how to prepare China intellectually for its new and expanding international role. The new great power reformism is created in part by this structural expectation, at the same time being informed by an understanding of China's historical status and destiny as a great power. Furthermore, the role of history does not lie simply in reminding Chinese elites of their country's past greatness and future prospects but also in providing a perceived contrast between China's supposed peaceful foreign policy and the aggressive modern Western one. This has led to a strong desire to proclaim a Chinese development route different from that of the West—a route determined by historical and cultural resources that would *reform* world politics in a more peaceful, cooperative, and harmonious direction.

Confucianism is perhaps the most effective cultural resource that can be used to substantiate this claim, and it is not surprising that the Chinese government and analysts have exploited it in promoting a new benevolent pacifism. Undoubtedly, there is something genuine and noble in China's insistence on the peaceful nature of its foreign policy. In the modern era, this has been a result of the "century of humiliation" and the visceral psychological impact it has had on generations of Chinese elites: because of what China had suffered in the past, it is said to condemn the evil of hegemony and cherish the value of peace.[44] But at the same time the paci-fist discourse also has important political and ideological functions for the current government. In addition to elevating China to the moral high ground, it is also meant to dissipate the fear and suspicion about a rising China and to create a friendly regional and international environment for its re-emergence. For example, the government and many analysts often try to refute the so-called China threat theory by falling back on assertions about China's "peaceful nature." Indeed, this desire to present China as a peaceful power to create a "China opportunity" thesis underpins all three components of the emerging exceptionalism. In this sense, exceptionalism is in part a product of the ideological discourse to facilitate China's rise— and an example of the use of history and culture to discursively counter structural pressures from the international system.

The sources of harmonious inclusionism are the most intriguing. The Confucian influence is easy to see, but what is striking is that this principle is completely silent on China's own position in a "harmonious world" other than that it would work with other countries to create a world based on accommodation and inclusion. Harmonious inclusionism, then, seems to have been developed for a China that wants to claim some moral author-ity and discourse power in modern international relations but is unclear about its fundamental position, value, and purpose in world politics. It is an ambiguous discourse structured materially by China's current status as a rising power facing the potential danger of a balancing coalition against it. How this principle might evolve when China's international position improves in the future is uncertain. The contemporary PRC professes no sinocentrism of either the imperial or the revolutionary kind, but it is well worth asking whether a new sort of sinocentrism might emerge when Beijing is in a more privileged structural condition. Might not history and culture be used differently in a different structural context to serve a new purpose, as seems to be the case historically?

The construction of an exceptionalist argument

Even if we know the conditions for the rise of Chinese exceptionalism and the sources of its current shape, we still have not explained how it has come into being. How is China's exceptionalism constructed? Strikingly, the gov-ernment and some intellectuals have taken an undifferentiated West as the Other in constructing the uniqueness of the Self, producing a discourse about the West as exploitative and aggressive and China as benevolent and peaceful. This is a process of essentializing both the Western and Chinese traditions through selective use of historical narratives. China's exceptionalism is partly constructed through selecting certain aspects of history and culture to fit exceptionalist narratives, and in the process to create myths. This is no surprise: the power of history lies in its rich offerings to myth making, and the Chinese are particularly noted for their use of traditions in the present.[45]

The problem is that, contrary to the exceptionalist claim to a uniquely peaceful and benevolent China, historically China has in fact possessed multiple strategic traditions. To the exceptionalism about one Confucian pacifist–defensive approach we should add a multiplicity of other foreign policy traditions including realpolitik, as has been demonstrated by historians and political scientists alike.[46] The pacifist claim is a vast simplification of the complexity of Chinese history contributing to its mythical quality. This is not to say it is entirely mythical or that it is entirely selective. Exceptionalist ideas, because they are noteworthy and durable, must have some important factual basis. However, Chinese exceptionalism is based on myths as well as facts.

Why then are so many Chinese intellectuals still enamored by exceptionalist ideas, if they do not rest on a solid historical ground? Part of the answer has already been suggested: because they are both mythical and factual, those who want to find support for them will always be able to find it if they look hard enough. Ideology may be another factor. The idea of a peaceful and benevolent China was a powerful political ideology in imperial China,[47] entrenched further by the myth-making tradition of Chinese historical writing.[48] In the modern era this ideology has gained a nationalist dimension in the desire to distinguish China from Western powers, and thus is all the more difficult to dispel. To many inside China, it has simply appeared unpalatable, unfashionable, and even unpatriotic to question China's benign nature, to expose the less savory elements of China's past, or to entertain the notion that China might also have been power-political just as Western powers have been. Too many Chinese intellectuals hold a uniquely and excessively benign view of Chinese history. An ideology of such a distinguished pedigree—buttressed by certain facts, supported by successive governments, perpetuated by a political historiography, and infused by modern nationalism—has suppressed thinking critical of the exceptionalist myth.

Yet this explanation is incomplete without a core element—the power of the Confucian tradition in Chinese history. Examining the main intellectual sources of exceptionalist writings, we find a clear Confucian lineage from its founding days in ancient China through its dominance as a political ideology in imperial China to its vicissitudes in the modern period. Thus, apart from habitual references to classic Confucian sayings, we see the distinguished modern historian Qian Mu's classic Confucianism-informed study on Chinese culture, written in 1941, still widely cited today.[49] For example, Li Shaojun, the CASS scholar mentioned earlier, acknowledging the lack of expertise in traditional China's foreign policy, bases his claims about Chinese peacefulness almost entirely on this work.[50] To a lesser extent, this is also the case with the work of Liang Shuming—famously dubbed "China's last Confucian"—on comparing Eastern and Western cultures first published in 1921.[51] Very similar arguments about China's propensity for peace were deployed in the postwar "new Confucian" Tang Junyi's work on the "spiritual value of Chinese culture."[52] A bewildering array of Chinese analysts in the mainland are now rediscovering and developing these arguments in various permutations. Contemporary China's exceptionalism, by emphasizing peace, harmony, and inclusion, is preeminently a Confucian exceptionalism blended with liberal ideas of international cooperation, one that was difficult to foresee in the Maoist period but is to be expected given the revival of Confucianism in China today.

IMPLICATIONS OF CHINA'S EXCEPTIONALISM

What has this exceptionalism meant for China's foreign relations? What would an exceptionalist foreign policy look like? Has this exceptionalism influenced China's foreign policy in any way, in terms of both language and behavior? And has it faced any major intellectual competitors in China's intellectual landscape?

An exceptionalist foreign policy

If China's foreign policy is guided by exceptionalism, what would such a policy look like? This question may be best answered by comparing China's exceptionalism with the much-noted American exceptionalism. Historically American exceptionalism has displayed two contradictory forms: a tendency to "unfold into an exemplary state separate from the corrupt and fallen world, letting others emulate it as best they can," and a competing one to "push the world along by means of regenerative intervention."[53] The first tendency is often characterized as passive, defensive, and isolationist; the second as active, offensive, crusading, and militaristic.

When one focuses attention on the offensive side of American exceptionalism, its contrast with Chinese exceptionalism can be made to seem glaring. While America claims the superiority of its ideals about democracy and freedom, China professes respect for and tolerance of all political values and systems without putting its own doctrines at the center. While America's sense of mission and self-righteousness induces it to cast foreign policy in moralistic and Manichean terms, China claims to have a foreign policy of peace and accommodation with all countries. While the missionary aspect of American foreign policy induces it to promote American values and remake the world in its image, China professes to strive for a world of harmony and diversity. While America would not shy away from spreading its institutions and values to the world, and to impose them by force if necessary (as in the case of the 2003 Iraq War), China claims to be satisfied with national defense and pursuit of its unique brand of benevolent pacifism. While America at times seeks to revolutionize world politics using unilateralist means, China claims only to want to reform world politics by developing itself into a new kind of great power.

The key ideals of China's emerging exceptionalism are put forward as peace and accommodation, and in themselves they are indeed very noble. They suggest, as various Chinese scholars are quick to assert, the pacifist and cooperative nature of China's foreign policy. China is said to be able to become a new kind of great power different from the Western model. It would allegedly see other countries as the object of varying degrees of cooperation rather than that of conquest and domination as in Western history.[54] It claims to reject the imposition of a particular ideology or value system to the exclusion of others, and such respect for diversity is said to derive from China's traditional cultural principle of "*li bu wang jiao*" (the Chinese do not go to foreign lands to teach ritual).[55] This principle is said to have further developed into the doctrine of "*hua bu zhi yi*" (the Chinese do not govern foreign peoples), thus giving rise to a further claim that China has historically renounced expansion and conquest as a foreign policy objective.[56]

Moreover, China would allegedly have no intention of exporting one ultimate value or system to the outside world, and such general passivity— the absence of any missionary impulse to export and impose—is also held to be rooted in China's cultural precept of "leading by example" ultimately traceable to Confucius's idea of exemplification.[57] This contrasts with what China perceives as a Western preference for "domination by spiritual or military conquest." Whereas Western powers claimed a *mission civilisatrice* in spreading their ideas to the rest of the world, traditional China, it is argued, did not consider it had the responsibility, let alone mission, to actively transform the *yi* (culturally inferior foreign peoples) into the *hua* (cultural Chinese).[58] If the transformation occurred, it was not because of China's forceful imposition but because of China's serving as a model and others' emulation of it.[59] With an understanding of this historical and intellectual background, contemporary China asserts that, having inherited this noble legacy, it would reject missionary universalism and prefer the harmonious coexistence of all political and cultural systems. Examples of this are plentiful. For example, in an October 2012 speech to Tsinghua University in Beijing on the current international situation and the Diaoyu Islands dispute, Le Yucheng, a high-profile assistant to the Foreign Minister, remarked that China, with neither a tradition of expansion nor an intention to follow the hegemonic path of Western powers, would strive for the peaceful development of cooperation and mutual interests with other countries. But, he added, even though China would not expand at the expense of others' interests, it should at least protect its own interests and safeguard the sovereignty of its territorial waters. Exceptionalism, then, was used as a justification for China's forceful policies toward territorial disputes by presenting China as a defensive and cooperative power.[60]Some observers, moreover, see a direct lineage between the old precept of "leading by example" and the new principle of harmonious inclusionism. The "harmonious world" discourse is seen to embody China's effort to develop itself into a sort of self-sacrificing great power for world harmony: the purpose is not to transform the world but to create an attractive model through self-improvement so that others may be moved by China's call for harmony and emulate it.[61]

Foreign policy behavior

Is there, then, a match between this ideal image of an exceptionalist foreign policy and China's actual foreign policy record? An important part of China's official policy discourses, especially those from the highest level of authority and at the broadest level of generality such as government white papers and leaders' major speeches, is an exceptionalist discourse about policy principles. Behaviorally, however, even if a match between exceptionalist principles and behavior can be identified, the causality in the match will still require testing, since such behavior may well have resulted from factors other than exceptionalism. The empirical test will need to weigh the influence of exceptionalism against other policy ideas as well as against material–contextual factors such as changes in relative power. Since this chapter is primarily concerned with Chinese exceptionalism as an ideational phenomenon, such tests will have to await future studies.

Several general observations, however, can be made at this point. First, to reinforce the analytical point just made, it is hard to claim a direct causal link between the exceptionalist principles and actual policy behavior. To do so is to claim exceptionalism as the sole or the most important source of policy. That is obviously false. Certainly American exceptionalism and ideology are not determinative of its foreign policy.[62] Exceptionalism suggests one possible influence on policy while actual behavior is determined by many other factors, including both competing policy ideas that might suggest very different policy positions (more on this below) as well as material–contextual factors that might pull policy toward other directions. For example, the beginning of China's reform era witnessed the Sino-Vietnamese war of 1979, a decision inexplicable from a pacifist perspective. And in fact, the PRC "has resorted to the use of military force more often than any other regional or middle-ranking power in the world."[63] Historically China's foreign policy has frequently deviated from its exceptionalist ideals, failing to uphold in practice exalted cultural principles. It is yet to be seen how closely current and future Chinese foreign policy can align with these ideals; in the meantime, we should view exceptionalism as one policy idea among many competing ones.

Second, although the myth of China's exceptionalism may further reduce our confidence in the match between behavior and principle, this does not mean that myth will have no impact on policy thinking. Myths always have meaning and significance for some present purpose.[64] The effect of myth on policy, as with the influence of ideas on behavior, can go in multiple directions and it is impossible to pin down without the specification of further conditions. But it can surely be hypothesized, though difficult to confirm, that contemporary Chinese exceptionalism has to some extent restrained the realpolitik impulse of China's foreign policy. In fact, if Beijing can uphold the ideals and consistently translate the themes of peace and harmony into behavior, then the myth might have beneficial consequences for world order. In this sense, another useful way to analyze Chinese exceptionalism is to see it as a normative theory for China's foreign policy.[65] The possibility of exceptionalist ideas being used for the construction of Chinese theories of foreign policy and international relations, which is a rising intellectual trend in China,[66] further suggests the usefulness of such a perspective. The myth of Chinese exceptionalism means that it cannot stand as a viable empirical theory since it does not stand on a solid factual basis. Viewed as a normative theory, however, it acquires a new function as an idea competing for policy influence against other ideas. Our criteria for evaluating its usefulness as a normative theory then shift to the question of what desirable future it envisions for China.

Third, reversing our perspective from the question of the influence of exceptionalism on policy, we may find that contemporary China's exceptionalism, perhaps due to its developing nature, is in fact more reflective of the problems and tensions internal to China's foreign policy. One problem is its overall defensiveness and self-righteousness, indicative of a self-centered view of how China's foreign policy should be conducted and how the outside world should view it. The exceptionalist discourse betrays a persistent desire to present a particular view of China's past behavior and why the outside world should accept such a view as the true representation of Chinese history and culture. There is a palpable sense of self-protection against what Beijing projects as foreign misunderstanding, prejudice, and misapprehension.

Exceptionalism is also reflective of an important internal contradiction within China's worldview. Specifically, China's strong desire to regain its historical great power status, underpinned by a fundamentally statist and nationalist logic, contradicts the inclusionist rhetoric. In other words, China's "great power mentality" may ironically compromise its proclaimed reformism, pacifism, and inclusionism, as it has professed that it would take whatever measures necessary to fulfill its historical destiny, regardless of any Western attempt to obstruct it. The conflict between statism based on perceived national interests and inclusionism based on cultural principles is a key contradiction underlying current Chinese foreign policy: a tension that has existed in China's worldview since at least the late Qing, when China had to choose or strike a balance between traditional cultural principles and modern nationalist statecraft.[67]

Intellectual competitors

The place of exceptionalism in China's intellectual landscape is important to elucidate at this stage and I do so, briefly, in what follows. Describing the intellectual debates and competition currently taking place will reinforce the point that exceptionalism is not a reliable predictor of China's foreign policy, since there are a number of other important intellectual schools in China's foreign policy. At the same time, via this comparison, it will help to further distinguish Chinese exceptionalism as a policy idea and a normative theory for China's foreign policy.

David Shambaugh has recently developed a useful typology of Chinese discourses on China's international identities, from "Nativism" at one end through "Realism," "Major Powers," "Asia First," "Global South," and "Selective Multilateralism" to "Globalism" at the other end.[68] One problem, however, is that this classification lumps together intellectual sources of policy positions ("Nativism" and "Realism") with policy positions themselves ("Major Powers," "Asia First," "Global South," "Selective Multilateralism," and "Globalism"). I propose a somewhat different typology based on the intellectual foundations upon which different policy discourses are based.

At the left end of the spectrum of China's foreign policy discourses today is what Shambaugh has identified as Nativism, or Leftism—the latter a term more commonly used inside China. This intellectual movement includes three related but not identical schools of thought. The first is the remnants of the old leftism of the Maoist revolutionary China, with orthodox Marxist views of class struggle and international conflict. The second is the so-called new leftism that has become prominent since the 1990s. With Western educational backgrounds and informed by Western critical theories, many new leftists take an "academic" approach to criticizing existing policies, in contrast to the populist approach of the old leftists. Although mainly focused on China's domestic reform policies, they also decry the inherent inequality and injustice of the existing international system and the "new imperialism" that the West has allegedly been waging against China. The third school is extreme or radical nationalism. Although all major schools in China's intellectual discourses today are informed by one type of nationalism or another, the extreme nationalists stand out as the most thorough converts of the leftist and patriotic historiography propagated by the Chinese Communist Party (CCP) and the accompanying belief in the necessity of the eventual redress of the historical injustices China has suffered in the modern world. This extreme nationalism finds most of its expressions online and is dominant neither within Chinese nationalism nor within the larger intellectual currents in China today.[69] Leftism is marked by the distrust of the outside world, the insistence on China's absolute sovereignty and autonomy, and the belief in the necessity of waging political, economic, military, and ideological struggles against the West.[70]

Next to Leftism is a kind of Assertive Nationalism that has gained traction since the 1990s,[71] with Wang Xiaodong as an influential originator of and speaker for this movement. Chinese nationalism is a very complex intellectual and political phenomenon with varying sources and contents.[72] Most Chinese analysts can be seen as one type of nationalist or another, and nationalism can range from its radical extreme at one end through its assertive variant to the moderate version at the other end. Assertive Nationalism does not yet seem to command the mainstream opinion in China today, but it is growing more vocal and vociferous with the rise of Chinese power. While it does not have the xenophobic quality of extreme nationalism, neither does it show the restraint and moderation of some of the other schools. What it asserts, in essence, is that first, China should take being the world's superpower as its international ambition, with achieving economic wealth and military strength as the key pathways; second, the Chinese people need to rediscover and redevelop the "martial spirit" that has allegedly been lost since the latter days of imperial China. In this view, pacifist exceptionalism would simply lead to China's decay and collapse; China's rise must be grounded on a firm resolve to use force when necessary, and therefore developing material, particularly military, capabilities must take center stage in China's grand strategy. Third, these nationalists perceive international politics as a brutal business. China should actively prepare for struggle and conflict with other states, especially against Western hegemony. Deriving their intellectual inspiration from a combination of Chinese and Western history, Social Darwinism and realpolitik theories of international politics, assertive nationalists argue that China should actively prepare for struggle and conflict with other, particularly, Western states.[73]

Moving further along the continuum is a powerful school that might be broadly characterized as Realpolitik, the idea that state policies follow from interest and necessity, not morality and justice.[74] China has been called the "high church of realpolitik in the post-Cold War world,"[75] and realpolitik has a long tradition in Chinese history.[76] The analysis of this Chinese realpolitik, however, can be fine-tuned by differentiating among three subschools. The first might be called the Geopolitics School, basing its analysis on theories of geopolitics originating in Europe in the late nineteenth century and focusing its attention on China's land and sea power.[77] The second might be called "Offensive Realism," not entirely corresponding to the propositions of academic offensive realism,[78] but with a general view that Beijing needs to forcefully advance its national interests where conditions permit.[79] The third can be called "Defensive Realism," again not entirely identical with defensive realism in academic IR,[80] but generally believing that China needs to pursue security cooperation rather than confrontation with other states.[81] So far this seems to have been the position of the majority of Chinese analysts as well as the government.[82] The current debate on whether or not to abandon Deng Xiaoping's strategic injunction of *Tao Guang Yang Hui* can in part be seen as a reflection of the competition between Defensive and Offensive Realism within Chinese IR.[83]

The next point on the spectrum is what I call a new Traditionalism that is rapidly emerging in China's international relations. Trying to find ideas and lessons for China's foreign policy from its past, many intellectuals are now fervently studying China's historical and cultural records relevant to its foreign policy. Their interests converge on two particular topics: the thinking and practice of the Spring and Autumn and Warring States period (770–222 B.C.) in ancient China as it seems akin to the interstate competition of modern international relations,[84] and the foreign relations of imperial China—variously described under the rubric of the "tribute system" or the "*tianxia* system"—as it apparently promises to enrich the foreign policies of a rising China.[85] This intellectual movement is expanding its following. Although united by a common purpose, scholars pursue separate analytical agendas focusing on different aspects of China's history and culture and thus produce different arguments. Some are exceptionalist as analyzed here—indeed, exceptionalism informs or is reinforced by their research. Others take a more eclectic approach emphasizing the need for both peace and force. Still others are trying to uncover a Chinese realpolitik tradition, apparently conveying the message that Beijing needs to practice more power politics during its rise.[86] What distinguishes the new Traditionalism from the other schools is that it no longer seeks major intellectual inspirations from Western theory and history but rather from China's own indigenous sources.

Finally, there is the Liberal school, stressing the role of international institutions and norms, economic interdependence, and globalization in China's engagement with international society. This school might also be subdivided, with the strong version embracing international institutions and global governance and the weak version favoring selective engagement, corresponding roughly to what Shambaugh has classified as "globalism" and "selective multilateralism," respectively.[87] Though China's liberal IR scholars hold varying views across a number of issue areas, they generally agree that Beijing needs to engage with international society, seek cooperation and accommodation, and advance its interests while making contributions. They are usually influenced by liberal, constructivist, and English school theories of international relations.[88]

For many Chinese analysts, these intellectual sources—Leftism, Assertive Nationalism, Realpolitik, Traditionalism, and Liberalism—are neither mutually exclusive nor incompatible in shaping their thinking. Assertive Nationalism and Realpolitik, for example, have a great deal in common in their understandings about China's international relations. Ordinarily one will find an important figure influenced by several of these sources simultaneously. The Tsinghua University scholar Yan Xuetong, formerly a staunch offensive realist, is now developing a Traditionalist agenda.[89] The Peking University scholar Wang Jisi could be described as both a defensive realist and liberal.[90] Even Liu Mingfu, a professor at the National Defense University of the People's Liberation Army (PLA), and

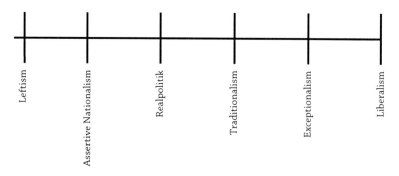

Figure 2.1
Intellectual spectrum of China's foreign policy discourse.

whose work is described in greater depth in chapter 1 in this volume, sub-scribes to a view very similar to the exceptionalism analyzed here, even while championing the buildup of China's military power.[91] One article advocating an inclusionist rising strategy is apparently influenced by Defensive Realism, Exceptionalism, and Liberalism simultaneously.[92] Classifying individual thinkers will prove more difficult than classify-ing the intellectual sources of their thinking. Nevertheless, knowing the sources is important for understanding the intellectual background of China's foreign policy.

Where does exceptionalism fit in this intellectual spectrum and how does it compare with its rivals? From a policy position and in terms of its intel-lectual underpinnings it may be placed somewhere between Traditionalism and Liberalism. As can be seen from Figure 2.1, exceptionalism's most seri-ous challenges come from Leftism, Assertive Nationalism, the Geopolitics and Offensive Realist variants of Realpolitik, and some quarters of Traditionalism. Defensive Realism and Liberalism share some policy posi-tions with exceptionalism, such as the emphasis on international coopera-tion and accommodation, but they are likely to challenge its pacifist and inclusionist myth, as are all the other schools.

However, this positioning of exceptionalism demonstrates little about the influence and merits of these intellectual currents. Exceptionalism dominates the official policy discourse and commands a notable following among the intellectuals, but it is only one among six major intellectual schools. It has all the problems described previously, yet how serious and consequential these problems are must be evaluated against those of its rivals. Among the various schools and subschools outlined here, which one would we prefer as the more desirable guide for China's foreign pol-icy? All have their own problems and promises, but exceptionalism seems at least more palatable than some of them as a normative theory for China's foreign policy. For example, a liaison among Leftism, Assertive Nationalism, and Realpolitik, if formed, could make for an isolationist and aggressive China. Given the very real problems of exceptionalism, however, we should encourage the development of a "critical exceptionalism" among Chinese intellectuals, so that they can begin to interrogate some of the questionable assumptions underlying the current version and help Beijing to deliver the exceptionalist promises by remedying its problems. It seems that such an evolution, though it may not be the best, is at least not the worst direction for Chinese foreign policy in the future.

CONCLUSION

This chapter has explored a set of interrelated questions about contemporary China's exceptionalism in international relations: what are its manifestations, why and how does it contribute to China's contemporary political project, and what might be the implications for China's foreign relations? Chinese exceptionalism is defined by great power reformism, benevolent pacifism, and harmonious inclusionism. While resting on an important factual basis, it is constructed by mixing facts with myths through selective use of China's vast historical and cultural experiences. It is better seen as a normative theory for China's foreign policy, whose merits can be compared with those of the other intellectual schools of China's foreign policy.

Exceptionalism reveals a prominent aspect of China's foreign policy traditions and provides a first window into the historical and emerging ideas that relate to China's view of international relations. As the opening chapter to this volume suggests, by being an essential part of China's worldview, exceptionalism can become an important source for policy ideas, offer the ingredients for the supposed construction of Chinese theories of international relations, and provide a lens through which to view emerging Chinese visions of international relations. This phenomenon is particularly important to uncover in the light of China's resurgence. However, exceptionalism should be seen as one among six major intellectual schools of China's foreign policy, one that may become increasingly influential as a result of the continuing revival of tradition in today's China. From the perspective of exceptionalism, a not-so-fanciful question about the future of China's foreign policy is: since China is already positioning itself as a sort of "Confucian great power," are we going to see, with the further success of China's rise, a new and different sort of sinocentric Confucian China practicing benevolent hegemony in East Asia? It is of more than theoretical interest to note that prominent Chinese scholars are already drawing on ancient Chinese thought to promote a future policy resembling hegemony, or what they prefer to term "humane authority."[93]

NOTES

1. Barry Buzan, "China in international society: Is 'peaceful rise' possible?" *Chinese Journal of International Politics*, Vol. 3, No. 1 (January 2010), pp. 5–36, at p. 21.
2. Samuel S. Kim, "Chinese Foreign Policy in Theory and Practice," in *China and the World: Chinese Foreign Policy Faces the New Millennium, 4th ed.*, edited by Samuel S. Kim (Boulder, CO: Westview, 1998), pp. 3–33, at p. 3.
3. Chris Alden and Daniel Large, "China's exceptionalism and the challenges of delivering difference in Africa," *Journal of Contemporary China*, Vol. 20, No. 68 (2011), pp. 21–38.
4. K. J. Holsti, "Exceptionalism in American foreign policy: Is it exceptional?" *European Journal of International Relations*, Vol. 17, No. 3 (2011), pp. 381–404.
5. Zhao Tingyang, *Tianxia Tixi: Shijie Zhidu Zhexue Daolun* [*The Tianxia System: An Introduction to the Philosophy of a World Institution*] (Nanjing: Jiangsu Jiaoyu chubanshe, 2005); Zhao Tingyang, *Huai Shijie Yanjiu: Zuowei Diyi Zhexue de Zhengzhi Zhexue* [*Investigations of the Bad World: Political Philosophy as the First Philosophy*] (Beijing: People's University Press, 2009).
6. Yan Xuetong, *Ancient Chinese Thought, Modern Chinese Power* (eds. Daniel A. Bell and Sun Zhe, trans. Edmund Ryden) (Princeton, NJ: Princeton University Press, 2011); Yan Xuetong and Xu Jin, *Zhongguo Xianqin Guojiajian Zhengzhi Sixiang Xuandu* [*Pre-Qin Chinese Thoughts on Foreign Relations*] (Shanghai: Fudan University Press, 2008); Yan Xuetong and Xu Jin et al., *Wangba Tianxia Sixiang ji Qidi* [*Thoughts of World Leadership and Implications*] (Beijing: World Knowledge Press, 2009).
7. Pan Wei, ed., *Zhongguo Moshi: Jiedu Zhonghua Renmin Gongheguo de 60 Nian* [*China Model: Reading 60 Years of the People's Republic*] (Beijing: Zhongyang bianshi chubanshe, 2009).
8. Paul Evans, "Historians and Chinese World Order," in *China and International Relations: The Chinese View and the Contribution of Wang Gungwu*, edited by Zheng Yongnian (London: Routledge, 2010), pp. 42–57, at p. 55. See also Jeffrey W. Legro, "What China will want: The future intentions of a rising power," *Perspectives on Politics*, Vol. 5, No. 3 (September 2007), pp. 515–34; Mark Leonard, *What Does China Think* (London: Fourth Estate, 2008).
9. Robert Gilpin, *War and Change in World Politics* (Cambridge: Cambridge University Press, 1981).
10. Legro, "What China Will Want."
11. See, for example, Buzan, "China in International Society," p. 22.
12. Ying-shih Yü, "The radicalization of China in the twentieth century," *Daedalus*, Vol. 122, No. 2 (Spring 1993), pp. 125–50.

13. Rana Mitter, *A Bitter Revolution: China's Struggle with the Modern World* (Oxford: Oxford University Press, 2004).

14. See Merle Goldman, *China's Intellectuals: Advise and Dissent* (Cambridge, MA: Harvard University Press, 1981).

15. Quansheng Zhao, "Policy-making Processes of Chinese Foreign Policy: The Role of Policy Communities and Think Tanks," in *Handbook of China's International Relations*, edited by Shaun Breslin (London: Routledge, 2010), pp. 22–34.

16. Leonard, *What Does China Think?* pp. 7, 17.

17. See David Shambaugh, "Coping with a conflicted China," *The Washington Quarterly*, Vol. 34, No. 1 (Winter 2011), pp. 7–27.

18. Dingding Chen and Jianwei Wang, "Lying low no more? China's new thinking on the Tao Guang Yang Hui strategy," *China: An International Journal*, Vol. 9, No. 2 (September 2011), pp. 195–216.

19. Feng Zhang, "China's new thinking on alliances," *Survival*, Vol. 54, No. 5 (October-November 2012), pp. 129–48.

20. More details are in Zhang, "The rise of Chinese exceptionalism."

21. Ren Jiantao, "Reshaping national ethos: A shift from the humble mentality of a weak nation to the dignified attitude of a world power," *Open Times*, 2009/09, pp. 133–41, at p. 135.

22. Zhao, *Tianxia Tixi*.

23. Zhang Zhizhou, "Zai Jueqi Beijing xia Goujian Zhongguo Ziji de Waijiao Zhexue" ["Constructing China's diplomatic philosophy against the background of the rising of China"], *Guoji Luntan* [*International Forum*], Vol. 9, No. 1 (January 2007), pp. 26–31, at p. 29.

24. Wang Zhengyi, "Chengwei Zhishi de Shengchanzhe" ["Becoming a knowledge producer"], *Shijie Jingji yu Zhengzhi* [*World Economics and Politics*], 2006/03, p. 1.

25. Wang Jun, "Daguo Fuxing yu Zhongguo Chuantong Ziyuan de Fajue" ["Great power reemergence and the excavation of China's traditional resources"], *Shijie Jingji yu Zhengzhi* [*World Economics and Politics*], 2006/05, p. 1.

26. See, for example, He Fangchuan, *He Fangchuan Jiaoshou Shixue Lunwenji* [*A Collection of Professor He Fangchuan's Papers on History*] (Beijing: Peking University Press, 2007), pp. 206, 308.

27. Li Shaojun, "Lun Zhongguo Wenming de Heping Neihan: cong Chuantong dao Xianshi —dui 'Zhongguo Weixie' Lun de Huida" ["On the peaceful orientation of Chinese civilization: From tradition to reality—A reply to the 'China Threat' theory"], *Guoji jingji pinglun* [*International Economic Commentary*], 1999 (1–2), pp. 30–3.

28. Zheng Bijian, "China's 'peaceful rise' to great power status," *Foreign Affairs*, Vol. 84, No. 5 (Sept./Oct. 2005), pp. 18–24. See also Bonnie S. Glaser and Evan S. Medeiros, "The changing ecology of foreign policy making in China: The ascension and demise of the theory of 'peaceful rise,'" *China Quarterly*, Vol. 190 (June 2007), pp. 291–310.

29. PRC State Council, *China's Peaceful Development Road* (Beijing, 2005). Available: http://www.gov.cn/zwgk/2005-12/22/content_134060.htm; PRC State Council, *China's Peaceful Development* (Beijing, 2011). Available: http://www.gov.cn/zwgk/2011-09/06/content_1941258.htm.

30. Dai Bingguo, "Persisting with Taking the Path of Peaceful Development." Available on the website of China's Foreign Ministry: http://www.fmprc.gov.cn/chn/gxh/tyb/zyxw/t774662.htm [January 5, 2011].

31. Fei Xiaotong, "Creating a harmonious but different world community: A speech at a conference of the IUAES," *Sixiang Zhanxian*, Vol. 27, No. 6 (2001), pp. 1–5, at p. 5.
32. Hu Jun, "'*He er Butong*': Zouxiang Yongjiu Heping de Zhexue Tujing" ["'Harmony with difference': A philosophical pathway to perpetual peace"], *Xin Shiye* [New Horizon], (2005/3), pp. 65–7.
33. William A. Callahan, "Remembering the future—Utopia, empire, and harmony in 21st-century international theory," *European Journal of International Relations*, Vol. 10, No. 4 (2004), pp. 569–601.
34. Ding Xiaowen, "'Zhonghe' sixiang yu Zhongguo waijiao" ["The idea of 'Zhonghe' and Chinese foreign policy"], *Guoji wenti yanjiu*, 2005/05, pp. 28–31, at p. 29.
35. President Jiang Zemin's Speech at the George Bush Presidential library, October 24, 2002. Available: http://www.fmprc.gov.cn/chn/pds/ziliao/zyjh/t7651.htm [December 24, 2009].
36. Ruan Zongze, "Hexie Shijie Yinling Zhongguo Waijiao Xinshidai" ["Harmonious world is leading a new era in Chinese diplomacy"], *Liaowang* [Outlook], January 9, 2006, p. 3.
37. The text can be found in Xinhua Yuebao, ed., *Shizheng Wenxian Jilan, 2006.3–2007.3 [Compilation of Current Affairs Literature]* (Beijing: People's Publishing House, 2007), pp. 964–67.
38. Wang Gonglong, "'Hexie Shijie': Guoji Zhixu de Xin Gouxiang he Xin Fanshi" ["'Harmonious world': A new conception and new paradigm for international order"], *Xiandai Guoji Guanxi [Contemporary International Relations]*, 2007/03, pp. 56–62.
39. The text can be found in Xinhua Yuebao, ed., *Shizheng Wenxian Jilan, 2004.3–2006.3 [Compilation of Current Affairs Literature]* (Beijing: People's Publishing House, 2006), pp. 1647–50.
40. See William A. Callahan, "Chinese visions of world order: Post-hegemonic or a new hegemony," *International Studies Review*, Vol. 10, No. 4 (2008), pp. 749–61; Feng Zhang, "The tianxia system: World order in a Chinese utopia," *Global Asia*, Vol. 4, No. 4 (Winter 2010), pp. 108–12.
41. Zhao, *Huai Shijie Yanjiu*, pp. 320–21.
42. Two foundational works are Kenneth N. Waltz, *Theory of International Politics* (Reading, MA: Addison-Wesley, 1979); and Alexander Wendt, *Social Theory of International Politics* (Cambridge: Cambridge University Press, 1999).
43. Rosemary Foot, "Chinese strategies in a US-hegemonic global order: Accommodating and hedging," *International Affairs*, Vol. 82, No. 1 (2006), pp. 77–94, at p. 80; Yong Deng, "Hegemon on the offensive: Chinese perspectives on US global strategy," *Political Science Quarterly*, Vol. 116, No. 3 (2001), pp. 345–46.
44. See Zheng Bijian, *The Evolution of an Idea: On the Origin, Basis, Content and Prospect of China's Peaceful Development Road* (Beijing: Central Party School Press, 2006), p. 263. Also see the PRC's first premier and foreign minister Zhou Enlai's remarks to this effect, in the PRC Foreign Ministry and the CCCPC Party Literature Research Office, eds., *Zhou Enlai Waijiao Wenxuan [Selected Diplomatic Works of Zhou Enlai]* (Beijing: Central Party Literature Press, 1990), p. 92.
45. Wang Gungwu, *To Act is to Know: Chinese Dilemmas* (Singapore: Eastern University Press, 2003), p. vi.
46. Michael H. Hunt, "Chinese Foreign Relations in Historical Perspective," in *China's Foreign Relations in the 1980s*, edited by Harry Harding (New Haven: Yale University Press, 1984), pp. 1–42; Arthur Waldron, "Chinese Strategy from the Fourteenth to the Seventeenth Centuries," in *The Making of Strategy: Rulers, States, and War*,

edited by Williamson Murray, Macgregor Knox, and Alvin Bernstein (Cambridge: Cambridge University Press, 1994), pp. 85–114; Alastair Iain Johnston, *Cultural Realism: Strategic Culture and Grand Strategy in Chinese History* (Princeton, NJ: Princeton University Press, 1995).

47. Peter Lorge, *War, Politics and Society in Early Modern China, 900–1795* (London: Routledge, 2005).

48. Wang Gungwu, "Early Ming Relations with Southeast Asia: A Background Essay," in *The Chinese World Order: Traditional China's Foreign Relations*, edited by John K. Fairbank (Cambridge, MA: Harvard University Press, 1968), pp. 34–62

49. Qian Mu, *Zhongguo wenhuashi daolun* [*Introduction to the History of Chinese Culture*] (Beijing: Commercial Press, 1994).

50. Li, "Lun Zhongguo Wenming de Heping Neihan."

51. Liang Shuming, *Dongxi wenhua jiqi zhexue* [*Eastern and Western Cultures and Their Philosophies*] (Beijing: the Commercial Press, 1999).

52. Tang Junyi, *Tang Junyi quanji, di si juan* [*Collected Works of Tang Junyi*, Vol. 4] (Taipei: Xuesheng Shuju, 1991).

53. Anders Stephanson, *Manifest Destiny: American Expansionism and the Empire of Right* (New York: Hill and Wang, 1995), p. xii. See also Stanley Hoffmann, "American Exceptionalism: The New Version," in *American Exceptionalism and Human Rights*, edited by Michael Ignatieff (Princeton, NJ: Princeton University Press, 2005), pp. 225–40, at p. 226; John Gerard Ruggie, "American Exceptionalism, Exemptionalism, and Global Governance," in *American Exceptionalism and Human Rights*, edited by Michael Ignatieff (Princeton, NJ: Princeton University Press, 2005), pp. 304–38, at p. 305; Michael H. Hunt, *Ideology and U.S. Foreign Policy* (New Haven: Yale University Press, 1987), p. 191; Eric A. Nordlinger, *Isolationism Reconfigured: American Foreign Policy for a New Century* (Princeton, NJ: Princeton University Press, 1995), p. 185.

54. Zhao, *Huai shijie yanjiu*, p. 89.

55. Ibid., p. 124.

56. Pan Wei, "The Chinese Model of Development" (delivered as a lecture at the Foreign Policy Center, London, October 2007), p. 3. Available: http://fpc.org.uk/fsblob/888.pdf [December 25, 2009].

57. Ying-shih Yü, *Ying-shih Yü Wenji, Di Er Juan:Zhongguo Sixiang Chuantong jiqi Xiandai Bianqian* [The Collected Works of Ying-shih Yü, Vol. 2: China's traditional thought and its modern transformation] (Guilin: Guangxi Normal University Press, 2004), p. 251.

58. Luo Zhitian, *Zaizao Wenming de Changshi: Hu Shi Zhuan (1891–1929)* [*The Attempt to Recreate Civilization: A Biography of Hu Shi, 1891–1929*] (Beijing: Zhonghua Shuju, 2006), p. 15; Luo Zhitian, *Biandong Shidai de Wenhua Lüji* [*Cultural Journey of a Changing Time*] (Shanghai: Fudan University Press, 2010), p. 7; Ren Xiao, "Traditional Chinese Theory and Practice of Foreign Relations: A Reassessment," in *China and International Relations*, edited by Zheng Yongnian (London: Routledge, 2010), pp. 102–16. Some Western scholars endorse this. See, for example, David C. Kang, "Civilization and State Formation in the Shadow of China," in *Civilizations in World Politics: Plural and Pluralist Perspectives*, edited by Peter J. Katzenstein (New York: Routledge, 2010), pp. 91–113.

59. Chih-yu Shih, "The West is not in the west: Identifying the self in oriental modernity," *Cambridge Review of International Affairs*, Vol. 23, No. 4 (December 2010), pp. 537–60, at p. 548.

60. Le Yucheng, "The Current International Situation and the Diaoyu Islands Dispute," Speech to Tsinghua University on October 16, 2012. Available: http://www.21ccom.net/articles/qqsw/zlwj/article_2012101969391.html [November 15, 2012].
61. Shih, "The West is not in the west."
62. Hunt, *Ideology and U.S. Foreign Policy*.
63. Samuel S. Kim, "Chinese Foreign Policy in Theory and Practice," in *China and the World: Chinese Foreign Policy Faces the New Millennium*, 4th ed., edited by Samuel S. Kim (Boulder, CO: Westview, 1998), pp. 3–33, at p. 14. For statistical data see Alastair Iain Johnston, "China's militarized interstate dispute behaviour 1949–1992: A first cut at the data," *China Quarterly*, No. 153 (March 1998), pp. 1–30.
64. Henry Tudor, *Political Myth* (London: Pall Mall Press, 1972).
65. On normative theory as opposed to empirical theory, see Milja Kurki and Colin Wight, "International Relations and Social Science," in *International Relations Theories: Discipline and Diversity*, 2nd edition, edited by Tim Dunne, Milja Kurki, and Steve Smith (Oxford: Oxford University Press, 2010), pp. 14–35.
66. Proponents of a "China school" in international relations include Qin Yaqing, "Why is there no Chinese international relations theory?" *International Relations of the Asia-Pacific*, Vol. 7, No. 3 (2007), pp. 313–40; Qin Yaqing, "Theoretical problematic of international relationship theory and the construction of a Chinese school," *Social Sciences in China* (English edition) (Winter 2005), pp. 62–72; Qin Yaqing, "Guoji Guanxi Lilun Zhongguo Xuepai Shengcheng de Keneng he Biran" ["A Chinese school of international relations theory: Possibility and inevitability"], *Shijie Jingji yu Zhengzhi* [*World Economics and Politics*], No. 3 (2006), pp. 7–13; Zhu Feng, "Zhongguo Tese de Guoji Guanxi yu Waijiao Lilun Chuangxin Yanjiu—Xin Yicheng, Xin Kuangjia, Xin Tiaozhan" ["Innovative research on international relations and foreign policy theories with Chinese characteristics—New agenda, new framework, new challenges"], *Guoji Zhengzhi Yanjiu* [*International Politics Quarterly*], No. 2 (2009), pp. 1–14.
67. See Luo, *Biandong*, pp. 90–112.
68. Shambaugh, "Coping with a conflicted China."
69. These schools are discussed in Xiao Gongqin, "Dangdai Zhongguo liuda shehui sichao: lishi yanbian yu weilai zhanwang" ["Six major social currents in contemporary China: historical evolution and future prospects"], originally published in *Lingdaozhe* [*The Leader*]. Available: http://21ccom.net/articles/zgyj/gqmq/2011/0606/36930.html [November 17, 2011].
70. Views often found in the Leftists' main website Utopia: http://www.wyzxsx.com/.
71. I use the term "Assertive Nationalism" in a more restricted sense than that of Allen S. Whiting, "Assertive nationalism in Chinese foreign policy," *Asian Survey*, Vol. XXIII, No. 8 (August 1983), pp. 913–33.
72. See Michel Oksenberg's perceptive comment in "China's confident nationalism," *Foreign Affairs*, Vol. 65, No. 3 (1986), pp. 501–23, at pp. 503–05. For more recent works, see Christopher R. Hughes, *Chinese Nationalism in a Global Era* (London: Routledge, 2007); Suisheng Zhao, *A Nation-State by Construction: Dynamics of Modern Chinese Nationalism* (Stanford, CA: Stanford University Press, 2004); Peter Hays Gries, *China's New Nationalism: Pride, Politics, and Diplomacy* (Berkeley: University of California Press, 2005).
73. See Wang Xiaodong, *Tianming suogui shi daguo* [*Being a Greater Power is China's Heavenly Destiny*] (Nanjing: Jiangsu Renmin Chubanshe, 2009).

74. Friedrich Meinecke, *Machiavellism: The Doctrine of Raison d'État and Its Place in Modern History* (London: Transaction Publishers, 1998).

75. Thomas J. Christensen, "Chinese Realpolitik," *Foreign Affairs*, Vol. 75, No. 5 (September/October 1996), pp. 37–52.

76. Johnston, *Cultural Realism*.

77. See, inter alia, Ye Zicheng, *Luquan fazhan yu daguo xingshuai: diyuan zhengzhi huanjing yu Zhongguo heping fazhan de diyuan zhanlüe xuanze* [*The Development of Land Power and the Rise and Decline of Great Powers: The Geopolitical Environment and the Geopolitical Strategic Choice for China's Peaceful Development*] (Beijing: New Star Press, 2007); Zhang Wenmu, *Shijie diyuan zhengzhi zhong de zhonguo guojia anquan liyi fenxi* [*Analysis of China's National Security Interests in World Geopolitics*] (Jinan: Shandong renmin chubanshe, 2004); Ni Lexiong, *Wenming de zhuanxing yu Zhongguo haiquan: cong luquan zouxiang haiquan de lishi biran* [*Civilizational Transformation and China's Sea Power: The Historical Inevitability of Moving from Land Power to Sea Power*] (Beijing: Xinhua chubanshe, 2010). See Christopher R. Hughes, "Reclassifying Chinese nationalism: The *Geopolitik* turn," *Journal of Contemporary China*, Vol. 20, No. 71 (September 2011), pp. 601–20.

78. John J. Mearsheimer, *The Tragedy of Great Power Politics* (New York: W. W. Norton, 2001).

79. Yan Xuetong's works, especially those before 2005 when he turned his attention to ancient Chinese thought, reflect this. See Yan, *Guoji zhengzhi yu Zhongguo* [*International Politics and China*] (Beijing: Peking University Press, 2005).

80. See Shiping Tang, *A Theory of Security Strategy for Our Time: Defensive Realism* (Basingstoke: Palgrave Macmillan, 2010).

81. Wang Jisi's works often have this flavor. See Wang, *Guoji zhengzhi de lixing sikao* [Rational reflections on international politics] (Beijing: Peking University Press, 2005).

82. China's security policy during the reform era has been said to reflect defensive realism: Tang Shiping, "From Offensive to Defensive Realism: A Social Evolutionary Interpretation of China's Security Strategy," in *China's Ascent: Power, Security, and the Future of International Politics*, edited by Robert S. Ross and Zhu Feng (Ithaca, NY: Cornell University Press, 2008), pp. 141–62. Also see Shambaugh, "Coping with a conflicted China," p. 22; Daniel Lynch, "Chinese thinking on the future of international relations: Realism as the Ti, rationalism as the Yong?" *The China Quarterly*, Vol. 197, No. 3 (2009), pp. 87–107.

83. See also Shambaugh, "Coping with a conflicted China," pp. 12–3.

84. See, inter alia, Yan, *Ancient Chinese Thought*; Yu Li and Li Tao, "Zhongguo guojiajian daoyi sixiang tanben suyuan—jiyu xianqin zhuzi guojiajian daoyi sixiang de duibi fenxi" ["An exploration of the original Chinese interstate moral thoughts: a comparative analysis of pre-Qin philosophers"], *Shijie jingji yu zhengzhi* [*World Economics and Politics*], No.3 (2011), pp. 66–99; Wang Rihua, "Zhongguo chuantong de guojiajian xinren sixiang jiqi qishi" ["Trust among states in traditional China and its implications"], *Shijie jingji yu zhengzhi* [*World Economics and Politics*], No. 3 (2011), pp. 100–21.

85. See, inter alia, Zhao, *Tianxia Tixi*; Feng Weijiang, "Shilun 'tianxia tixi' de zhixu tezheng, cunwang yuanli ji zhidu yichan" ["The Tianxia system: Characteristics, logic, and legacy"], *Shijie jingji yu zhengzhi* [*World Economics and Politics*], No. 8 (2011), pp. 4–29; Fangyin Zhou, "Equilibrium analysis of the tributary system," *Chinese Journal of International Politics*, Vol. 4, No. 2 (2011), pp. 147–78; Li Baojun

and Liubo, "'Chaogong-cefeng' zhixu lunxi" ["Analyzing the 'tribute-investiture' order"], *Waijiao Pinglun* [*Foreign Affairs Review*], No. 2 (2011), pp. 109–21.

86. Shi Yinhong's work reflects this: "Wuzhuang de zhongguo: qiannian zhanlüe chuantong jiqi waijiao yiyun" ["An armed China: a millennial strategic tradition and its diplomatic implications"], *Shijie jingji yu zhengzhi* [*World Economics and Politics*], No. 6 (2011), pp. 4–33.

87. Shambaugh, "Coping with a conflicted China," pp. 17–21.

88. See, for example, Wang Yizhou, *Tanxun quanqiu zhuyi guoji guanxi* [*International Relations in a Globalized Perspective*] (Beijing: Peking University Press, 2005); Qin Yaqing, *Quanli, zhidu, wenhua: guoji guanxi lilun yu fangfa yanjiu wenji* [*Power, Institutions and Culture: Essays on International Relations Theory and Methodology*] (Beijing: Peking University Press, 2005).

89. Yan, *Ancient Chinese Thought*.

90. Wang, *Guoji zhengzhi de lixing sikao*.

91. Liu, *Zhongguo meng*.

92. Wang Yiwei, "Chaoyue heping jueqi—zhongguo shishi baorongxing jueqi zhanlüe de biyaoxing yu kenengxing" ["Beyond peaceful rise: The necessity and possibility of China's inclusive rise"], *Shijie jingji yu zhengzhi* [*World Economics and Politics*], No. 8 (2011), pp. 140–54.

93. Yan, *Ancient Chinese Thought*.

ᴄᴧᴐ

The Domestic Sources of China's "Assertive Diplomacy," 2009–10

Nationalism and Chinese Foreign Policy

ROBERT S. ROSS

The sources of post-1949 Chinese foreign policy have been a central focus of scholarship on China's role in international politics. Studies of the Maoist era frequently stressed the importance of such domestic factors as ideology or factional politics in policy making. In contrast, studies of post-Mao Chinese foreign policy have stressed the Chinese leadership's preoccupation with China's interest in a peaceful international environment conducive to China's development of an advanced and powerful economy. Scholars have argued that, for the most part, national interest considerations have informed post-Mao Chinese policy making.

After thirty years of foreign policy stability, however, domestic factors once again play an influential role in Chinese foreign policy. But whereas in the Maoist era ideology and factional politics affected policy making, in recent years Chinese nationalism has challenged Chinese leaders' ability to focus on Chinese national security. As the Introduction to this volume argues, as China's power has grown, so too have Chinese citizens' expectations of the government as it operates in the international sphere, constraining its choices and shaping its responses. This was clear in 2009–10, when Chinese foreign policy appeared to change dramatically. Over the prior thirty years China's "peaceful rise" strategy had established cooperative and friendly relations with nearly every country in the world. But by the end of 2010 a more contentious Chinese foreign policy had elicited widespread suspicion of Chinese intentions and of its greater capabilities in East Asia, South Asia, and Europe. China's new diplomacy elicited a countervailing U.S. policy toward China that stressed greater strategic cooperation with countries on China's periphery.

This chapter explains this development in Chinese foreign policy as the result of domestic political change. It argues that traditional realist explanations for greater foreign policy assertiveness, strategic challenges, or improved military capabilities cannot explain the contentious turn in Chinese foreign policy in 2009–10. Instead, we need to pay greater attention to the expression of ideas, particularly nationalist ideas that have affected China's diplomacy and have pressured the leadership to adopt a more assertive diplomatic posture. It also suggests that nationalism has now emerged as a long-term factor affecting Chinese foreign policy.

The first part of this chapter discusses the turn in Chinese diplomacy and argues that there had not been either a significant challenge to Chinese security or a significant change in Chinese capabilities that might explain the alteration in Chinese diplomacy. The second part of the chapter discusses the emergence of significant economic problems in China in 2009–10 and the spread of digital communication technologies, which together challenged the legitimacy of the Chinese Communist Party (CCP) and domestic stability—a point that is elaborated further in chapter 7 of this book, which deals with the issue of human rights. The third part of the chapter discusses Chinese nationalism in what I identify as the crucial turning point of 2009–10 and considers two case studies in 2010 in which nationalism influenced Chinese policy. The conclusion of the chapter considers the implications of Chinese domestic politics for future Chinese policy making and for regional stability.

CHINA'S NEW FOREIGN POLICY AND REALIST EXPLANATIONS

In 2009–10 China adopted a series of diplomatic initiatives that together amounted to a new trend in Chinese policy and a departure from China's post-Mao emphasis on "peaceful rise." These initiatives included China's March 2009 naval harassment of the U.S. Navy reconnaissance ship *Impeccable* operating in China's exclusive economic zone in the South China Sea; difficult negotiations with the United States over U.S. President Barack Obama's visit to China; heavy-handed resistance to negotiation at the December 2009 Copenhagen Climate Change Conference[1]; hard-line responses to the January 2010 U.S. decision to sell arms to Taiwan, including a threat to impose sanctions on U.S. companies that have defense cooperation agreements with Taiwan; strident protests against U.S.–South Korean naval exercises in international waters in the Yellow Sea; excessive hostility to the Japanese detention in September 2010 of the captain of a Chinese fishing boat for operating in Japanese-claimed waters; harsh and persistent opposition in December 2010 to Liu Xiaobo's selection as the Nobel Peace Prize recipient[2]; and increasingly forceful assertion of its economic and territorial claims in the South China Sea.

One possible realist explanation for China's diplomatic turn is that in 2009–10 China encountered heightened challenges to Chinese national interests that required forceful responses. But China's diplomacy has created a disproportionate increase in tension over relatively minor issues. The contrast with past Chinese moderation is striking. Whereas China had tolerated from 2000 to 2008 the challenge that Taiwan's leader Chen Shui-bian posed to Chinese sovereignty over Taiwan, the most sensitive issue in Chinese diplomacy, in 2010 it strongly challenged, for example, the United States over routine naval surveillance activities in the South China Sea and naval exercises in international waters in the Yellow Sea, and Japan over its detention of a fishing boat captain for ramming a Japanese coast guard ship.

Another possible realist explanation for China's contentious diplomacy is its development of greater military capabilities and a corresponding ability to develop a more assertive diplomacy that could challenge the U.S.-dominated maritime order and realize long-held Chinese national interests. But in 2009–10 China had yet to develop significant new military capabilities that can explain China's new diplomacy. China's naval capability remains dependent on its advanced diesel submarines. It first deployed Russian Kilo-class submarines in the mid-1990s. By 2000 China's submarine force had already begun to pose significant challenges to U.S. naval operations in the western Pacific Ocean. Although China has developed its own capable diesel submarines, the Yuan and Song-class submarines, these ships have simply augmented China's existing capability.[3]

China's surface fleet is developing, but it has yet to offer the People's Liberation Army (PLA) Navy a new maritime capability. In August 2011 China launched its first aircraft carrier, the ex-Russian Varyag, which China bought from Ukraine in 1998. But China has not yet developed aircraft for the carrier.[4] Management of the carrier and its support vessels will also challenge the PLA Navy's operational abilities. China is developing new missile systems that may eventually affect U.S. security in maritime theaters. It has tested an anti-ship ballistic missile (ASBM) on land and it has developed various long-range surveillance technologies. Nonetheless, the ASBM is a program, not a capability.[5] China's anti-piracy naval operations off the coast of Somalia remain primitive. Its protection of its fishing claims in the South China Sea has depended on lightly armed coast guard ships. Its space program is making progress, but the PLA has yet to develop an operational capability that can significantly challenge U.S. space-based communication capabilities. China will eventually develop more advanced military capabilities, but China's contentious diplomacy in 2009–10 cannot be explained by its acquisitions of new maritime capabilities.

In the absence of a correlation between changing foreign policy factors and China's diplomatic turn, analysis must turn to a domestic explanation for policy change. There is a correlation between Chinese domestic change and Chinese foreign policy change.

CHINESE ECONOMIC AND SOCIAL INSTABILITY, 2009-10

In 2009–10 China's economy experienced significant disruptions that affected the welfare of many urban and rural Chinese people. Significant economic instability challenged the CCP's performance-based legitimacy. Simultaneously, Chinese society experienced the onset of the "social networking revolution," which undermined the communist party's government control of information dissemination, contributed to mass awareness of Chinese national problems, and facilitated organization of anti-government demonstrations. This combination of economic and social change contributed to leadership preoccupation with maintaining stability, a point concurred with by Gudrun Wacker in chapter 7.

China's mismanagement of the 2008 financial crisis

As the global financial crisis deepened in mid-2008, Chinese leaders had hoped that the Chinese economy would not be affected. But in October 2008 they realized that reduced global demand for Chinese exports would contribute to a significant decline in Chinese economic growth and significant unemployment. They responded with a 4 trillion renminbi stimulus program.[6] The stimulus package contributed to continued economic growth, but it failed to significantly moderate Chinese unemployment while it contributed to significant inflation and other macroeconomic problems.

In the last quarter of 2009 Chinese inflation began to increase. In early January 2010 the central bank increased banks' reserve requirement ratio, trying to constrain lending and inflation. It raised the rate again in February and April. In February, Premier Wen Jiabao acknowledged that "product prices" could "undermine social stability." But whereas in November the inflation rate was 0.6 percent, in April 2010 it accelerated at its fastest pace since 2009 and in May *People's Daily* warned that inflation could climb to 5 percent in 2010, far exceeding the government's target of 3 percent inflation. In May a record number of Chinese reported that prices were "too high to be acceptable." Despite continued efforts to restrain bank lending, inflation increased throughout 2010.[7] Of particular concern was food inflation. Vegetable prices in April 2010 increased approximately 25 percent since the previous April. Garlic prices had increased ten times over this period. This trend continued through May and June. In May the price of tea had increased 20 percent over the previous year.[8]

Housing inflation was also a mounting concern. As early as 2009 Chinese economists were speculating when the property bubble would burst. In November, Wu Jianmin, one of China's most distinguished economists, warned that excessive lending and the resulting speculation was contributing to an "asset bubble" and that the "frothy property market" was a "sign of a new crisis." By February 2010, Premier Wen Jiabao acknowledged that housing prices "have risen too fast" and he vowed that the government would curb housing inflation. In April the government imposed restrictions to restrain speculative investment in housing. Nonetheless, housing inflation continued to soar.[9]

The 2008 stimulus weakened financial and government institutions. It led to a record number of bank loans in 2009. There were three problems with these loans. First, many of these loans were to enterprises that could not repay them. By 2010 the Chinese banks had more nonperforming loans on their books than at any time since the 1990s. Second, many of the loans were made to Chinese localities that incurred massive local government debt that could not be repaid, undermining local economies throughout China. This issue began to attract leadership attention in early 2010 and by June 2010 it had become a serious problem.[10] Third, national banks and localities made loans almost exclusively to state-owned enterprises. Thus, the stimulus did little to help the private sector, the most dynamic part of the economy, and led to the expansion of the less-productive state sector in the national economy. Chinese observers characterized this trend as the "advance of the state sector and the retreat of the private sector" (*guojin mintui*). By March 2010 Chinese commentators were concerned that the growth of the state sector would undermine long-term gross domestic product (GDP) growth and the prospect for employment.[11]

As China's economy experienced high inflation, unemployment and social inequality emerged as sources of instability. In December 2009 Premier Wen Jiabao reported to the Central Economic Work Conference that "the employment situation remains grim." In March 2010 he reported that unemployment in 2010 "will still be serious" and that the government faced "unemployment pressure of 200 million." The government was especially concerned by unemployment among college graduates, a potential source of urban instability. In 2009 there were over 7 million unemployed college graduates. The government invested 42 billion renminbi to develop employment for college graduates in rural areas.[12]

As Chinese unemployment and inflation increased, inequality also increased. *People's Daily* reported in May 2010 that China's "income divide" had reached a "dangerous point." It cited World Bank statistics that put China's Gini coefficient in 2009 at 0.47, "among the highest in the world," and that such inequality could "brew strong negative feelings against the affluent." It warned that "the alarm bell is ringing. Beijing must not, and cannot afford to ignore it." *Global Times* reported that urban-rural income ratio had grown from 2.56:1 in 1997 to 3.33:1 in 2009 and it issued similar warnings of a potential crisis.[13]

Social instability, social networking, and the party's preoccupation with stability

Over the decade prior to the world financial crisis, the Chinese leadership had become increasingly concerned about social instability and challenges to party control. The number of "mass incidents" had increased over the decade, reflecting the party's inability to ameliorate economic and social problems that gave rise to mass discontent. As Andrew Walter argues in chapter 6, it is this domestic context that is essential to consider when analyzing the Chinese leadership's reaction to external pressure to help address global economic imbalances.

However, after the 2008 financial crisis, the situation deteriorated yet further. The number of mass incidents in China increased from 120,000 in 2008 to over 180,000 in 2010.[14] The failure of the 2009 stimulus package to ameliorate significantly unemployment thus led to ever greater leadership concern for social instability. The Chinese Academy of Social Sciences (CASS) reported that as a result of the global financial crisis, "the employment situation in society is becoming grim, which constitutes a latent threat to social stability." The escalation of mass incidents in 2009 was also worrisome because the level of mass violence directed against the authorities had "increased and spread." The CASS report described the Shishou incident, in which 70,000 people faced off against the People's Armed Police, as the "most serious street riot since the founding" of the People's Republic of China (PRC). CASS also associated the significant increase in crime in

2009, including a nearly 16 percent increase in criminal cases, a 16 percent increase in "order disrupting" cases, and a 15 percent increase in violent crime, to elevated levels of rural unemployment, the growth of the "idle" and "marginalized" population, and the formation of "outlaw gangs."[15]

Wu Bangguo's Work Report to the Standing Committee of the National People's Congress and Wen Jiabao's government work report delivered to the March 2010 session National People's Congress stressed the importance of social stability. The reports called for the expansion of the rural pension program and job creation for college graduates and rural migrant workers. Wen's report called for a nearly 9 percent increase in the budget of the People's Armed Police, the party's domestic security force, a greater increase than that for the PLA.[16] A Tsinghua University report observed that the party's increasing inability to cope with social conflict had led to the party's "growing sensitivity" to the problem.[17]

The leadership's preoccupation with maintaining stability was exacerbated by the spread of the internet and microblogging. In 2007, internet postings first exposed the nation to numerous incidents of local government corruption and violence against citizens. The government had lost control of the news and the internet had turned local news into national news that affected the reputation of the central leadership. Moreover, the internet had become an instrument for people to organize large-scale "mass incidents" against official malfeasance. The first such digitally organized incident occurred in March 2007 (well before the 2011 "Arab spring"), when several thousands of residents of Xiamen responded to a weblog by massing to protest against the construction of a chemical factory that could have a serious environmental impact. Beginning in 2008, the government stepped up its efforts to control public opinion through greater censorship of the internet. Nonetheless, the party has been unable to prevent independent dissemination of news and the "outing" of corrupt public officials and the wealthy elite, including in 2012, knowledge of the accumulated wealth of the families of Hu Jintao's successor, Xi Jinping, and Wen Jiabao. The number of internet users in China increased by nearly 60 percent during 2009 and in November 2009 a CASS report found that the internet was a main force for exacerbating "heated social incidents."[18]

THE GROWTH OF NATIONALISM AND CHINESE FOREIGN POLICY

Nationalism has been a persistent feature of Chinese politics for over a century. In the PRC, leadership-driven Maoist ideological nationalism influenced China's policy toward the Soviet Union in the 1960s and 1970s. In the post-Mao era, following the declining salience of ideology in politics, the leadership used nationalism, especially anti-Japanese nationalism, to sustain the CCP's legitimacy. This trend accelerated in the 1990s following the June 4, 1989, CCP's violent repression of mass protests in Beijing and the party's subsequent development of the "patriotic education campaign."[19] But throughout this period mass nationalism had a marginal impact on foreign policy.[20] Into the first decade of the twenty-first century, the leadership had maintained dominant control over public opinion and mass activities and the vast majority of urban and rural Chinese focused on China's economic development and the opportunities for individual economic advancement, rather than on politics or foreign policy.

From 2008 to 2010, not only did China's economic and political situations radically change, but nationalism emerged as a more pervasive political force. This new trend reflected the spread of nationalist sentiment to many sectors of urban society and the implications of the internet for wide dissemination of nationalist sentiment and for the organization of independent nationalist protests.

A major source of growing nationalism was popular Chinese understanding of China's international status during the global financial crisis. As Rosemary Foot's Introduction to this volume notes, many Chinese were seeking direct evidence that the country's economic successes were resulting in tangible gains in relationships with outsiders. Whereas the Chinese leadership experienced heightened insecurity during 2008–10, during this same period many Chinese believed that the Western financial crisis was the culmination of thirty years of economic growth and of China's rise to great power status. Whereas in 2008 the United States entered into a significant recession, in 2008 and 2009 China's economy grew at 10 percent. Moreover, the Chinese people witnessed the apparent modernization of the PLA. Although many PLA military modernization programs remained in development, China's anti-satellite tests, anti-piracy missions in the Gulf of Aden, tests of advanced aircraft, expanding naval exercises in the western Pacific Ocean, aircraft carrier program, and cyber capabilities all indicated to many Chinese that the PLA was catching up with the U.S. military. That catching up, in turn, suggested to many Chinese that China could develop a more assertive role in international politics.

But whereas in the past nationalism was primarily confined to young Chinese and to some soldiers in the PLA, in 2009–10 such sentiment spread to Chinese business people, academics—including some whose views are discussed in chapters 1 and 2 in this volume—and elite politicians. This trend contributed to a major debate over the continued relevance of Deng

Xiaoping's 1989 sixteen-character statement that China should "maintain a low profile, hide brightness, not seek leadership, but do some things" (*taoguang yanghui, bu dang tou, yousuo zuowei*). Not until State Councilor Dai Bingguo authoritatively reaffirmed the importance of China's foreign policy of "peace and development" in December 2010 did the debate begin to die down.[21]

China's traditional media was a prominent outlet for nationalist views, including China Central Television and such official central-government newspapers as *People's Daily, China Youth Daily,* and *Global Times,* as well as provincial newspapers. But the expansion of the internet accentuated the role of nationalism in Chinese policy making. A wide range of Chinese people, including retired military officers and leading intellectuals, used the internet to voice strident demands for noncompromising Chinese positions on a wide range of foreign policy issues, including bilateral policies, defense policy, and foreign economic policy.[22] Just as the internet had facilitated mass protests in the Chinese interior against government corruption and economic policies, it might also be used to organize large-scale and nationalist protests in Beijing and other cities against foreign governments. Such protests against foreign governments might evolve into destabilizing anti-Chinese government protests, should the protesters believe that the Chinese government had failed to adequately resist foreign pressures.

In the context of nation-wide economic instability, the erosion of the party's performance-based legitimacy and declining party control over society, the dissemination on the internet of broad-based and increasingly strident nationalist sentiment increased the salience of nationalism in policy making. The impact of nationalism in Chinese foreign policy was evident in China's reaction to U.S.–South Korean naval exercises in July 2010 and to Japan's arrest of the captain of a Chinese fishing boat in September 2010.

China, the sinking of the Cheonan, and U.S. naval exercises in the Yellow Sea

On March 26, 2010, the South Korean naval ship Cheonan sunk; forty-six South Korean sailors died. On May 20, following escalating North Korea–South Korea tension, the South Korean government announced that its investigation had established that the Cheonan had been sunk by a North Korean torpedo. On May 25, the United States announced that it would hold joint naval exercises with South Korea. Then, on June 2, South Korean "sources" reported that the U.S. aircraft carrier *George Washington* would participate in the joint exercises in the Yellow Sea, contiguous to China's northeast coastline.[23]

This would be the largest U.S.–South Korean exercise since 1976. The United States also initiated flights over South Korea of its F-22 Raptor, its most advanced military aircraft. Chinese sources reported it was the first time that a U.S. aircraft carrier had exercised in the Yellow Sea since 1994.[24] Nonetheless, China maintained a low-profile diplomatic posture. Chinese Foreign Ministry officials, Ministry of Defense officials, and other government officials did not publicly comment on U.S. military activities or on the planned U.S.–South Korean exercise throughout June and into early July. Chinese television, newspapers, and websites were also restrained. If Chinese leaders objected to U.S. policy, including the presence of a U.S. carrier in the Yellow Sea, they had decided to work quietly through diplomatic channels.

China's diplomatic posture fundamentally changed on July 1, when PLA Chief of Staff General Ma Xiaotian publicly said that the Yellow Sea "is very near Chinese territorial waters and we are very much opposed to such an exercise."[25] This statement critical of the United States by a senior Chinese general provided "political cover" for public Chinese discussions of U.S. policy and unleashed a wave of anti-American nationalist sentiment. On July 6, *Global Times* cited an arms control researcher that U.S. military activities "exert negative influence" on Sino–U.S. military relations. That same day the foreign ministry spokesman was asked about Ma Xiaotian's comments regarding the exercises. After six weeks of silence, he now replied that China was "seriously concerned" about the U.S. plans.[26] The next day, a *Global Times* editorial encouraged a nationalist outcry. It argued that a public protest by the Chinese people would bolster Chinese diplomacy. That same day, Major General Luo Yuan argued that the planned exercises required development of the theory of the "United States military threat." On the same site, a researcher from the Chinese Ministry of Defense's Institute of Strategic Studies argued that the exercises in the Yellow Sea would be an "out-and-out provocation." Dai Xu, a "military expert," alleged that the exercise would challenge China's economic lifeline, "just like a knife . . . aimed at the heart." China must "draw a red line." On July 16, *People's Daily* carried an interview with General Luo, who declared that the U.S. military exercise would pose "a direct security threat to China's heartland" and that China should have a "sense of crisis" and that it should "prepare for the worst."[27]

For two weeks following Ma Xiaotian's statement, statements by senior Chinese military officers continued to legitimate strident anti-American nationalism by Chinese "netizens" and by commentators in government publications. One netizen argued that "China should show the determination we had in the anti-Japanese war and fight the Americans." A fellow nationalist declared, "Let's sink the USS *George Washington*. All Chinese people support you." A frustrated netizen asked "The US is at our doorstep, where are our advanced weapons?" Another insisted that China will "demonstrate its capability to attack and destroy any [trespassing] naval vessel." Some netizens recommended that China use its reputed ASBM capability to sink the USS *George Washington*. A posting on the *People's Daily* forum included alleged "photos" of a U.S. aircraft carrier engulfed in flames. The posting elicited gratifying online rumors that the carrier had just been bombed.[28]

Chinese newspapers were similarly nationalist. An article in *Guangming Wang* argued that the United States is "menacing our North China Plain" and that the planned U.S.–South Korean naval exercise will "constitute a threat to our important ports and cities..., as well as to our maritime transportation routes." In *Guangzhou Ribao*, Tang Xiaosong, director of the International Security and Strategic Studies Center at Guangdong Foreign Language and Trade University, reflected the popular view that China's time to challenge the United States had now come. He argued that "The United States is in an awkward position: Following the financial crisis, its national strength has declined and it is in a relatively weak phase, needing China's support and cooperation. This is precisely the best time for China to be tough, and the conditions are there for this."[29]

The combination of China's hypernationalist political environment with increasingly severe economic and social instability elicited China's hard-line and unprecedented diplomatic posture against U.S. naval exercises in international waters in the Yellow Sea. On July 8, two days after his first statement of China's serious concern regarding the planned U.S.–South Korea naval exercise, the foreign ministry spokesperson issued a more serious warning against the United States. He expressed China's "grave concern" and declared that China is "firmly opposed to foreign military vessels and planes conducting activities in the Yellow Sea...that undermine China's security interest." On July 13, the spokesperson reaffirmed China's "grave concern" and he insisted that China's position is "unequivocal." On July 15, he said that Chinese leaders "resolutely oppose warships and military aircraft from any country conducting activities that affect China's security interest in the Yellow Sea."[30]

Only after the United States stated on July 21 that an aircraft carrier would participate in the July exercise but that it would not enter the Yellow Sea did the foreign ministry diminish its hostility to the exercise. On that day the spokesman merely expressed China's "concern."[31] But by that time

Chinese diplomacy had already created an image of an "assertive" China that had tried to use its improving great power capabilities and its international status to coerce other countries to change their established policies to suit China's interests. This image damaged China's reputation in Asia, where countries began to reconsider China's commitment to "peaceful rise" intentions. Beijing's heavy-handed diplomacy also damaged China's relationship with South Korea. It had challenged South Korean confidence that rising China would both constrain North Korea and not threaten South Korea. South Koreans thus placed greater emphasis on the U.S.–South Korean alliance for its security.

China and Japan's arrest of a Chinese fisherman

On September 7, 2010, the Japanese Coast Guard detained a Chinese fishing boat and its crew for fishing in Japanese territorial waters within twelve miles of an island chain claimed by both Japan and China (Senkaku Islands in Japan; Diaoyu Islands in China) and for ramming the Japanese coast guard ship with the fishing boat. Japanese detention of Chinese fisherman had occurred before, but the next day the Japanese coast guard took the unusual step of formally arresting the boat captain Zhang Qixiong and Japan informed the Chinese ambassador that "Tokyo would enforce its domestic laws" against the captain. On September 9, Japanese prosecutors assumed authority over the case.

Japan's exercise of its domestic law in disputed waters increased Japan's challenge to China's sovereignty over the disputed islands.[32] Nonetheless, similar to its response to U.S.–South Korean exercises in the Yellow Sea, China's reaction was disproportionate to the challenge to Chinese interests and it undermined China's interest in cooperative Sino-Japanese relations. Chinese policy reflected the leadership's concern for popular nationalism. But unlike China's delayed nationalist response in June–July to the planned U.S.–South Korean naval exercise in the Yellow Sea, in September popular Chinese nationalism reacted almost immediately to the arrest of the fishing captain. Moreover, Chinese nationalism was more extreme than in July, reflecting the *a priori* widespread Chinese anger at Japan's occupation of China in the 1930s and 1940s and the effect of China's patriotic education campaign on popular attitudes toward Japan.[33]

On September 8, the day that Japanese officials formally arrested Zhang, approximately forty Chinese protesters met at the Japanese embassy in Beijing. That same day, Chinese writers began a campaign for a hard-line Chinese policy. An editorial in *Global Times* insisted that if Japan deals with the captain unilaterally, rather than through talks with China, then the East China Sea is "in danger." The next day, Feng Zhaokui, a leading Chinese specialist on Japan, warned that "Now it is no longer the era in which China can be bullied at will." *Global Times* reported that protest banners at the Japanese embassy called for "Japan, get out of the Daioyu Islands. Get out" and the comment of one protester that the arrest of the captain is "a form of illegal kidnapping."[34]

Chinese netizens voiced increasingly strident demands that China defend its sovereignty over the islands and they called for mass demonstrations to commemorate the "September 18" incident, the date in 1931 when Japanese forces occupied all of Manchuria.[35] After September 7, "Diaoyu islands" and "Zhang Qixiong" had become the most searched terms on the Chinese internet and Chinese online news portals had been overwhelmed with demands that Japan immediately and unconditionally release Zhang.[36] Soon after the arrest, nationalist anger at Japan escalated. Among the strident anti-Japanese postings, one netizen's post on the *People's Daily* website charged Japan with "naked aggression." Another netizen posted that the "only way is to fight back strongly, there is no other choice." A third netizen wrote, "kill the devils." One angry netizen wanted to "blow up the Japanese son of a bitch's turtle sons."[37]

Chinese nationalism reflected the widespread belief that China had become a great power and that it no longer had to compromise with Japan. For example, one netizen wrote that "the Chinese people are no longer the Chinese people that could be slaughtered by anyone." Another, on the Chinese Foreign Ministry's website, asked: "Do we have to wait until the next Nanjing Massacre happens...[and] continue to tolerate?" According to another netizen, Japan was "trying to test China's bottom line."[38]

Moreover, the week before the anniversary of the September 18 incident, Chinese nationalist netizens circulated proposals for public protests.[39] Although the Chinese authorities had deleted online discussion of protests and blocked searches for "Diaoyu," protests took place at Japanese diplomatic offices in Beijing, Shanghai, and elsewhere in China. In Beijing approximately 100 protesters gathered at the Japanese embassy. They shouted "down with little Japan" and "free our captain." Another group protested in front of the Chinese foreign ministry. It called out "down with the traitors to the motherland" and it called on China to "retake the Diaoyu islands."[40] That same day, Major General Luo said that Japan must release the Chinese crew "unconditionally" and that there was "no room for compromise." China, he said, "will not pay for peace with compromise and concession." He argued that the September 18 protests were "fair" and "reasonable" responses to Japanese policy.[41]

Nationalist demands for retaliation intensified after September 20, when Japan extended the detention on Zhang Qixiong. In an interview with *Global Times*, Major General Peng Guanqian argued that China must "intensify counter-measures and give Japan tit-for-tat." Feng Zhaokui called for economic sanctions against Japan, including Chinese government purchase of the Japanese yen to force its appreciation to slow Japan's exports.[42] During this period "millions" of Chinese went online to express their anger. Many netizens called for a boycott of Japanese goods and for the Chinese government to adopt stronger measures. For example, one wrote that the "dignity" of the "Chinese nation" was at stake. Another wrote that "I hope the Chinese government adopts an even tougher attitude .... Don't let the public lose confidence."[43]

Preoccupied with significant domestic economic and social instability, the Chinese government appeased China's nationalists with hard-line diplomacy at the expense of China's diplomatic relationship with Japan. On September 7, the Chinese Foreign Ministry expressed its "grave concern" at Japan's detention of the Chinese fishermen and the Chinese ambassador to Japan lodged "solemn representations" to the Japanese Foreign Ministry. And within twenty-four hours of the incident, Chinese Assistant Foreign Minister Hu Zhengyue and Vice Foreign Minister Song Tao each "summoned" Japanese Ambassador Uichiro Niwa to the foreign ministry to protest Japanese actions and to demand the release of the crew.[44] After Japan arrested the captain and the Japanese prosecutor took over the case, Chinese demands intensified. On September 9, the Chinese Foreign Ministry spokesmen insisted that it is "absurd, illegal and invalid that Japan applies its domestic laws to Chinese fishermen operating in those waters, and absolutely unacceptable to China." The next day Chinese Foreign Minister Yang Jiechi summoned the Japanese ambassador and demanded that Japan "immediately and unconditionally" release the crew. China also postponed talks with Japan regarding joint development of a contested gas field in the East China Sea. Then early morning September 11, State Councilor Dai Bingguo summoned the Japanese ambassador for an "urgent meeting" and he "solemnly expressed" China's "grave concerns and serious and just position." He warned Japan that should the conflict continue, tension could escalate. Dai urged Japan "not to misjudge the situation, to make a wise political resolution, and to immediately return the Chinese fishermen...." On September 13, after Japan had the ship's crew released but continued to detain Zhang Qixiong, the Japanese ambassador was summoned for his fifth meeting since his country had detained the Chinese ship. Vice Foreign Minister Liu Zhenmin conveyed China's demand that "Japan immediately release and send back the Chinese boat captain." Adding actions to words, China moved drilling equipment to a disputed natural gas field in the East China Sea, despite Japan's opposition to Chinese unilateral exploitation of the field.[45]

After the September 18 protests in Beijing, Shanghai and elsewhere and as Japan faced a ten-day deadline to decide whether or not to indict Zhang Qixiong, China increased its pressure. On September 19, the Chinese foreign ministry spokesmen warned for the first time that China was prepared to take "strong counter measures" if Japan "obstinately clings to its own course and doubles its mistakes." That evening Chinese Vice Foreign Minister Wang Guangya summoned the Japanese ambassador to express China's "strong indignation" and declared that the incident had "severely damaged" relations. Wang warned that China would take "strong counter-measures" if Zhang were not immediately released.[46] China then imposed sanctions against Japan. It suspended bilateral exchanges with Japan at and above the provincial and ministerial levels, including a meeting between the Japanese and Chinese premiers at the annual United Nations General Assembly meeting in New York; it halted discussions with Japan regarding expansion of civil aviation rights and coal mining; it canceled a Japanese youth group's visit to the Shanghai World Expo; and it canceled a major initiative plan for Chinese tourism in Japan. On September 20 China announced that it had sent "marine surveillance ships" to strengthen Chinese law enforcement in "relevant waters to safeguard China's maritime rights and interests" and that "law enforcement ships" had been "dispatched to cruise in the area and protect fishermen and their boats."[47]

On September 20 Japan released the video of the September 7 collision. The video revealed that the Chinese fishing boat was responsible for the collision. It had circled back and then sailed into the Japanese Coast Guard ship.[48] Nonetheless, on September 22 Chinese Premier Wen Jiabao spoke out for the first time on the dispute. He said that the disputed islands are China's "sacred territory" and that "I strongly urge the Japanese side to release the skipper immediately and unconditionally." He warned that "If Japan clings to its mistake, China will take further actions." On September 24, Chinese authorities arrested four Japanese nationals from the Fujitsu Corporation for allegedly "illegally filming defense targets" in a military zone.[49]

In the afternoon of September 24, Japan released Zhang Qixiong from prison and allowed him to leave Japan. But China continued to posture for its domestic audience. On September 25, the Ministry of Foreign Affairs declared that Japan "must apologize to and compensate the Chinese side for the incident." On September 28 it refused a request from the Japanese ambassador for a meeting to discuss the four detained Japanese citizens.

Beijing released three of the four detained Japanese citizens on September 30, but it only released the fourth Japanese citizen on October 10.[50]

CONCLUSION: NATIONALISM AND GREAT POWER CONFLICT

The two case studies examined in this chapter establish that contentious Chinese diplomacy and the corresponding instability in regional affairs reflected the insecurity of the Chinese leadership arising from China's deteriorating economic and social conditions and its appeasement of strident nationalism. The PRC leadership's domestic objectives, rather than China's national foreign policy objectives, informed China's foreign policy, illustrating the interpenetrated nature of these two spheres.

Nationalism has been a frequent determinant of foreign policy choices. Scholars, however, have taken some time to realize its importance in post-Mao China. China's authoritarian political system has enabled China's leaders to develop foreign policy relatively free from domestic nationalist constraints. But the emerging social consequences of economic instability, combined with the advent of digital communication technologies, have increasingly challenged the leadership's ability to sustain political stability and created incentives to develop a nationalist foreign policy. In this respect, in a comparative historical perspective, China's nationalist foreign policy reflects similar domestic dynamics that shaped the nationalist foreign policies of Wilhelm Germany and of Imperial Japan—with important caveats that I discuss next.

Domestic trends in China since 2010 suggest that nationalism will continue to be influential in Chinese foreign policy. China's economic growth rate has significantly slowed, contributing to heightened unemployment. Poor governance, including widespread corruption, land confiscations, and cover-ups of official malfeasance, continues to undermine support for the CCP. Moreover, the internet remains a critical source of information for the Chinese people and its contribution to independent social activism continues to grow. The October 2012 demonstrations in Ningbo against the construction of a petrochemical plant underscored the leadership's vulnerability to anti-government activities. Moreover, since 2012 there has been greater elite conflict, reflected in the "Bo Xilai affair" and the intensified elite differences prior to the 18th Party Congress held in November 2012. Intensified elite conflict has further undermined the leadership's ability to insulate foreign policy from popular nationalist pressures. The October 2012 Sino–Japanese dispute over the Japanese government's purchase of disputed islands elicited violent anti-Japanese nationalist demonstrations throughout China, which contributed to China's disproportionate retaliation against Japanese policy. Nonetheless, twenty-first-century China is fundamentally different from Wilhelm Germany and Imperial Japan. Germany and Japan were led by nationalist leaders who wielded military supremacy over other great powers to achieve overly expansive foreign policy objectives. China remains a militarily weak great power and its leaders are cautious politicians fixated on domestic stability and have responded to nationalist sentiment to sustain their legitimacy rather than mobilize mass nationalism for foreign policy expansionism. These differences are decisive for explaining the impact of Chinese nationalism on Chinese foreign policy, great power conflict, and regional stability.

The domestic conditions that affected China's 2010 diplomacy will continue to beset the Chinese leadership and challenge regional stability for many years. High inflation and high unemployment will likely persist, corruption and inequality will remain endemic to China's one-party system, popular discontent will be pervasive, and digital communication technologies will continue to outpace the CCP's capacity to maintain control over information and independent organization. These conditions will continue to promote a nationalist Chinese foreign policy. In these conditions, not only will sustained great power cooperation and regional stability require Chinese leaders to resist the temptation to use foreign policy to enhance their domestic legitimacy, but they will also require the United States and China's East Asian neighbors to acknowledge China's fundamental maritime weakness and to respond with restraint, rather than with alarm, to Chinese nationalism.

NOTES

1. Chapter 8 in this volume explores China's climate change negotiating behavior in greater detail and over a longer time period.
2. See chapter 7 in this volume for further detail on the award of the Nobel Peace Prize to Liu Xiaobo.
3. For a discussion of China's naval ships, see Ronald O'Rourke, *China Naval Modernization: Implications for US Naval Capabilities—Background and Issues for Congress*, Congressional Research Service, Report for Congress, RL33153 (updated July 22, 2011). On China's acquisition of Russian submarines and its development of indigenous technologies, see Bernard D. Cole, *The Great Wall at Sea*, 2nd ed. (Annapolis, MD: Naval Institute Press, 2010), ch. 5.
4. Evan S. Medeiros, Roger Cliff, Keith Crane, and James C. Mulvenon, *A New Direction for China's Defense Industry* (Santa Monica, CA: Rand Corporation, 2005), ch. 4.
5. Eric Hagt and Matthew Durnin, "China's Antiship Ballistic Missile: Developments and Missing Links," *Naval War College Review*, Vol. 62, No. 4 (Autumn 2009), pp. 87–115; Owen R. Cote, Jr., "Assessing the Undersea Balance," SSP Working Paper WP11–1 (Cambridge: Massachusetts Institute of Technology, 2011), pp. 16, 14, 23–24.

6. On the stimulus, see Wang Hu and You Chunjie, "Interpretation of the five hot topics of the Central Economic Work Conference," *Jiefang Ribao* [Online], December 9, 2009, in Open Source Center (OSC), doc. no. CPP20091210038005.

7. *Xinhua News Agency*, October 30, 2009, in OSC, doc. no. CPP20091030968206; Xin Zhimin, "Nov CPI Grows First Time Since Jan," *China Daily* [Online], December 12, 2009, in OSC, doc. no. CPP20091212968034; *Xinhua News Agency*, January 12, 2010, in OSC, doc. no. CPP20100112968253; *Xinhua News Agency*, February 12, 2010, in OSC, doc. no., CPP20100212968163; *Xinhua News Agency*, May 2, 2010, in OSC, doc. no. CPP20100502968115; "Chinese Premier Pledges Efforts to Control Housing Prices, Inflation," *Xinhua News Agency*, February 27, 2010, in OSC, doc. no. CPP20100227968161; *Xinhua News Agency*, May 12, 2010, in OSC, doc. no. CPP20100512968038; "Inflation could rise to 5%: Economist," *People's Daily* [Online], May 10, 2010, in OSC, doc. no. CPP20100510787004; *Xinhua News Agency*, June 17, 2010, in OSC, doc. no. CPP20100617968187; *Xinhua News Agency*, August 18, 2010, in OSC, doc. no. CPP20100818968185.

8. Kang Juan, "Surging prices stoke inflation fears," *Global Times* [Online], May 12, 2010, in OSC, doc. no. CPP20100512722002; Shan Juan, "Price hikes in certain basic goods fuel inflation fears," *China Daily* [Online], June 5, 2010, in OSC, doc. no. CPP20100605968028; *China Daily* [Online], June 5, 2010, in OSC, doc. no. CPP20100605968028.

9. "China counts down to the next bubble burst," *Caijing* (Finance) [Online], August 5, 2010, in OSC, doc. no. CPP20090805968025; *Xinhua News Agency*, November 17, 2010, in OSC, doc. no. CPP20091117968202; "Chinese premier pledges efforts to control housing prices, inflation," *Xinhua News Agency*, April 30, 2010, in OSC, doc. no. CPP20100430968249.

10. *China Daily* [Online], January 15, 2010, in OSC, doc. no. CPP20100115968234; *China Daily* [Online], June 2, 2010, in OSC, doc. no. CPP20100602968112; *Xinhua News Agency*, June 15, 2010, in OSC, doc. no. CPP20100615968178; *Xinhua News Agency*, June 23, 2010, in OSC, doc. no. CPP20100623968230; Wang Tao, "Massive local government debts trigger controversy," *Jingji Cankao Bao*, June 30, 2010, in OSC, doc. no. CPP20100630308002; Shi Hongxiu, "Government financing platform and local government debt," *Zhongguo Jingji Shibao* [Online], July 6, 2010, in OSC, doc. no. CPP20100706308002. On the banking sector, see Carl E. Walter and Fraser J. T. Howie, *Red Capitalism: The Fragile Financial Foundation of China's Extraordinary Rise* (Singapore: Wiley, 2010).

11. Hu Xingdou, "It is suggested that the 'two sessions' review situation of state owned enterprises advancing as private sectors retreat," *Guangming Ribao* [Online], February 24, 2010, in OSC, doc. no. CPP20100225610002; *Zhongguo Fazhan Guancha* [Online], March 9, 2010, in OSC, doc. no. CPP20100330308003. On China's financial bias toward state-owned enterprises, see Huang Yasheng, *Capitalism With Chinese Characteristics: Entrepreneurship and The State* (Cambridge: Cambridge University Press, 2008).

12. *Xinhua News Agency*, December 7, 2009, in OSC, doc. no. CPP20091207072001; *Xinhua News Agency*, March 5, 2010, in OSC, doc. no. CPP20100305968122; *Xinhua News Agency*, March 22, 2010, in OSC, doc. no. CPP20100322312008; *Liaowang*, January 18, 2008, in OSC, doc. no. CPP20100125710007.

13. Li Hong, "Income divide reaches dangerous point," *People's Daily*, May 10, 2010, in OSC, doc. no. CPP20100512787004; Guo Qiang, "Income gap rings alarm," *Global Times*, May 27, 2010, in OSC, doc. no. CPP20100527722001. See the discussion of "urgency" in *Guoji Xianqu Daobao* [Online], July 14, 2010, in OSC, doc. no. CPP20100730671001.

14. Doyle McManus, "China—Economic juggernaut, running scared," *Los Angeles Times*, September 19, 2010. Available: http://articles.latimes.com/2010/sep/19/opinion/la-oe-mcmanus-column-china-20100919; "Chinese village activist's death suspicious: daughter," *Reuters*, December 16, 2011. Available: http://www.reuters.com/article/2011/12/16/us-china-unrest-villager-idUS-TRE7BF0T920111216. For an authoritative discussion of the extent of mass demonstrations and the party's efforts to promote stability, see Zhou Baogang, *Zhuntixing Shijian: Yufang, Chuzhi Gongzuo Fanglue* [*Mass Incidents: General Work Plan for Prevention and Management*] (Beijing: Zhongguo Gongan Daxue Press, 2008) (*neibu faxing*).

15. Fan Zaiqin, Song Erdong, and Yan Congbing, "Analysis, Forecast of China's Social Situation," in Ru Xin, Lu Xueyi, Li Peilin, Chen Guangjin, Li Wei, and Xu Xinxin, *Blue Book of China's Society—Society of China: Analysis and Forecast* (2010) (Beijing: Chinese Academy of Social Sciences, December 2009), in OSC, doc. no. CPP20100301442001.

16. *China Daily* [Online], March 5, 2010, at OSC, doc. no. 2-1-0305968161; Willy Lam, "Powerful interests stifle China's reforms," *Asia Times*, March 2010. Available: http://www.atimes.com/atimes/China/LC20Ad01.html; Wu Bangguo's report is available at OSC, doc. no. CPP20110318968076; Wen Jiabao's report is available at OSC, doc. no. CPP20110305046001.

17. Zhuang Qinghong, "New thinking on stability presented by Qinghua University Sociology experts," *Zhongguo Qingnian Bao*, April 19, 2010, in OSC, doc. no. CPP20100512636002.

18. *People's Daily* [Online], January 16, 2010, in OSC, doc. no. CPP20100116705009; *Nanfang Dushi Bao* [Online], December 22, 2009, in OSC, doc. no. CPP200912236300. For an authoritative party discussion of the imperative of leading public opinion, including on the internet, see *Yulun Yindao Yishu: Lingdao Ganbu Ruhe Miandui Meiti* (*The Art of Guiding Public Opinion: How Leading Cadres Deal with the Media*) (Beijing: Xinhua Chubanshe, 2010). The implications of digital communications technologies for party control are discussed in Xiao Qiang, "The Rise of Online Public Opinion and Its Political Impact," in *Changing Media, Changing China*, edited by Susan L. Shirk (New York: Oxford University Press, 2011), pp. 202–24. On more recent developments, see Xiao Qiang, "The battle for Chinese internet," *Journal of Democracy*, Vol. 22, No. 2 (April 2011), pp. 47–61.

19. Suisheng Zhao, *A Nation-State by Construction: Dynamics of Modern Chinese Nationalism* (Palo Alto: Stanford University Press, 2004); Susan L. Shirk, *China: Fragile Superpower: How China's Internal Politics Could Derail Its Peaceful Rise* (New York: Oxford University Press, 2007); He Yinan, "History, Chinese nationalism and the emerging Sino-Japanese conflict," *Journal of Contemporary China*, Vol. 16, No. 50 (2007), pp. 1–24; William A. Callahan, *China: The Pessoptimist Nation* (New York: Oxford University Press, 2010).

20. James Reilly, *Strong Society, Smart State: The Rise of Public Opinion in China's Japan Policy* (New York: Columbia University Press, 2011).

21. For a discussion of this Chinese policy debate, see Dong Wang, "Eying the Crippled Hegemon: China's Grand Strategy Thinking in the Wake of the Global Financial Crisis," Paper presented to the 2010 Annual Meeting of the American Political Science Association, Washington, DC, September 2–5, 2010; Zhao Suisheng, "Chinese foreign policy under Hu Jintao: The struggle between low-profile policy and diplomatic activism," *The Hague Journal of Diplomacy*, Vol. 5, No. 4 (2010), pp. 357–78; David Shambaugh, "Coping with a conflicted China," *Washington*

Quarterly, Vol. 34, No. 1 (Winter 2011), pp. 7–27. Dai Bingguo, "Adhere to the Path of Peaceful Development," December 6, 2010. Available: http://china.usc.edu/ShowArticle.aspx?articleID=2325. Also see Wang Jisi, "The issue of China's international positioning and the strategic idea behind the idea of 'hiding our capacities and biding our time,'" *Guoji Wenti Yanjiu*, March 13, 2011, in OSC, doc. no. 20110413671003.

22. See, for example, Simon Shen and Shaun Breslin, eds., *Online Chinese Nationalism and China's Bilateral Relations* (Lanham, MD: Lexington Books, 2010). On defense policy, see Robert S. Ross, "China's naval nationalism: Sources, prospects, and the American response," *International Security*, Vol. 34, No. 2 (Fall 2009), pp. 46–81.

23. Mark Landler, "Diplomatic storm brewing over the Korean peninsula," *New York Times*, May 20, 2010; David Sanger and Thom Shanker, "Pentagon and U.N. chief put new pressure on N. Korea," *New York Times*, May 25, 2010. Available: http://www.nytimes.com/2010/05/25/world/asia/25korea.html; Jung Sung-ki, "S. Korea, US to stage joint naval exercise next week," *Korea Times*, June 2, 2010. Available: http://www.koreatimes.co.kr/www/news/nation/2010/06/205_66957.html.

24. Kim Deok-hyun, "Joint South Korea-US military drills begin as warning to North Korea," *Yonhap News*, July 25, 2010; Choe Sang-hun, "As tensions rise, US and South Korea begin naval drills," *New York Times*, July 26, 2010; "Major General Luo Yuan discusses joint military exercise in the Yellow Sea," *Renmin Wang*, July 13, 2010, in OSC, doc. no. CPP20100713787008.

25. "China 'very opposed' to US-Korea Yellow Sea drill," *Sunday Morning Post*, July 4, 2010, in OSC, doc. no. CPP20100705718012; Liu Bin, "'Explosive contact': Chinese and US Navies stand off in Yellow Sea," *Nanfang Zhoumo* [Online], July 7, 2010, in OSC, doc. no. CPP20200709788015.

26. Li Jing, "US subs reach Asian ports," *Global Times* [Online], at OSC, doc. no. CPP20100706722009; *Xinhua News Agency*, July 6, 2010, at OSC, doc. no. CPP20100706968196.

27. Editorial, "A test of Chinese people's diplomacy," *Global Times*, July 7, 2010, in OSC, doc. no. 20100708722013; Liu Yueshan, "People's Liberation Army Major General Luo Yuan says that US aircraft carrier can be used as live target," *Wen Wei Po* [Online], July 7, 2010, in OSC, doc. no. CPP20100707788008; "'Explosive contact'"; "Why China opposes US-South Korean military exercises in the Yellow Sea," *People's Daily*, July 16, 2010, in OSC, doc. no. CPP20100719787007; "Major General Luo Yuan discusses joint military exercise in the Yellow Sea."

28. Liu, "People's Liberation Army Major General Luo Yuan"; "China and inter-Korean clashes in the Yellow Sea," *Asia Report*, No. 200 (2011). Available: http://www.crisisgroup.org/~/media/Files/asia/north-east-asia/200%20—%20China%20and%20Inter-Korean%20Clashes%20in%20the%20Yellow%20Sea.pdf; Yang Yi, "Navigating stormy waters: The Sino-American security dilemma at sea," *China Security*, Vol. 6, No. 3 (2010); Peter Lee, "China turns netizen anger on Seoul," *Asia Times*, July 16, 2010, at OSC, doc. no. CPP20100716715029. On Luo Yuan's statements, see, for example, *Feng Huang Wei Shi Tzu Hsun Tai*, July 21, 2010, in OSC, doc. no. CPP20100723715035.

29. Wang Xiyi, "Chinese government takes 'tough line'; US carrier turns around," *Guangzhou Ribao* [Online]; July 17, 2010, in OSC, doc. no. CPP20100725138004.

30. Ministry of Foreign Affairs of the People's Republic of China, July 8, 2010, in OSC, doc. no. CPP20100721467004; Ministry of Foreign Affairs of the People's

Republic of China, July 13, 2010, in OSC, CPP20100721467005; Ministry of Foreign Affairs of the People's Republic of China, July 15, 2010, in OSC, doc. no. CPP20100715364001.

31. *Xinhua News Agency*, July 21, 2010, in OSC, doc. no. CCP20100721005008. Also see Foreign Minister Yang Jiechi's July 23 comments to Secretary of State Hillary Clinton, *Xinhua News Agency*, July 23, 2010, in OSC, doc. no. CPP20100723045009. Later that year in November a U.S. aircraft carrier did participate in a U.S.–South Korean exercise in the Yellow Sea.

32. For a time-line of the major events, see *Agence France Presse*, September 22, 2010, in OSC, JPP20100922969063.

33. Reilly, *Strong Society, Smart State*; He Yinan, "History, Chinese Nationalism and the Emerging Sino-Japanese Conflict"; Callahan, *China: The Pessoptimist Nation*.

34. *Xinhua News Agency*, September 8, 2010, in OSC, doc. no. CPP20100908968233; editorial, "Diaoyu Islands a dangerous game," *Global Times* [Online], September 8, 2010, in OSC, doc. no. CPP20100908722004; *Wen Wei Po*, September 9, 2010, in OSC, doc. no. CPP20100909794004; Guo Qiang, "Experts assess impact of islands dispute," *Global Times* [Online], September 9, 2010, in OSC, doc. no. CPP20100909722002.

35. For this paragraph and next paragraph, I am grateful for the online research carried out by Ciqi Annabel Chua.

36. Zhongguo Tongxun She, September 18, 2010, in OSC, doc. no. CPP20100918066006; *Xinhua News Agency*, September 24, 2010, in OSC, doc. no. CPP20100924968216.

37. Strong Nation Forum, September 7, 2010. Available: http://bbs1.people.com. cn/postDetail.do?view=1&id=102619602&bid=1; Sina Forum, September 11, 2010. Available: http://club.news.sina.com.cn/thread-581329-1-1.html; Tianya Forum, September 8, 2010. Available: http://bbs.city.tianya.cn/tianyacity/ content/5154/1/1383.shtml.

38. Sina Forum, September 27, 2010. Available: http://club.news.sina.com.cn/thread-591709-1-1.html; FMPRC Forum, December 20, 2010. Available: http://bbs .fmprc.gov.cn/detail.jsp?id=360237; QQ Forum, September 21, 2010. Available: http://bbs.news.qq.com/b-1000087807/23748.htm.

39. *Zhongguo Tongxun She*, September 18, 2010, in OSC, doc. no. CPP2010091806-6006;

40. *Agence France Presse*, September 18, 2010, in CPP20100918968045; *Jiji Web* (Japan), September 18, 2010, JPP20100919164001.

41. *Zhongguo Tongxun She*, September 18, 2010, in OSC, doc. no. CPP2010091806-6004.

42. *Huanqiu Wang*, September 20, 2010, in OSC, doc. no. 20100920671003.

43. *Xinhua News Agency*, September 20, 2010, in OSC, doc. no. CPP20100920968174; *BBC Monitoring*, September 22, 2010, in OSC, doc. no. CPP20200922950001.

44. Ministry of Foreign Affairs of the People's Republic of China, September 7, 2010, in OSC, doc. no. CPP20100907364001; *Xinhua News Agency*, September 8, 2010, in OSC, doc. no. CPP20100908071003; *Xinhua News Agency*, September 8, 2010, in OSC, doc. no. CPP20100908968215.

45. Ministry of Foreign Affairs of the People's Republic of China, September 9, 2010, in OSC, doc. no CPP2010091346001; *Xinhua News Agency*, September 10, 2010, in OSC, doc. no. CPP20100910968159; *Xinhua News Agency*, September 10, 2010, in CPP20100910968249; *Xinhua News Agency*, September 11, 2010, in OSC, doc. no. CPP20100911138004; *Kyodo News* , September 12, 2010, in

OSC, doc. no. JPP20100912969003; *Agence France Presse*, September 15, 2010, in CPP20100915968051; *Kyodo News*, September 16, 2010, in OSC, doc. no. CPP20100916969110.

46. *Xinhua News Agency*, September 19, 2010, in OSC, doc. no. FEA2010091-9009462.

47. *China Daily* [Online], September 20, 2010, in OSC, doc. no. CPP20100920968012; Ministry of Foreign Affairs of the People's Republic of China, September 21, 2010, in OSC, doc. no. CPP20100921364001; *Kyodo News*, September 20, 2020, in OSC, doc. no. JPP20100920969037; *Agence France Presse*, September 22, 2010, in OSC, JPP20100922969063.

48. Among other locations, the video is available at www.youtube.com. See, for example, http://www.youtube.com/watch?v=1YxIFxkNXlc&feature=related.

49. *Xinhua News Agency*, September 22, 2010, in OSC, doc. no. CPP20100922-968052.

50. *Xinhua News Agency*, September 25, 2010, in OSC, doc. no. CPP20100924508015; *Asahi Shimbun* [Online], September 28, 2010, in OSC, doc. no. JPP20100928969012; *Kyodo News*, September 30, 2020, in OSC, doc. no. JPP20100930969170; *Asahi Shimbun* [Online], October 11, 2010, in OSC, doc. no. JPP20101011969006.

PART TWO

Transnationalism

CHAPTER 4

⌒⋎⌒

Immigrant China*

FRANK N. PIEKE

The international migration order has changed fundamentally in the last twenty years. First came a surge in new immigration to the developed countries in North America, Europe, and Oceania, soon followed by immigration in more recently developed countries, particularly in East and Southeast Asia. We are currently at the brink of a third phase of change, where the world's emerging economies demand a prominent role, not only as countries of origin but also, and increasingly, as countries of destination for international migrants.[1] With all the fear that surrounds immigration and the clamor for ever more stringent controls and restrictions the world over, it is often ignored that this major phenomenon of transnationalism—migration—is itself an important driver of development and economic growth. The future of the world will be determined by competition not only over resources, markets, and capital but also over human beings, the most precious commodity of all. The resulting new patterns of spatial and social mobility will create forms of diversity that combine or clash the world over with established ideas and interests vested in, for example, nations, ethnic groups, or local communities.

This chapter focuses on China's relationship with these new patterns of mobility and explores the nature and implications of this fundamental shift by the first, largest, and arguably most important of the twenty-first century's so-called emerging powers. China's development has given rise

---

* A longer version of this chapter was published in Frank N. Pieke and Elena Barabantseva, eds., "Old and new diversities in contemporary China," *special issue of Modern China*, Vol. 38, No. 1 (2012), pp. 40–77.

to massive flows of both domestic migration and international emigration abroad. Since the start of the reforms, these domestic and transnational flows suggest that the People's Republic of China (PRC) is developing into a crucial hub of the global migration order.[2] However, what is less often noted, both in China itself and by other global actors, is the radical changes currently taking place that potentially will have an even greater impact in the next five, ten, or twenty years: China is rapidly also becoming an important destination of international migrants. These migrants into China, attracted by the promise of a better life, are beginning to fill specific gaps in the labor market created by economic and social development and demographic trends.[3] In twenty years from now, China will be a country defined by its cities rather than by its countryside, and the latter no longer will be able to act as a limitless reservoir of labor migrants for the lower-end jobs in urban manufacturing, construction, and services.

In the short to medium term, the rise of China as a major immigration country is mostly predicated on the continued growth of its economy and its gradual transition to an urban, service-based economy. The role and especially the timing of demographic factors are less clear. In 2003 for the first time China began to experience shortages of *internal* migrant labor as there are only a few people left in rural China under the age of 30 who still work in agriculture. According to China's leading labor economist, Cai Fang and his collaborators, this is because China has started its demographic transition and can no longer rely on an inexhaustible supply of labor to drive further economic growth.[4] Shortages of labor do indeed drive up migrant workers' wages, a trend that has continued apace despite a short blip caused by the economic crisis in late 2008 and early 2009.[5] In 2010 and 2011, sometimes violent strikes and protests by migrant workers were reported widely in Guangdong, revealing the strong bargaining power of migrant laborers in the area and causing speculation that the end of China's labor-intensive, export-processing growth strategy might be near.[6] In response, local employers are turning to illegal Vietnamese labor immigrants to fill the gap left by domestic migrants (*mingong huang*).[7]

This is very likely only the beginning of a fundamental restructuring of the Chinese labor market. According to Athar Hussain, the imbalances caused by the one-child policy, some of the consequences of which are discussed more fully in chapter 5 in this volume, only in the long term (over fifteen years from now) will lead to truly massive shortages of working-age people. Before that, China will in fact continue to benefit from the dividend of the one-child policy of a relatively small number of under-age children that have to be supported by the working-age population The number of people of working age will continue to rise and then stabilize, while the size of the elderly population will only gradually increase. Meanwhile, the number of under-age dependents will continue to shrink. However, once the imbalances caused by mandatory family planning fully kick in, their consequences will rapidly become increasingly severe.[8] Moreover, China's alarmingly unbalanced sex ratio will mean that there will continue to be many more men than women, creating a demand for women (mainly as wives, but also as concubines or prostitutes, as chapter 5 attests) that will fuel international migration.

In recent years, the media and a few academic researchers have started reporting on groups of nonethnic Chinese immigrants, such as Muslim, South Asian, or African traders, foreign students, South Korean middle-class settlers, foreign expatriates, and North Korean refugees. However, with a very few exceptions,[9] none of these studies approach foreigners in contemporary China more generically as an immigration issue that is leading to the formation of ethnic communities, comparable in this regard to most if not all of the countries in the developed world, including many East and Southeast Asian countries. The mind-set that China is a country of emigration, not immigration has created a huge blind spot in the perception of China's global role.[10]

This chapter is intended as a first step. It gives basic information on the history of post-1949 immigration and the numbers and types of immigrants who have come to the PRC. The main part of the discussion is devoted to an analysis of the perceptions and policies within the Chinese administration of foreign immigration, residency and employment. I conclude that China faces considerable challenges in reaching a long-term, sustainable accommodation with foreign immigrants, with potentially significant consequences for other aspects of cultural, ethnic, and religious diversity, and for China's relations with the governments of these foreign immigrants.[11]

ORIGINS AND GROWTH OF IMMIGRATION TO CHINA

In 1949, the year of the victory of the Chinese Communist Party (CCP), more than 200,000 foreigners (*waiguo qiaomin*, or *waiqiao*) lived in China. This foreign presence was the most visible aspect of what the party perceived to be China's 100 years of humiliation since the Opium Wars at the hands of foreign imperialist and capitalist aggressors. Immediately after victory, the party proceeded, in the words of Party Chairman Mao Zedong, "first to clean out the rooms before inviting new guests" (*dasao ganjing wuzi zai qingke*). In 1955, with only 7,833 foreign residents remaining, a new system was put in place to accommodate the travel and stay of New China's "foreign guests" (*waibin*) and "foreign friends" (*waiguo pengyou*): delegates, visitors, students, businesspeople, and apparently even some tourists. Although loosely modeled on the Soviet Union, the PRC's "foreign affairs" (*waishi*) system was unique in the world in the meticulous differences between foreigners and Chinese that it created in all spheres of life. Aspects of this system continue to exist, still informing attitudes toward foreigners within the state and among the general population.[12]

The most important foreign presence in the new China of the 1950s was the thousands of experts sent by the Soviet Union and its allies to help China industrialize and set up a socialist planned economy. With the growing rift between China and the Soviet Union after 1956 these experts were withdrawn. In the 1960s and especially from 1964, restrictions on foreigners were increased, including for instance foreigners' checkpoints.[13] At the start of the Cultural Revolution, China had become a hermetic state that few foreigners could travel to, and just a few diplomats, journalists, students, and businesspeople from countries that recognized the PRC remained, in addition to overseas Chinese who had fled Indonesia after the anti-Chinese movements there.

In the 1970s, after the end of the "revolutionary" phase of the Cultural Revolution (1966--69), a gradually rising number of foreigners began to arrive in conjunction with the opening up of Chinese society and normalization of China's international relations. After the death of Mao in 1976 and the official start of the "Four Modernizations" in 1978, the number of foreign visitors to China rose quickly. In 1978, 1.02 million foreigners entered China, a number that rose to 3.29 million in 1985 and 16.7 million in 1999.[14] In the 1970s and 1980s foreigners who resided in China for a longer period of time consisted of four main categories: degree students mainly from developing countries (especially Africa and North Korea) and Chinese-language and culture students mainly from the developed world; expatriate businesspeople, journalists, and diplomats; and foreign-language teachers and other "foreign experts" hired by Chinese state employers. Foreign residence in all categories was still strictly controlled by state agencies rather than by market forces or other factors beyond the economic plan. Only the further growth and maturation of the market economy in the 1990s and 2000s created the conditions for autonomous immigration and settlement. Liberalization of housing, employment, trade, investment, health care, and education allowed not only Chinese but also foreigners to make their own choices where to work and live.

Until the 2010 population census, which for the first time included foreign residents, the most immediately available and internationally

comparable data on the number of immigrants in China were those com-
piled by the United Nations (UN). According to the UN, China's foreign
population was 245,700 in 1960, rising to 376,400 in 1990 and 590,300
in 2005.[15] No information is given on what exactly these figures refer to,
but they most likely only include foreign nationals and ignore Chinese
from Taiwan, Hong Kong, and Macao living in China. This seems to be
confirmed by the 2010 population census that yielded a total number of
593,832 foreigners, which excluded 170,283 Taiwanese, 234,829 Hong
Kong residents, and 21,201 Macao residents for a total of 1,020,145 foreigners in the PRC.[16] Although this, for the first time, gives comprehensive
and reliable figures on the number of foreigners, the census may well have
severely undercounted the numbers involved. As we will see later in this
chapter, many foreigners in China either reside illegally or else have only
short-term visas, forcing them frequently to travel in and out of the country, thus being visible to the administration only as visitors rather than
residents.

International migrants still are only a minute fraction of China's huge
population. However, foreigners are highly concentrated in specific parts
of the country, such as Guangzhou, Shanghai, or Beijing. In these places,
foreigners have become a long-term and important aspect of the urban
landscape and, with an absolute number of over one million, the scale and
variety of immigration in China already defies easy and unambiguous characterizations. As a start, three broad and overlapping categories of immigrants can be distinguished: (1) cross-border migrants; (2) students; and
(3) middle-class professionals, businesspeople, and traders.

Cross-border migrants

China's international borders no longer divide and separate. North Korea
provides perhaps the clearest example. The famine there in the mid- to late
1990s led to a flood of emigrants into China. The PRC government has
treated these Koreans as illegal entrants and with little sympathy. In 2002,
Human Rights Watch and other human rights groups reported massive
roundups, detentions, and repatriations of North Koreans, and a crackdown on religious and human rights groups that assisted them.[17] The issue
is made more complex because of the large ethnically Korean population
that lives in China just across the border from North Korea. Many North
Koreans were taken into rural Korean households and even were irregularly registered as members of these households by the local authorities. In
addition, North Korean women were trafficked for marriage across China,

reportedly for a price of about 10,000 Yuan.[18] At present, China continues to be a major transit country for smuggled North Koreans en route to
South Korea.

China's border areas are becoming part of larger cross-border regions
defined by complex relationships of co-ethnicity, religion, legal trade and
illegal smuggling, marriage, employment, study, immigration and emigration, crime, and (particularly in the case of Xinjiang) terrorism.[19] Today,
probably more than at any other time since the establishment of the PRC,
people living close to the border continue to maintain contact with their
relatives and co-ethnics and move freely across the border, with or without a permit.[20] One particular issue that concerns local authorities is the
inflow of women from the other side of the border as wives for local co-
ethnic men. These women and their children are permanent members of
their communities in China, yet they have no legal status and are a major
headache locally in the enforcement of state family planning.[21]

Students

China has become a magnet for fee-paying foreign students. In 2007 the
number of foreign students was 190,000, or more than five times as many
as in 1997.[22] Major state and private investment in the tertiary educational
sector has made Chinese universities competitive in the lucrative international student market. As China's global role increases, firsthand knowledge of Chinese language and culture becomes a more important asset,
attracting ever larger numbers of students to China. The majority of such
students take short-term courses specifically tailored to foreigners.

China has also become the choice of many degree students, mainly from
Southeast and South Asia. In 2008, 50,468 foreign students were enrolled
in undergraduate and 10,743 in postgraduate programs.[23] Some of this is
part of the government's "soft power" strategy,[24] but many students apply
to Chinese universities also because of the combination of good-quality
education, reasonable fees, and geographic proximity.

Professionals, businesspeople, and traders

China's cities attract ever larger numbers of businesspeople and professionals from the developed world. The communities of middle-class and
elite resident foreigners are no longer numerically dominated by expatriate employees of foreign multinationals, international organizations,

diplomatic missions, and "foreign experts" hired by Chinese state enterprises or organizations.[25] Large numbers of foreigners have independently taken up long-term residence in search of local employment (with either a Chinese or foreign firm), cheaper living costs, or to set up their own business. In addition, we should also include in this category the very diverse group of traders from Russia, Central, South and Southeast Asia, the Middle East, and Africa. To all of these foreigners, China is the land of opportunity, not just a stopover on an international career.

In the eyes of many Chinese, (white) Westerners are the paradigm of what are known as *yang dagong* (foreign workers).[26] However, numerically this category of foreign residents is in fact dominated by hundreds of thousands of middle-class Taiwanese, Hong Kong Chinese, South Koreans, Japanese and Southeast Asians, and, of course, returning Chinese nationals and former Chinese nationals.[27]

Policy-oriented articles on foreigners in China often begin by stating that China's growth, World Trade Organization (WTO) membership, and general opening up have created a need for highly skilled foreign labor despite China's own very large labor force. China is said to need, for instance, high-level managers, engineers, or employees with the skills necessary to operate in an international business environment.[28] This is in line with the 1996 "Rules for the Administration of Employment of Foreigners in China" that limit foreigners to employment that cannot be filled by Chinese. Furthermore, article 34 of these regulations explicitly forbids Chinese individual economic organizations or individual citizens from hiring foreign workers, limiting foreign employment to foreign and state and larger private enterprises. However, this is honored mostly in the breach, an important cause of the "*san fei*" (three illegalities) problem that the authorities are struggling to resolve and which is discussed in the section on "fortune seekers" below.

Despite their spread beyond areas designated specifically for foreigners, many groups of immigrants who share a common background tend to concentrate in one particular city or neighborhood and/or specialize in a particular type of employment or business. Such clustering (for instance, through chain migration or professional specialization) is an important feature of settlement of foreign communities in for instance Guangzhou,[29] a pattern reminiscent of the settlement of certain domestic rural–urban migrants in contemporary China, such as the well-known "Zhejiang Village" in Beijing.[30] In some cases, this has enabled the emergence of an ethnic infrastructure. In Beijing, 80,000 or so mainly middle-class South Koreans live in the city's Wangjing district, supporting a large and well-equipped Korean school, restaurants, shops, and travel agents.[31]

The very large communities of Taiwanese in Shanghai, Shenzhen, and Dongguan have established many schools that teach for Taiwanese degrees, while Dongguan even has a Taiwanese hospital.[32] Taiwanese migrants are able to capitalize on a combination of an international background and native language and cultural skills. The Chinese government in practice actively encourages their migration. Entry and one-year residence visas as well as work permits are much easier to obtain than for other foreigners; since 2005, work permits are given without the normal restrictions on foreign employment.[33] Taiwanese migration, together with migration from Hong Kong and Macao and return migration of (former) Chinese nationals, is a phenomenon that complicates the notion of a divide between international and domestic migration.

Much smaller communities of traders exist from Russia, Central, South and Southeast Asia, the Middle East, and Africa.[34] Immigrant traders tend to create and exploit highly specific niches where dense co-ethnic networks and access to specific overseas markets give them a competitive advantage. The group of foreign traders that are by far the best researched are the Africans in Guangzhou, partially because of the visibility of what is locally known as "Chocolate City" (*Qiaokeli cheng*) and partially also as a corollary of the recent interest in the connections between China and Africa, including Chinese migration to the continent.[35] Guangdong, as the manufacturing center of the global economy, is a magnet for traders and procurement agents, while Africa has emerged as a natural market for cheap manufactured goods from China. Starting with a few enterprising students some fifteen years ago, currently about 30,000 Africans operate in Guangzhou purchasing manufactured goods for export to their home country either from wholesale markets or directly from factories in the Pearl River Delta.

China's affluence and opportunities attract more and more Chinese professionals and businesspeople. The majority of highly educated professional Chinese may currently still choose to stay abroad. However, they are a huge talent pool that China will continue to be able to draw on in the years to come. In government policy, Chinese students and scholars abroad (*liuxue renyuan*) are kept completely separate from the overseas Chinese, despite the fact that they are often lumped together under the heading of the "new migrants" (*xin yimin*) and that the PRC's overseas Chinese office (*Qiaoban*) is formally responsible for both.[36] Overseas Chinese leave China predominantly from rural areas, are unskilled and in a very real sense deemed superfluous in China itself. Their return migration is not a priority. The same cannot be said about Chinese students and scholars abroad: their leaving is considered a loss to China that can only be repaired by their eventual return.[37] The accumulated number of foreign students and scholars abroad in the eleven years between 1996 and 2006 was 1,067,000, of whom 275,000 have returned to China.[38] The overwhelming majority of students and scholars that return do so to Shanghai, Beijing, and southern Jiangsu. Shanghai alone accounted for a full one-third of all returnees, or 50,000, by 2002, with Beijing not far behind at 40,000 by 2003.[39]

Returnees are very prominent among academics and senior administrators in higher education and research institutions, especially the more prestigious and better funded ones. National and local governments and university administrations strongly encourage students and scholars abroad to return to China to take up academic employment, encouraging them with a range of privileges and perks (salary, housing, research funds) regardless of foreign permanent residence status or even citizenship. This has led to considerable tension between the "sea turtles" (*haigui pai*) and "locals" (*bentu pai*), although at least some of these privileges may seem more extreme than they might actually be.[40] However, the strong drive to build "world class universities" made this an unequal contest, and, as Rosen and Zweig conclude, "the battle is over and the returnees have 'won.'"[41]

Returnees in China are a new and growing elite group drawn from upwardly mobile middle-class families, while only relatively few members derive from the old political elite.[42] Their impact on Chinese society extends beyond the world of universities and research. Chinese administrations actively recruit among overseas graduates and scholars and encourage them to set up businesses or contribute their knowledge, skills, and patents to partnerships with Chinese businesses. To woo potential investors, governments frequently organize conventions or fairs, creating what Xiang Biao has called an elaborate "ritual economy of 'talent.'"[43] Saxenian has shown how Chinese engineers and entrepreneurs from Silicon Valley have accelerated the development of the information technology sector in China.[44]

"FORTUNE SEEKERS" AND PROBLEMS OF IMMIGRATION

As some of the examples given previously already show, neatly dividing foreign immigrants into categories such as "students," "traders," "businesspeople," "professionals," and "cross-border migrants" hardly exhausts the reality on the ground. Migrants are highly enterprising and proactive in exploring the opportunities that China has to offer, and as a result there is very considerable overlap and spillover between all these categories. From the perspective of the Chinese authorities, the dynamic nature of migration has created a further category of immigrant that does not come to China for bona fide business, study, or employment but opportunistically in search of wealth or survival. Few such "fortune seekers" (*taojinzhe*, literally "gold panners") bring any skills or capital to China, and "many are people from poor countries without a profession, income, skills, or health guarantee."[45] In short, these migrants are deemed not to come to China to contribute to its modernization but merely to take advantage of the country's new prosperity.

Filipinos are often given as an example of "fortune seekers." Among richer and upwardly mobile Chinese families, Filipino domestic workers and home tutors have become increasingly common. These families want their children to learn English to give them better opportunities in school, in university, and later in life, and they employ Filipinos for this purpose.[46] This practice is particularly widespread in Shenzhen, Shanghai, and Beijing and most likely has entered China from Hong Kong and Taiwan where Filipino domestic workers have long been common.[47]

Fortune-seeking illegal migrants are not limited to poor national or ethnic groups. For instance, one other example of fortune seekers given repeatedly is young Westerners, who use their student status for residence purposes only and in fact make a living masquerading as foreign experts or scholars, giving English-language classes or lectures about Western culture, society, and business to gullible Chinese audiences.[48]

In fact, almost every group of immigrants in China is internally stratified, having both highly successful professionals and businesspeople (although some of these might in fact not have full and proper paperwork either, a point I return to later) and more marginal groups without formal jobs or fully registered businesses. Instead, new immigrants rely on their own resources and personal contacts, causing the growth of residentially concentrated urban "villages" (*cun*) or "cities" (*cheng*), such as the Burmese and Vietnamese in Guangxi and the South Koreans in Beijing.[49] Here we see the beginnings of the "ethnic enclave" pattern of immigrant settlement found among many immigrant groups the world over, where the institutional infrastructure and employment offered by a co-ethnic community provides new arrivals with the chance to get established and ultimately become successful too.[50]

Currently, foreigners still have certain privileges that are partially a leftover of the time that all foreigners in China were "foreign guests" (*waibin*) and partially because China needs their "talent" and contribution. In their discussions on fortune seekers and illegal immigrants, Chinese authors often conclude that such migrants do not deserve such courtesies but should rather be considered similar to the "floating population" (*liudong renkou*) of domestic rural–urban migrants. Foreign fortune seekers allegedly compete with China's own huge labor force for jobs. The "foreign floating population" (variously termed *jingwai liudong renkou*, *waiguo liudong renkou*, or *waiguo liudong renyuan*[51]) is a cause of increasing concern. However, as China's immigration policies still remain unformed, at the moment this is dealt with mainly as a public-order issue. Local police in places with many foreigners periodically carry out crackdowns on illegal foreigners, leading to fines, detentions, and even expulsions without providing a more structural solution.

Increasingly, the problem of the "foreign blind flow" (*waiguo mangliu*) is directly connected with that of the "three illegalities" (*san fei*) of illegal entry, residence, and work.[52] As in all countries, it is by its very nature impossible to quantify exactly how serious the issue of foreign illegality is, but it is certain that it has rapidly increased. In 2007, the head of the Jiangsu province border exit and entry bureau estimated that 30 percent of resident foreigners in the province were illegal.[53] In 2006, the Ministry of Public Security handled 36,000 *san fei* cases and repatriated 9,560 foreigners.[54]

In many Chinese analyses, the three illegalities and the foreign floating population are often discussed together with many other much more serious problems, including terrorism, organized and petty crime, drinking, drugs and violence, prostitution, and unemployment,[55] a list that is depressingly similar to observations on immigration in Western countries.[56] Crime in particular is singled out. In Yunnan along the Burmese border, foreigners and Chinese are involved in large-scale organized crime, including the smuggling of drugs and consumer goods, human smuggling, kidnapping, extortion, and murder.[57] Despite a step-up in law enforcement, crime in these areas is reported to have become more serious, because of increasing population mobility, economic development, lack of international cooperation, and ethnic and religious factors.[58] In the city of Guangzhou crime by foreign "floaters" is said to constitute a "hidden danger" (*yinhuan*) to public order in the city.[59]

EVOLUTION OF THE ADMINISTRATION OF FOREIGN ENTRY AND RESIDENCE

Despite the fact that a link is assumed to exist between fortune seeking, illegality, and criminality, most Chinese authors agree that the lack of compliance with China's regulations regarding foreign entry, employment, and residence should be separated from more serious law enforcement issues.[60] The illegality of many foreigners in China often has to do more with the lack of appropriate regulation, the continued restrictions on travel and other activities by foreigners, and a general lack of expertise and coordination within those branches of the administration that are responsible for foreigners. Even many professional and business migrants, the kind of people China says it wants, either have no choice but to bend the rules in order to live and work in China or else have little incentive to comply with the regulations. A 1998 article, for instance, points out that foreigners often do not want a work permit quite simply because that would make them liable to taxation in China.[61] With its entry into the WTO in December 2001, China also signed on to the principle that foreigners in China are entitled to the same treatment as Chinese citizens. Quite apart from the fact that this in reality still has not been achieved (for instance, many areas are still closed to foreigners), several Chinese sources expressed concern that the illegal status of foreigners in fact prevents the authorities from extending these rights to them.[62]

Although China is beginning to face issues that other destination countries have grappled with for much longer, it still lacks a clear legal and administrative framework and apparatus to deal with foreign entry, residence, and employment. As the Introduction to this volume notes, decisions made in one policy area can have many unintended effects in another policy realm and require the authorities to be alert to these widespread repercussions. At the moment, administrative responsibilities are scattered over numerous departments, such as public security, foreign affairs, human resources, foreign experts, commerce, and education. These departments not only do not work together, because each takes responsibility for only certain categories of foreigners (diplomats, experts, workers, businesspeople and investors, students, seafarers), but also even compete for turf and influence.

The vast majority of foreigners, even long-term residents, hold visas valid for at most a few years, while many simply move in and out of the country every few months to get a new visitor's visa or stay in China illegally. It is even more difficult to obtain work permits, particularly for foreigners who are self-employed or work for employers other than foreign-invested firms or state organizations. In response, in China's large cities a thriving market in visas and work permits has sprung up that are irregularly obtained by specialist travel agencies or "visa boys"; in fact, many employers and employees in China don't even bother with the bureaucratic maze around formal applications at all.[63]

China also faces a more fundamental policy gap. Currently, immigration in China is mainly regulated by three sets of laws and regulations: the Law on Control of the Entry and Exit of Aliens and the Law on Control of Exit and Entry of Citizens,[64] both promulgated in 1985; the Rules for the Administration of Employment of Foreigners in China of 1996; and, finally, the Regulations on Examination and Approval of Permanent Residence of Aliens in China of 2004. In addition, a large number of more specific national and local regulations and rules exist.[65]

In the management of foreign immigration, the creation of a separate Border Exit and Entry Management Bureau (*Churujing Guanli Ju*) within the Ministry of Public Security in 1983, followed by the promulgation of the 1985 law on the entry and exit of aliens, was somewhat of a watershed. Both the bureau and the law signaled a public move away from an exclusionary discourse and the recognition that the presence of foreigners was a normal aspect of social life that had to be regulated by law rather than politics.[66] In the 1990s this new normalizing discourse gradually evolved into the perception that China, in order to fulfill its modernizing ambitions, needs specific skills, knowledge, and expertise from foreigners, ultimately leading to the 1996 regulations on the employment of foreigners.

The next step in the process of gradual normalization of a foreign presence was the recognition that foreigners were there to stay. This led to the regulations on permanent residence of aliens in 2004, a policy modeled on the American green card system. In 2011, a new law was released requiring foreigners to participate (both allowing them to benefit as well as obliging them to contribute) in the public pension scheme in Beijing. However, the regulations on permanent residence are very strictly applied and such residence is reportedly mainly given to ethnic Chinese, mostly as part of a broader policy initiative to turn China's brain drain since 1978 into a brain and capital gain.[67]

As my Chinese sources readily admit, much of the current regulatory framework is already outdated, while the many existing laws, rules, and regulations of individual government departments and local administrations are not integrated. Particularly the 1996 regulations on foreign employment need to be replaced as they are still rooted in the perception that the employment of foreigners is temporary and needed only to fulfill specific skill and expertise requirements. New legislation will have to be based on the recognition that foreign employment in China is a permanent feature, including employment with small private enterprises and private individuals.[68] Another much debated issue is that of dual nationality, which China's current nationality law does not allow. This issue is particularly important in dealing with Chinese return migrants, many of whom have acquired a foreign nationality.[69]

At the moment, however, policy making is progressing only at a snail's pace. Despite apparent setbacks, a general agreement continues to exist on the need for a new comprehensive migration law and the establishment of either an immigration office separate from the ministries, or even a ministry of interior affairs, or else the appointment of a senior member of the State Council responsible for immigration affairs. However, the political impetus behind such a change has clearly waned. Apart from competition between departments currently in charge of aspects of foreigners' work, the political sensitivity of immigration is also frequently given as a reason for the lack of change. Creating a comprehensive immigration policy and administration would amount to stating publicly that China is becoming an immigration country, which, it is feared, would encounter widespread popular and administrative resistance. China still sees itself as defined by its huge population, and policies in many areas are still predicated on or justified by that fact. What would people think, for instance, if foreigners were freely allowed to live and work in China when so many local workers and university graduates still cannot find a job? And, most contentious of all, what about family planning? Would it be possible to continue to limit Chinese couples to just one child when the government openly adopts a pro-immigration policy?[70]

These arguments amount to a version that is specific to contemporary China of a problem that currently is almost universal across immigration countries. Immigration is economically beneficial yet politically explosive, frequently leading, as Stephen Castles points out, to "hidden agendas" in migration policies. Governments prefer either not to make any policy at all or, alternatively, to adopt formally restrictive policies or rhetoric, while simultaneously allowing immigration to continue through other measures or even simply illegally.[71]

Beyond the narrow issues of entry and employment, China will also have to find ways of dealing with a permanent foreign presence. As ethnic communities of foreigners based on common nationality, race, language, religion, or culture are beginning to grow, China is more obviously becoming an immigration country rather than a place where foreigners happen to live. With this, China, like other immigration countries, will have to find ways of permanently integrating these communities, dealing with questions of ethnic and race relations, religious and cultural pluralism, nationality and political rights, and the emergence of a second generation in ways never faced before. Beijing will also have to assess how these movements of people could affect government-to-government and transnational societal relations with these countries of origin.

Yiwu city's approach might give some indication where future policy in practice might go. Yiwu proudly presents itself as a laboratory for managing the peaceful co-residence of a multitude of visitors from elsewhere in China and abroad. In 2003, a city-wide video surveillance system was completed to help the police keep crime and conflict under control, while streamlined visa and residence procedures aim to facilitate the steady stream of foreign and domestic visitors.[72] Yiwu explicitly aims at the "integration in the community" (*rongru shequ*) and the creation of a "second home area" (*di'er guxiang*) with the objectives to treat foreigners as citizens, to fight and prevent crime and other illegal activities, and to promote the feeling "that Chinese and foreign families enjoy a natural bond like members of one family" (*Zhongwai jiating tong xiang tianlun*). To this aim, Yiwu experiments with an interesting mix of measures. The city allows selected foreigners to observe the city's people's congress and people's consultative conference and gives them the opportunity to raise suggestions during special feedback meetings. Yiwu also has equipped special stations at the administrative community (*shequ*) level for residence and visa formalities. Foreigners are involved in the running of certain test-point administrative communities where they live; Chinese-language training stations have been set up for foreigners, while their children are given the right to attend local schools. They are also given the same rights as Chinese in business and financial transactions, and they have freedom of religion. Special cultural activities are organized to promote Chinese and foreign understanding and friendship. Information networks have been set up with the participation of heads of residential blocks, landlords, personnel of associations, public security cadres, and local people's police to prevent and fight crime by and against foreigners. Finally, Yiwu aims its policies mostly at the administrative community level and seeks to concentrate its foreign population even more in those communities that already have a high concentration of foreigners.[73]

Inspiration for these measures seems to have been drawn from several different sources. Empowerment, recognition of equal rights, government service provision, and policing are part of a modern approach based largely on foreign templates. Conversely, celebration of cultural difference and friendship is more reminiscent of China's older minority and "foreign friends" policies. Finally, residential concentration and indirect administration through community leaders might be an echo of more specifically Chinese preferences in dealing with internal migrants in pre-1949 Chinese cities.

China still does not possess the regulatory framework and administrative capacity fully to deal with large-scale immigration, and the next few years are likely to be a window of debate and policy making that will determine what kind of immigration country China will become. Currently, the trend is toward a more integrated approach that facilitates the entry and stay of foreigners. The recognition that foreigners are there to stay also comes with the necessity to cater to their needs, such as education for their children and the right to profess their religion in churches, mosques, or temples. However, the normalization of immigration also means that foreign residents are only entitled to the rights that Chinese citizens enjoy as well, and should no longer get an especially privileged treatment.[74]

Yet in certain respects, the normalization of immigration will continue to be less than straightforward as it touches on some politically very sensitive issues. In these areas, foreigners are still treated on the basis of the old exclusionary discourse as carriers of subversive influences that may harm Chinese society and even the rule of the CCP. The most important example here is possibly religion. In 1994, the State Council issued the "Rules on the management of religious activities of foreigners in the People's Republic of China,"[75] which give them the right to conduct collective religious activities in specially designated locations. However, importation of religious materials that could be used to spread religion in China is explicitly forbidden. Moreover, in their implementation of the rules, local religious affairs authorities ban Chinese citizens from attending religious activities organized by foreigners.[76] It seems unlikely that this lingering sensitivity to foreign subversion will disappear completely. In addition, as we have seen, a new perception is emerging that not all immigration is necessarily a good thing. The growth of a "foreign floating population" is considered a burden on Chinese society, while immigration is also associated with terrorism, subversive activities, and international organized crime. As a result, an increasing emphasis on control and national security in addition to service and equal treatment is to be expected.

CONCLUSION

At present, China continues to be one of the world's most important sources of emigrants. There is little doubt that China will continue to play this role for at least the next ten years, and quite possibly even longer. Developed countries thus have little reason for immediate worry about the supply, or migration "pipeline," of migrant labor, without which their population would peak in 2020 and fall by 7 percent in the next three decades.[77] However, international migration specialists are already beginning to think about what happens next, when "China, India and South East Asia could well become massive players in the international migration system with relatively little 'notice.'"[78]

This chapter has given a glimpse of that future. As we have seen, China's prosperity and opportunity are already attracting a diverse range of immigrants as the country is developing into the center of gravity of the whole of East, Southeast, and Central Asia. With the increase in the number and diversity of immigrants, China is beginning to face the formation of more permanent immigrant communities, many of which are residentially clustered and occupationally specialized. Their impact on China's existing cultural, regional, and occupational diversity will have considerable reper- cussions for the kind of country China will be in ten or twenty years from now. Immigration is set to become a key policy concern for China, both domestically and, as competition for international migrant labor stiffens, in the international arena as well.

At present, the Chinese authorities have only rudimentary policy instru- ments to deal with the new flows of immigrants and the diversity that they engender. The policy initiatives and discussions outlined in the final section of this chapter, notably the experiments in Yiwu city, indicate that China's understanding of immigration is quite different from that of almost all developed Asian countries. Countries such as Japan, the Republic of Korea, Taiwan, Malaysia, Thailand, Singapore, and the Gulf states encourage immigration of the highly skilled, but allow unskilled labor immigration on highly restrictive temporary contract schemes.[79] Much more than in even some of the more extreme anti-immigration Western countries, such as the Netherlands, Switzerland, or Denmark, the state in Asia jealously guards the nation as a set of entitlements and rights that only native inhabitants are privileged to have.[80] This particularly exclusivist reading of the con- cept of nationalism often discriminates not only against immigrants but also against certain categories of native people—for instance, the ethnic Chinese in Malaysia or the hill tribes in Thailand, who are imagined as not or not fully belonging to the core national group that has monopolized the nation.

China certainly has its fair share of this form of nationalism, but the tra- ditional cultural and ethnic inclusivity of the Empire and socialist ideology and practice coupled with the country's size and diversity have put limits on its expression for most of the PRC's history. China, moreover, expects to play a leading role in the world. It accepts that this quite naturally attracts foreign immigrants to its shores. Even more, China acknowledges that its further development and globalization require the presence of foreigners both as temporary visitors and more permanent residents. The new Exit- Entry Administration Law adopted by the Standing Committee of the National People's Congress on June 30, 2012, can be taken as a further— but still tentative—step in this direction. The law is predominantly driven by public security and foreign affairs agendas, especially the clear regula- tion of entry, exit, residence, and employment of foreigners and curbing of illegal practices. Here the law is quite liberal as it emphasizes administrative punishment (mainly fines or extradition) rather than criminal persecution of transgressors. However, the law also contains (admittedly modest) provisions for the management of immigration that cater to the agendas of other government departments and businesses, such as education, human resources and social security, foreign experts, and commerce. This is most clearly the case with the special consideration given to foreign "talents" and investors throughout the law and with article 42, which explicitly allows work–study of foreign students and promises a "catalogue" of types of employment that are in need of foreign labor.[81]

Although by itself the new law remains insufficient as a comprehensive immigration law, it nevertheless clearly represents foreign immigration, employment, and residence as normal. China's policy makers see immigration as part of the emergence of China as East Asia's leading metropolitan area that requires much greater freedom of movement and cultural diversity than the smaller nation-states elsewhere in the region dare to imagine for themselves. However, we also have seen that a traditional socialist suspicion of foreigners and foreign influences still lurks in the background, now often fused with more contemporary concerns about national security and transnational crime.

The question we have to ask then is where China will look for inspiration in designing policies to respond to the country's foreign immigrants. Older policies for minority nationalities (*shaoshu minzu*) or the overseas Chinese (*Huaqiao*) are inadequate and hardly ever mentioned in Chinese discussions of foreign immigrants. Despite subsequent elaborations and adaptations, China's policies in these areas essentially date from the late 1970s and early 1980s. The key component of policy in both cases consisted of the bureaucratic creation and validation of ascribed social statuses. Minority people and overseas Chinese were given a specific and privileged place and special rights that simultaneously also defined and delimited their access to mainstream society. This, in fact, was fairly similar to the containment of and privileges given to foreigners until the 1990s.

Currently, policy making is more likely to go the other way, namely, the creation of legally defined rights and duties that are broadly identical for all residents of the PRC. Foreign immigration might very well set the direction and pace for more general policy initiatives in response to China's increasingly fluid and diverse social structure. Future research on diversity and migration would benefit, in particular, from growing sensitivity to questions revolving around this issue. As China's policies for migrant communities mature, how long will it take before the old overseas Chinese and national minority policies also come across as out of touch with reality? Will we eventually see the emergence of a general set of policies aimed at pluralism in the context of rapid mobility and social change that includes overseas Chinese, new returned Chinese emigrants, indigenous minorities, internal migrant communities, and international migrant communities?

NOTES

1. Demetrios G. Papademetriou, "Reflections on the international migration system: Introduction," *Canadian Diversity*, Vol. 6, No. 3 (2008), pp. 3–6.
2. Frank N. Pieke, "Community and identity in the new Chinese migration order," *Population, Space and Place*, Vol. 13, No. 2 (2007), pp. 81–94.
3. I will only focus here on the People's Republic. Taiwan, Hong Kong, and Macao have, of course, for much longer been destinations of immigrants. Because of their separate history and political systems, they are best considered separately from the PRC.
4. Cai Fang, Du Yang and Wang Meiyan, *Migration and Labor in China*, Human Development Research Paper 2009/09 (United Nations Development Programme, 2009), pp. 22–5.
5. Fang Cai, Yang Du, John Giles, Albert Park, and Meiyan Wang, "Shock and Recovery in China's Labor Market: Flexibility in the Face of a Global Financial Crisis," Review paper for East Asia PREM (The World Bank, 2010).
6. "Is China's labour at a turning point?" *The Economist* (June 12, 2010), p. 94.
7. Interview at the Guangzhou Police Officers Academy [*Guangzhou Jingguan Xueyuan*], June 25, 2010.
8. Athar Hussain, "Demographic Transitions in China and Its Implications," *World Development*, Vol. 30, No. 10 (2002), pp. 1823–34; Athar Hussain, Robert Cassen and Tim Dyson, "Demographic Transition in Asia and Its Consequences," *IDS Bulletin*, Vol. 37, No. 3 (2006), pp. 79–87.
9. For instance Zhang Li, "Ethnic congregation in a globalizating city: The case of Guangzhou, China," *Cities*, Vol. 25, No. 6 (2008), pp. 383–95.
10. Prasenjit Duara, "Asia redux: Conceptualizing a region for our times," *Journal of Asian Studies*, Vol. 69, No. 4 (2010), pp. 963–83.
11. I have systematically scanned Chinese, English, and French language materials up to and including 2009. In addition, in June 2010 I undertook a research trip to Beijing, Kunming, and Guangzhou to interview officials and researchers working on various aspects of foreign migration, employment, and residence.
12. This paragraph, including the Mao quote, is based on the official record on China's border management *Zhongguo jingcha xuehui churujing guanli zhuanye weiyuanhui* [Special Commission on Border Management of the Learned Society of the Chinese Police] *Gong'an churujing guanli da shi ji* [Record of main events in the public security management of border exit and entry], (Beijing: Qunzhong Chubanshe, 2003), pp. 2–6, 13–4; and Anne-Marie Brady, *Making the Foreign Serve China: Managing Foreigners in the People's Republic* (Lanham, MD: Rowman and Littlefield, 2003).
13. Zhongguo jingcha, *Gong'an churujing guanli da shi ji*, pp. 6–7.
14. Zhongguo jingcha, *Gong'an churujing guanli da shi ji*, pp. 7–8.
15. On the background and methodology of these data, see United Nations, Department of Economic and Social Affairs, Population Division, *Trends in*

International Migrant Stock: The 2008 Revision: CD-ROM Documentation [Online]. Available: http://www.un.org/esa/population/migration/UN_MigStock_2008. pdf [October 13, 2009]. Here I am using the UN figures as presented in table A in the statistical annex of United Nations Development Programme (UNDP), *Overcoming Barriers: Human Mobility and Development. Human Development Report 2009* (New York: United Nations Development Programme, 2009). The same data, including the figures on refugees, are also available online at http://esa.un.org/ migration [October 13, 2009].

16. The first census figures on foreign residents in China were made public on April 29, 2011. Available: http://www.stats.gov.cn/english/newsandcomingevents/ t20110429_402722638.htm [May 1, 2011].

17. Human Rights Watch, "The invisible exodus: North Koreans in the People's Republic of China," *Human Rights Watch*, Vol. 14, No. 8 (2002); see also "China: Crackdown on 'Illegal Immigrants' Aims at North Korean Refugees" [Online], March 27, 2002. Available: http://www.hrea.org/lists/refugee-rights/markup/ msg00029.html [September 16, 2008].

18. Li Guangsen and Gu Guoyong, "'Yibola houzi': jujiao waiguoren feifa rujing Zhongguo" ["'Ebola monkeys': focus on foreigners who illegally enter China"], *Jiancha fengyun*, Vol. 4 (2006), pp. 4–7.

19. On the latter, see Hao Chiyong, "Jiaqiang xibu diqu churujing guanli gongzuo sikao" ["Reflections on strengthening border exit and entry work in western areas"], *Gong'an yanjiu*, No. 96 (2002), pp. 109–12; Cui Yazhou, "Qiantan bianjing shaoshu minzu diqu chutu fankong zuozhan yuanze" ["Discussion on the principles of counter terrorism operations in border minority areas"], *Gong'an yanjiu*, No. 151 (2007), pp. 72–4.

20. Janet C. Sturgeon, *Border Landscapes: The Politics of Akha Land Use in China and Thailand* (Seattle: University of Washington Press, 2005).

21. He Yue, "Zhongguo xinan bianjiang jingwai liudong renkou de quyu guanli yan-jiu [Research on the regional management of the foreign floating population in China's southwestern frontier]," *Guizhou shehui kexue*, No. 228 (2008), pp. 38–43; see also Jing Changling, "Quanqiuhua shidai Zhongguo jingwai renkou taishi ji shehui wenti touxi [Penetrating the situation and social problems of China's foreign population in the time of globalization]," *Zhengfa xuekan*, Vol. 20, No. 3 (2003), pp. 56–62.

22. "Foreign student quota to expand," *China Daily*, July 29, 2008.

23. Kai Yu and Nian Cai Liu, *Tertiary Education at a Glance: China 2010* (Washington, DC: World Bank, 2010), p. 50.

24. Particularly in Southeast Asia; see Joshua Kurlantzick, *Charm Offensive: How China's Soft Power Is Transforming the World* (New Haven: Yale University Press, 2007), pp. 69–71.

25. This seems to be true even in Beijing, where most foreign and international organizations have their offices. A small sample survey of registered foreign workers in the city gives indications of clear differences in attitude toward work and life between expatriate and long-term resident foreigners. Unfortunately, the quality of the article's data, analysis, and data presentation allow few further conclusions; Zhao Yao and Yang Rui, "Waiguoren zai Jing gongzuo zhuangkuang yu tedian yan-jiu," *Laodong jingji yu renli ziyuan*, Vol. 1 (2009), pp. 114–18.

26. For instance, an article on *yang dagong* in the *Tianjin ribao* [Tianjin Daily] fea-tures three (European) white males; see "Yang dagong de kuaile shenghuo qinjin Zhongguo ge you suo ai [The happy life of foreign workers in China: to each his

own love]," *Tianjin ribao*, March 3, 2007. [Online]. Available: http://view.news. qq.com/a/20070517/000035.htm [September 23, 2008].

27. *70 wan Hanguoren changzhu Zhongguo: jiasu rongru Zhongguo shehui* [*700,000 Koreans live permanently in China: accelerated integration into Chinese society*] [Online]. May 17, 2007. Available: http://view.news.qq.com/a/20070517/000001. htm [September 23, 2008].

28. The most recent installment of this argument can be found in the 2010 *Guojia zhongchangqi rencai fazhan guihua gangyao (2010–2020)* [*National outline for medium- and long-term talent development (2010–2020)*] [Online]. Available: http://www.gov.cn/jrzg/2010–06/06/content_1621777.htm [July 29, 2010].

29. Li, "Ethnic congregation in a globalizating city."

30. Xiang Biao, *Transcending Boundaries. Zhejiangcun: The Story of a Migrant Village in Beijing* (Leiden: Brill, 2005); Li Zhang, *Strangers in the City: Reconfigurations of Space, Power, and Social Networks Within China's Floating Population* (Stanford: Stanford University Press, 2001).

31. Shana Sun Roberts, personal communication, 2007; see also Ariana Eunjung Cha, "Chasing the Chinese Dream," *Washington Post*, October 21, 2007: A16.

32. Sam Ng, "Taiwanese gold rush to China," *Asia Times Online*, June 30, 2004 [Online]. Available: http://www.atimes.com/China/FF30Ad04.html [September 16, 2008].

33. Yen-Fen Tseng, "Emerging Career Maps in New Times: Migration Patterns of Skilled Taiwanese to China," Paper presented at New Times? Economic Crisis, Geo-Political Transformation and the Emergent Migration Order, Centre on Migration, Policy and Society (COMPAS), annual conference, Oxford, September 21–22, 2009.

34. There are relatively many journalistic and scholarly accounts of Africans and Indians in China (see note 36 below). On Russians, to my knowledge no information exists except the statement that tens of thousands of Russians live in Shanghai and Beijing. See E. Wishnick, "Migration and Economic Security: Chinese Labour Migrants in the Russian Far East," in *Crossing National Borders: Human Migration Issues in Northeast Asia*, edited by Tsuneo Akaha and Anna Vassilieva (Tokyo: United Nations University Press, 2005), pp. 68–92, cited in Irina Ivakhnyuk, "Crises-Related Redirections of Migration Flows: The Case of the Eurasian Migration System," Paper presented at New Times? Economic Crisis, Geo-Political Transformation and the Emergent Migration Order, Centre on Migration Policy and Society (COMPAS), annual conference, Oxford, September 21–22, 2009, p. 18, and observations on Russian home ownership in Chinese cities in Su Yu, "Huanjing shushi lilü di Eluosiren zhengxian konghou mai Zhongguo fangzi" ["A comfortable interest rate environment rushes Russians to buy a house in China"], *Xinhuawang*, September 10, 2006 [Online]. Available: http:// view.news.qq.com/a/20070517/000018.htm [September 23, 2008]. At present, Middle Eastern traders merely get passing reference in a few Chinese sources, while I found only one report on Vietnamese traders in Guangzhou; see Huang Yunjing, "Yuenanren zai Guangzhou" ["The Vietnamese in Guangzhou"], *Dongnan Ya zongheng*, Vol. 2 (2009), pp. 74–8.

35. Brigitte Bertoncelo and Sylvie Bredeloup, "The emergence of new African 'trading posts' in Hong Kong and Guangzhou," *China Perspectives*, Vol. 1 (2007), pp. 94–105; Adams Bodomo, "The African trading community in Guangzhou: An emerging bridge for Africa–China Relations," *China Quarterly*, No. 203 (2010), pp. 693–707; He Yue, "Yunnan jingnei de waiguo liudong renkou taishi yu

bianjiang shehui wenti tanxi" ["Exploration and analysis of the situation of the foreign floating population inside Yunnan's border and problems of frontier society"], *Yunnan Shifan Daxue xuebao*, Vol. 41, No. 1 (2009), pp. 18–25; Hélène Le Bail, *Les grandes villes chinoises comme espace d'immigration internationale: le cas des entrepreneurs africains [China's Large Cities as Places of Immigration: The Case of African Entrepreneur]* (Paris: Centre Asie Ifri, 2009); Li, "Ethnic congregation in a globalizing city"; Michal Lyons, Alison Brown, and Zhigang Li, "The 'third tier' of globalization: African traders in Guangzhou," *City*, Vol. 12, No. 2 (2008), pp. 196–206; Evan Osnos, "The promised land: Guangzhou's Canaan Market and the rise of an African merchant class," *The New Yorker*, February 9–16, 2009, pp. 50–5; Heidi Østbø Haugen, "Chinese and African Traders: Different Types of Capital Employed in Transnational Economic Activity," Paper presented at the conference *Chinese in Africa/Africans in China*, Centre for Sociological Research, University of Johannesburg, August 27–28, 2009.

36. Pal Nyiri, *Mobility and Cultural Authority in Contemporary China* (Seattle: University of Washington Press, 2010).

37. Cheng Li, "Coming Home to Teach: Status and Mobility of Returnees in China's Higher Education," in *Bridging Minds across the Pacific: U.S.-China Educational Exchanges, 1978–2003*, edited by Cheng Li (Lanham, MD: Lexington Books, 2005), p. 79.

38. Wang Huiyao, *Dangdai Zhongguo haigui [Contemporary Chinese Returnees]* (Beijing: Zhongguo Fazhan Chubanshe, 2007), p. 7.

39. Li, "Coming Home to Teach," p. 90.

40. Luo Keren, Fei Guo, and Huang Ping, "China: Government Policies and Emerging Trends of Reversal of the Brain Drain," in *Return Migration in the Asia Pacific*, edited by Robyn Iredale, Fei Guo, and Santi Rozaria (Cheltenham: Edward Elgar, 2003), pp. 88–111.

41. Stanley Rosen and David Zweig, "Transnational Capital: Valuing Academic Returnees in a Globalizing China," in *Bridging Minds across the Pacific: U.S.-China Educational Exchanges, 1978–2003*, edited by Cheng Li (Lanham, MD: Lexington Books, 2005), p. 128; see also David Zweig, Chen Changgui, and Stanley Rosen "Globalization and transnational human capital: Overseas and returnee scholars to China." *China Quarterly*, No. 179 (2004), pp. 735–57.

42. Li, "Coming Home to Teach"; A.L. Saxenian, "From brain drain to brain circulation: Transnational communities and regional upgrading in India and China," *Studies in Comparative International Development*, Vol. 40, No. 2 (2005), pp. 35–61.

43. Xiang Biao, "A ritual economy of 'talent': Chinese and overseas Chinese professionals," *Journal of Ethnic and Migration Studies*, Vol. 37, No. 5 (2011), pp. 821–31.

44. Saxenian, "From brain drain to brain circulation."

45. Zhang Jie, "'Feiyong' xianxiang dui woguo sanfei anjian zhili de qishi" ["Lessons for the management of our country's cases of three illegalities from the phenomenon of 'Filipino employment'"], *Jiangxi Gong'an Zhuanke Xuexiao xuebao*, No. 115 (2007), p. 60.

46. Zhang Jie, "Cong 'Feiyong' xianxiang toushi shichang jingji tiaojian xia de waiguoren jiuye guanli" ["Perspective on the employment of foreigners under conditions of market reform from the perspective of 'Filipino employment'"], *Shandong Jingcha Xueyuan xuebao*, No. 95 (2007), pp. 110–12.

47. Nicole Constable, *Maid to Order in Hong Kong: Stories of Filipina Workers* (Ithaca, NY: Cornell University Press, 1997).

48. Zhang Jie, "Cong 'Feiyong' xianxiang," pp. 110–12; Zhang Jie, "Toushi waiguo-ren," p. 26.

49. Zhang Jie, "'Feiyong' xianxiang," p. 60.

50. On this point, see Li, "Ethnic congregation in a globalizating city"; for the original ethnic enclave argument, see Alejandro Portes and Robert L. Bach, *Latin Journey: Cuban and Mexican Immigrants in the United States* (Berkeley: University of California Press, 1985); Alejandro Portes and Leif Jensen, "What's an ethnic enclave? The case for conceptual clarity," *American Sociological Review*, Vol. 52 (1987), pp. 768–71.

51. See He Yue, "Yunnan jingnei de waiguo liudong renkou taishi yu bianjiang shehui wenti tanxi" ["Exploration and analysis of the situation of the foreign floating population inside Yunnan's border and problems of frontier society"], *Yunnan Shifan Daxue xuebao*, Vol. 41, No. 1 (2009), pp. 18–25.

52. Du Guoqiang, "Dangqian liudong renyuan fanzui zhuangkuang, yuanyin ji duice yanjiu—yi Guangzhou shi liudong renyuan fanzui wei qieru dian" ["Research on the circumstances, causes and policy responses to crime among the present floating population—crime among Guangzhou city's floating population as point of entry"], *Fazhi luntan*, Vol. 4 (2008), pp. 163–71; Huang Jin, "Guanyu jingwai renyuan feifa juliu wenti de sikao" ["Reflections on the problem of illegal residence by foreigners"], *Hunan Gong'an Gaodeng Zhuanke Xuexiao xuebao*, Vol. 15, No. 2 (2003), pp. 70–4; Zhuang Huining, "'San fei' waiguoren jiujing you duoshao" ["How many illegal foreigners actually are there?"], *Renmin gong'an*, Vol. 5 (2007), p. 24.

53. Zhuang Huining, "'Sanfei' waiguoren guanli kaoyan zhengfu nengli" ["Management of 'three illegal' foreigners tests the government's capacity"], *Renmin gong'an*, Vol. 5 (2007), pp. 28–9.

54. Zhuang Huining, "'San fei' waiguoren jiujing you duoshao."

55. Du Guoqiang, "Dangqian liudong renyuan"; see Hao Chiyong, "Jiaqiang xibu diqu"; Qi Jianxia, "'21 shijie churujing (yimin) guanli xueshu yantaohui' zhuti zongshu" ["Summary of the main themes at the 'Scholarly discussion meeting on border entry and exit (immigration) in the 21st century'"], *Shanghai Shangxue Yuan xuebao*, Vol. 10, No. 1 (2009), pp. 17–8.

56. The association of foreigners with violations of public order resonates strongly with popular images, and of course with the CCP's traditional suspicion of foreign subversion and spiritual pollution. For an early and more popular account of the foreign threat to social order, including illegal business practices, smuggling, extramarital sex, and prostitution, see Li Guoqing, "'Laowai' zai Hua fanzui xianxiang saomiao" ["Scan of the phenomenon of foreigners' crime in China"], *Liaowang*, Vol. 22 (1994), pp. 28–9.

57. Song Yun, Yang Xingcai, and Dong Qinzhen, "Ruili kuajing fanzui wenti" ["The problem of transborder crime in Ruili"], *Zhongguo xingshi jingcha*, Vol. 3 (2001), pp. 16–7.

58. Hu Ergui, "Lun hexie shehui jianshe zhong de bianjing zhi'an wenti—Yunnan bianjing diqu zhi'an diaoyan pingxi" ["A discussion of the question of public security of border areas during the construction of a harmonious society: A critical analysis of research on public security in Yunnan's border areas"], *Sixiang zhanxian*, Vol. 33, No. 4 (2007), pp. 119–20.

59. Du Guoqiang, "Dangqian liudong renyuan," p. 165; see also Zhang Jie, "Toushi waiguoren," p. 26.

60. For instance, Jiang Jianyun and Xu Jiyuan, "Jinnian lai Changsha shi shewai an(shi)jian de tedian, chengyin ji qita duice" ["Special characteristics, causes and other countermeasures of criminal cases (incidents) involving foreigners in Changsha in recent years"], *Hunan Gong'an Gaodeng Kexue Xuexiao xuebao*, Vol. 19, No. 3 (2007), pp. 58–62.

61. Lu Chunping, "Dui waiguoren feifa jiuye de xingwei jieding ji guanli duice" ["Demarcation and management policy of illegal employment behaviour of foreigners"], *Gong'an lilun yu shijian*, Vol. 5 (1998), pp. 45–7.

62. Jiang Jianyun and Xu Jiyuan, "Jinnian lai Changsha shi shewai an(shi)jian de tedian, chengyin ji qita duice" ["Special characteristics, causes and other countermeasures of criminal cases (incidents) involving foreigners in Changsha in recent years"], *Hunan Gong'an Gaodeng Kexue Xuexiao xuebao*, Vol. 19, No. 3 (2007), pp. 58–62; Wu Guangzhen, Zhang Jian, and Yan Wanhong, "'Sanfei' waiguoren weifa fanzui wenti" ["The problem of illegal foreigners breaking the law and committing crime"], *Zhongguo xingshi jingcha*, Vol. 5 (2008), pp. 16–7; Zhang Jie, "'Feiyong' xianxiang," pp. 58–61.

63. This observation on a black market in visas is based on my own informal conversations with foreign residents in Beijing over the past few years. My Chinese sources give ample support for the more general point that the current regulatory system is unworkable and forces many foreigners into illegality.

64. For a very elaborate discussion of the law on exit and entry of citizens and the more detailed laws and regulations that followed it, see Guofu Liu, *The Right to Leave and Return and Chinese Migration Law* (Leiden, The Netherlands: Martinus Nijhoff, 2007); for a more general discussion of China as an emigration country, see Xiang Biao, "Emigration from China: A Sending Country Perspective," *International Migration*, Vol. 41, No. 3 (2003), pp. 21–48.

65. As in other areas, transparency is not helped by the fact that many of the more specific rules are not publicly available but are for internal use only, in this case by public security organs. For a slightly outdated overview of the regulation of foreign residence, see Luo Hongguan, "Waiguoren juliu guanli de lilun yu shijian" ["Practice and theory of the management of foreign residence"], *Jiangsu Gong'an Zhuanke Xuexiao bao*, Vol. 5 (1999), pp. 62–9.

66. Zhongguo jingcha, *Gong'an churujing guanli da shi ji*, pp. 14–15.

67. Interview, Yunnan Province Foreign Expert Office, Kunming, June 24, 2010.

68. Zhang Jie, "Cong 'Feiyong' xianxiang toushi," p. 112.

69. Zhou Nanjing, *Jingwai Huaren guoji wenti taolun ji* [*Collection of Discussions on the Nationality Question of Overseas Chinese*] (Hong Kong: Xianggang Shehui Kexue Chubanshe Youxian Gongsi, 2005); Qi Jianxia, "21 shijie churujing (yimin) guanli," p. 18.

70. The information and opinions in this paragraph were recorded during interviews in June 2010. For the protection of the interviewees I will not identify the specific interviews involved.

71. Stephen Castles, "Why migration policies fail," *Ethnic and Racial Studies*, Vol. 27, No. 4 (2004), pp. 205–27; for a similar conclusion, see Wayne A. Cornelius and Takayuki Tsuda, "Controlling Immigration: The Limits of Government Intervention," in *Controlling Immigration: A Global Perspective*, edited by Wayne Cornelius, Takayuki Tsuda, Philip L. Martin, and James F. Hollifield (Stanford, CA: Stanford University Press, 2004), pp. 41–2.

72. Weng Li, "Liuzhu wailai yimin anju leye shi hexie chengshi de zhongyao biaozhi— Yiwu shi gong'an gongzuo geiren de qidi" ["Resident immigrants living peacefully

and working happily is an important goal of the harmonious city—enlightenment from Yiwu city's public security work"], *Gong'an xuekan—Zhejiang Gong'an Gaodeng Zhuanke Xuexiao xuebao*, No. 98 (2006), pp. 42–44, 53.

73. Li Zhiqiang, "Gong'an jiguan jingwai renyuan guanlide xin tujing: Yiwu shi chuangjian 'guoji shequ' de shijian yu sikao" ["A new route of public security in the management of foreigners: practice and reflections on the creation of 'international communities' in Yiwu city"], *Gong'an xuekan—Zhejiang Gong'an Gaodeng Zhuanke Xuexiao xuebao*, No. 97 (2006), pp. 36–8.

74. Xu Min, "Waiji renyuan guanli zhong de zhengfu juese" ["The role of government in the management of foreign nationals"], *Chuangxin yanjiu*, Vol. 3 (2008), pp. 27–8.

75. *Zhonghua Renmin Gongheguo jingnei waiguoren zongjiao huodong guanli guiding*, State Council document 144 (1994) [Online]. Available: http://www.sara.gov.cn/GB//zcfg/37d8114b-0a1c-11da-9f13–93180af1bb1a.html [September 19, 2009].

76. Zhu Liangmei, "Jiefang sixiang Zhizheng wei min Jianzheng Shanghai shi Zongjiao gongzuo 30 nian fazhan" ["Liberate thought Hold power for the people Witnessing 30 years of development of religious work in Shanghai"], *Zhongguo zongjiao*, Vol. 12 (2008), pp. 43–4; Ao Ligong, "Shudao xuqiu Qianghua fuwu Guifan guanli: Tianjin shi fuwu he guanli waiguoren jiti zongjiao huodong de jingyan ji sikao" ["Accommodate demand Strengthen service Standardize management: Experiences and thoughts on servicing and managing collective religious activities of foreigners in Tianjin city"], *Zhongguo zongjiao*, Vol. 3 (2009), pp. 68–70.

77. UNDP, *Overcoming Barriers*, p. 43.

78. Papademetriou, "Reflections on the international migration system," p. 6; see also Graeme Hugo, "Trends in Asia that will influence its future as a source of skilled migrants," *Canadian Diversity*, Vol. 6, No. 3 (2008), pp. 41–6; Ronald Skeldon, "Immigration futures," *Canadian Diversity*, Vol. 6, No. 3 (2008), pp. 12–7.

79. Useful overviews of the immigration policies in these countries are given in the papers presented at the Workshop on International Migration and Labor Market in Asia, organized by the Japan Institute for Labour Policy and Training, Japan Institute for Labor, Tokyo, February 17, 2006. All papers are available from the workshop's webpage http://www.jil.go.jp/english/events_and_information/06_0217_report.htm [February 3, 2012] .

80. Peter Geschiere, *The Perils of Belonging: Authochthony, Citizenship, and Exclusion in Africa and Europe* (Chicago: University of Chicago Press, 2009).

81. *Exit-Entry Administration Law of the People's Republic of China*, adopted at the 27th session of the Standing Committee of the Eleventh National People's Congress of the People's Republic of China on June 30, 2013. In my comments here I have also drawn on Liu Guofu's discussion of the law at the "Immigrant China" workshop at Angers, France, October 4–6, 2012.

CHAPTER 5

Transnational Consumers

The Unintended Consequences of Extreme Markets in Contemporary China

KARL GERTH

If there is any doubt that the changing appetites and desires of domestic populations have transnational political, societal, and cultural consequences, consider an American couple wanting to adopt a more readily obtainable, less expensive Chinese infant, which may lead to baby thefts in rural China that in turn require new Chinese state regulations and enforcement mechanisms. Or, consider the countless numbers of Chinese newlyweds who wish to eat shark fin soup at their reception banquets, which is leading to the extinction of shark species off the coast of Chile that in turn leads Chinese nongovernmental organizations (NGOs) and government officials to try to limit shark fin soup consumption and change its cultural significance within China. In such cases, the impact of consumer desires and their negative consequences stretches across thousands of miles, an ocean, and political boundaries. As such cases demonstrate, transnational consumption has had unintended consequences for the Chinese state and society, prompting regulatory and cultural adjustments that have only just begun.

Behind these cases are tens of millions of newly middle-class urban Chinese consumers who are catching up with their counterparts in wealthier countries. The measure of such "catching up" has changed dramatically over time. In the early twentieth century, electric fans, light bulbs, and even a Western-style bowler hat set one apart. During the Maoist era from 1949 to 1976, Chinese consumers sought four functional status symbols: bicycles, watches, sewing machines, and radios, known as "the four things that go round." As expectations rose in the 1980s, wealthier Chinese hoped to purchase "six big things": videocassette recorders, televisions, washing machines, cameras, refrigerators, and electric fans. By 2000, consumers desired even more expensive items, with air conditioning units becoming the most sought-after product by consumers in the country's eleven largest cities, followed by personal computers, mobile phones, color televisions, and video equipment. In the countryside, motorcycles topped the shopping lists of 10 million Chinese as motorized vehicles increasingly replaced human- or animal-powered transport such as bicycles and donkey carts. Chinese consumer desire has also expanded to the consumption of experiences, such as private education, leisure travel, and cultural events like the Beijing Olympics. Although China remains a nominally socialist country, consumerism has indeed now become deeply entrenched in Chinese life and a key driver of global economic development.

Yet the consequences of Chinese consumers' attempts to catch up with and overtake their counterparts in the leading consumer countries also create new challenges for their country and the world. While many areas of the world stand to reap benefits from China's embrace of consumerism, including new and expanding markets for their products, nobody yet fully understands the *collective* global implications of *individual* Chinese consumer choices. While many journalists, scholars, and critics have already found much to worry about China's ascendance—the outsourcing of manufacturing jobs, competition for oil and other vital resources, human rights violations, growing Chinese military budgets, and carbon emissions—they have generally overlooked the effects of something subtler but equally profound: China's rapid development of a consumer culture. Many consequences have been as positive as predicted, particularly for consumers around the world who have benefited from the low-priced goods churned out of Chinese factories. But capitalist countries have long looked to China not only for low-wage workers but for consumers to fuel another round of global economic growth, hoping that new demand from Chinese consumers would translate into global economic opportunities. Indeed, many multinational corporations now pin their hopes for future growth on consumers in rapidly developing countries such as China, where the American-based coffee chain Starbucks alone is tripling its number of stores between 2010 and 2015, from 500 to 1,500.[1]

Chinese consumer demand has created market problems within China as well as unintended problems arising worlds away. Once stimulated, Chinese consumption—like consumption based on long commodity chains in all contemporary economies—is not easily contained, creating transnational challenges along with opportunities. The problems created by the economic rise of China began innocently enough. Since the earliest days of the Deng Xiaoping era at the end of the 1970s, capitalist countries have welcomed China's policy of "opening to the outside world." In 1986, the American magazine *Time* named Deng its Man of the Year for leading "an audacious effort to create what amounts almost to a new form of society" that, in effect, would be much more "open" to capitalist manufactured goods, investment, and tourists.[2] Such expectations and hopes continued throughout the 1990s, when the Clinton Administration argued that delinking human rights from trade was a surefire way to develop both.[3] Since then, business leaders and politicians from across the political spectrum have looked to China to do its part to drive a new round of global economic growth by implementing policies promoting domestic consumption by Chinese consumers.

Starbucks is not alone. The recent history of multinationals investing in China—first in manufacturing, now in domestic services—is well-known. Since 1992, when Deng Xiaoping reassured international investors that China still welcomed foreign direct investment (FDI), tens of billions of dollars of FDI have flowed into China, making China the leading recipient of FDI in the developing world and one of the overall world leaders. But now it is becoming easier and more obvious to recognize the importance of Chinese *outbound* FDI. Witness the endless procession of trade missions to China from both developing and developed economies not to hawk national goods and services but increasingly to solicit Chinese FDI. According to a report by the Asia Society, $1 trillion in direct Chinese investment will pour into other countries by 2020.[4]

More difficult to track and acknowledge are the innumerable transnational linkages caused by Chinese consumers as they slowly begin to do what political and business leaders have hoped: buy and consume. While many of these linkages benefit all involved, others create complex problems not easily solved. This chapter examines those negative and largely unintentional transnational consequences of China's emergence as a consumer culture by examining four of what I am calling "extreme markets." As we shall see, these implications have in turn led to formal Chinese governmental attempts to regulate markets and in some cases to respond to international regulation of these markets.

What the Chinese have seen as fit to market and therefore to consume has changed dramatically over the past century. Under Mao, Chinese leaders attempted to eliminate markets in general and those markets deemed extremely exploitative in particular, making it difficult or impossible, for example, to hire the services of a wet nurse, buy a bride, or sell a child. But as the state withdrew from many areas of private life and started creating new market incentives following the rise of Deng Xiaoping in 1978, China witnessed the return of pre-Communist-era markets for seemingly anything that one could buy and sell, including infants, wives, sex slaves, human hearts, and endangered species. These extreme markets illustrate how, once unleashed and prodded into action, Chinese consumers and consumer markets have unintended consequences that resist control by the Chinese government, other states, and international institutions that otherwise benefit from increased Chinese consumer demand.

FROM MAO TO MARKETS

China has had an ambiguous relationship with transnational markets. With the establishment of the People's Republic of China (PRC) in 1949, Mao Zedong announced that China had "stood up," meaning that the country, which had been dominated by foreign imperialist powers for the previous hundred years, would now control its own destiny. For its first thirty years, as market economies from America to Japan were developing modern consumer societies, the PRC tried to develop its industrial economy with as little integration as possible into those capitalist economies and exercised its sovereignty by limiting the availability of consumer goods and channeling scarce resources to heavy industry. The state's priorities at this time were *productivist*: to make or facilitate the making of things that make more things—"producer goods" such as steel and chemicals—rather than things that could be used directly—"consumer goods" like bicycles and toothpaste.

But this all changed with the death of Mao in 1976 and the rise of Deng Xiaoping in 1978. China's leaders decided that "opening to the outside world" (meaning the capitalist world) was essential to secure the technology and investment necessary to develop its economy. The Mao era's go-it-alone approach had, they decided, outlived its usefulness, and the risks of creating inequality within China and dependence on capitalist countries seemed outweighed by the potential gain. Observance of the obvious economic gains enjoyed by other East Asian neighbors reinforced this path. Thus, with Deng's rise to power, the country's leaders began to dismantle the state-controlled planned economy and society to prepare the soil in which foreign investors were invited to plant the seeds of market-led growth. Following the examples set by Japan, Taiwan, Chile, South Korea, and Singapore, Deng created a market economy mixed with authoritarian centralized control that he called "socialism with Chinese characteristics." The resulting massive expansion of industrialization was nurtured by a reliance on exports, foreign investment, and technology transfer to China through joint ventures with foreign companies. But China's leaders still attempted to restrict access to imported consumer goods and limit the influence of consumers on economic growth. This was born of a desire not so much to limit consumerism as to channel it, to ensure that the result was long-term growth in national wealth rather than an outrush of Chinese capital to buy consumer goods. Yet as markets have replaced the state as the supplier of goods and services, the state's power to limit or direct consumer spending has also waned, creating an opening for the reemergence of extreme markets.

As urban Chinese lifestyles become more like those of consumers in developed states, it is easy to forget just how recent the Chinese policies designed to promote consumer spending are. Since the 1990s, the country's leaders have understood that the massive budget and trade deficits of its biggest trading partner, the United States, were unsustainable and have wanted to decouple their economy from an over-reliance on economic growth fueled by exports. Even before the 2008 global economic crisis, they recognized that it was only a matter of time before American and European consumer markets were saturated with inexpensive Chinese imports and heavily indebted Western consumers would be less able to pay for lifestyles based on consuming more and more. Chinese leaders now began to view stimulating consumer desire not as a wasteful end point, the death of production, but rather as the starting point of production. This leaves unanswered, however, what China and the rest of the world should and can do when these new consumers have desires that create unintended negative consequences such as extreme markets.

MARKETS FOR CHINESE BABIES AND WIVES

It is easy to identify the domestic and global forces that create specific extreme markets within China. Take the markets for babies and wives. Culture and economic conditions there have long made sons far more valuable to families than daughters. In the traditional Han Chinese household, when a daughter "married out" of her birth family, she became part of her husband's kin. This represented a real transfer of wealth: a daughter ceased being her father's property, becoming instead her husband's. Consequently, daughters were liabilities for the families that raised them; sons were assets, as sons and their wives were expected not only to share the work of the family but to care for elderly parents. For several thousand years, Confucianism thus promulgated the idea that failing to have a male heir was the most unfilial act.

Yet the extreme market for babies and wives is also an unintended consequence of specific political policies. China's One Child Policy, introduced in 1979 to counteract the economic pressures of the uncontrolled population growth encouraged by Mao Zedong, further heightened the preference for male children. Under this policy, the Chinese government began penalizing families for having more than one child, a policy that, when enforced, gave couples only a single chance to secure a male heir and thereby a caretaker in their old age. This traditional role took on renewed importance as the consequence of other policies ending state-provided health care and retirement benefits. As boys became even more desirable and girls less so, female infanticide, long a way to dispose of unwanted girls, increased precipitously. When ultrasound scanning became more widely available in the 1980s, providing parents with a reliable, inexpensive way to determine the sex of fetuses, tens of millions of Asian parents elected to abort female fetuses. Even though the Chinese state banned ultrasound testing in an effort to stop sex-selective abortion in 2004, the market soon provided a growing number of for-profit "maternity clinics" and back-alley stalls performing the tests for only a few dollars and offering abortions for $15 to $120. As with other extreme manifestations of market behavior, buying and selling such services is difficult to stop, with sellers often staying one step ahead of enforcers, such as taking advantage of China's new car culture to introduce mobile backseat gender ultrasounds.[5]

The market for ultrasound services and abortions has led to an alarming gender imbalance in China, which now has about 120 boys for every 100 girls, rising to 144 to 100 in some areas, and 152 male second children for every 100 females.[6] And of the girls who are born, across the country a disturbing number are being abandoned, becoming wards of the state in Chinese orphanages.

At first glance, this skewed gender balance may seem merely a Chinese domestic issue. But since the early 1980s, the demand for adoptable babies in foreign markets has created new links between China and transnational markets, particularly consumers in the United States. In the 1990s, the increasing availability of contraceptives and abortion and acceptance of single mothers in the United States meant that millions of American couples with fertility problems faced a declining number of American babies available for adoption. Even when available, adopting an American baby could easily cost more than $30,000 and might take years to complete. Thus, American couples increasingly began to look abroad for less expensive and easier places to adopt children. By 2000, American couples were import-ing 20,000 children per year from Asia and Central and Eastern Europe. Between 1991, when China began to relax its adoption laws to address the growing number of abandoned girls, and 2010, China became the world's primary supplier of adopted children, sending more than 62,000 to the United States and another 10,000 to other countries.[7] Just between 1991 and 1992, the number of Chinese children adopted by Americans rose from a mere 61 to 206, and by 2005, when the number of Chinese adoptees peaked, the United States granted nearly 8,000 orphan visas for Chinese children, making up a third of all foreign adoptions.[8] Of these, 95 percent were girls.

Thus, American demand has helped create markets within China. Assuming that each adopting family paid an average of $15,000 to $20,000 for the entire process, Americans paid Chinese orphanages $24 million in 2005 alone.[9] Travel agencies began to shuttle adopting foreign families to sightseeing spots in Beijing, then on to the provinces handling inter-national adoptions. Five-star hotels in cities across China have become hubs for foreigners with new Chinese babies. The best known of these is the White Swan Hotel in Guangzhou, whose rooms, lobbies, and elevators are regularly filled with multiethnic families waiting to obtain U.S. visas for their new babies. The surrounding streets are lined with shops selling silk infant clothing and renting strollers. Each family staying at the hotel receives a special "Going Home Barbie Doll," the iconic blond-haired and blue-eyed plastic figure holding a Chinese baby.[10]

The surplus of mostly girl babies in China has served multiple American markets, including career women, affluent single people, and homosexual couples. By 2006, however, waiting lists of up to two years, bad press, and abuse led Chinese authorities to introduce new rules that excluded homo-sexual couples, older couples, the obese, those medicated for depression, and families with a net worth of under $80,000.[11] Since then, the num-ber of imported Chinese babies has halved to under 3,000 a year by 2011, though China still remains the top baby exporter to the United States. As a result, Americans have returned to South Korea, which remains a leader in international adoptions, and are also adopting babies from Guatemala, which temporarily replaced China as the number-one exporter in 2008, with Russia, Ethiopia, the Ukraine, Kazakhstan, and India also in the mix.[12] The baby export industry may soon follow the example of shoe manufac-turers and shift out of China and into even less expensive, less regulated labor markets such as Vietnam.

But foreign demand is not solely to blame for this extreme market, which is also partially an outgrowth of a domestic black market in babies serving Chinese customers. Because orphanages impose age and residency restrictions on domestic adoptions, buying a baby and legalizing the adoption process with bribes are often more convenient and less expensive than facing fines imposed under the One Child Policy.[13] The international adoption market has skewed the domestic market, however, especially after 2001 when the China Center of Adoption Affairs (CCAA, est. 1996) ended restrictions over the number of international adoptions and orphanage directors, recognizing the high international market value of each adoptee, began to make hundreds of thousands of dollars through mandatory $3,000 "donations" from adoptive parents. To generate more supply, some orphanages began to buy babies from surrounding orphanages not engaged in international sales. The market value even tempted desperately poor parents to sell their newborns and induced a few orphanage directors to pay for abducted infants, sometimes with the complicity of local officials enforcing the One Child Policy.[14] In one case uncovered by a leading Chinese financial magazine, officials from family planning agencies forcibly removed infants from households that had violated the One Child Policy and refused to pay a 6,000 yuan fine, providing an important source of revenue for local governments in Hunan province. The local officials then sold the babies to an orphanage for 1,000 yuan.[15]

The profit in stolen babies is enough for some to risk the penalties. According to the confessions of baby abductors, one can earn $36 to $60 per child, in a country with an average income of approximately $100 a month. Middlemen sell children to orphanages for $400 or more. The baby market is carefully calibrated: the end purchaser pays some $1,200 for "substandard goods" (girls) and over $2,000 for "quality goods" (boys). Likewise, healthy babies fetch more than unhealthy ones, and good-looking babies cost more.[16] In another sign of a maturing market, organized gangs are replacing family rings and freelancers in the child-theft business.[17] For instance, Liang Guihong, a 56-year-old woman who claimed to find homes for abandoned infants, was sentenced to fifteen years in prison for leading a gang that had sold seventy-eight infants in 2005 alone.[18] Babies have even been offered for auction on eBay's Chinese website, Eachnet, with an asking price of 28,000 yuan ($3,450) for boys and 13,000 yuan ($1,603) for girls.[19]

The exact size of this illegal market is unclear. In 2012, officials admitted that police stations across China had broken up over 9,000 groups of traffickers and rescued some 80,000 women and babies over the previous three years.[20] Likewise, Chinese media routinely include news stories on the arrests of child traffickers. In 2005, police busted a ring of twenty-seven traffickers who since 2002 had abducted or bought some 1,000 children and sold them to orphanages in Hunan province for $400 to $538 each. Unsuspecting American families then made mandatory contributions of $3,000 per baby, the highest of the many fees involved to adopt these children. As with other illegal market activities, local officials were often complicit and defense attorneys argued that the babies were abandoned, and heads of orphanages have tried to cover their tracks with forged reports confirming abandonment. Although China has strict regulations to avoid baby selling and Western countries refuse to permit adoptions through baby selling, lucrative market incentives make the practice all but impossible to stop.[21] The Hengyang orphanage in Hunan, a major provider of children for Americans, was caught buying babies in 2005, leaving adoptive parents uncertain if they had adopted a stolen baby rather than rescued an impoverished orphan.[22]

China often receives international media criticism for its adoption market, which puts pressure on national officials to impose restrictions, make arrests, pass laws prohibiting baby buying, and forbidding the resale of purchased babies on international markets. Parents of missing children say the state should also work to eliminate the market by severely punishing the consumers, those who buy children. At least one police officer interviewed agreed, adding that the costs of investigating and retrieving even a few abducted babies greatly exceeds local policing budgets.[23] This lack of enforcement is a consistent problem with the regulation of all Chinese markets. While baby buyers, for instance, are subject to a three-year jail sentence, few ever see jail.[24] And, of course, this extreme market within China also reflects problems within the other countries involved, creating transnational regulatory headaches and personal heartbreak. The market within China would not be the same without the complicity of foreign consumers willing to look the other way or to too readily believe stories of "abandoned" babies. In such countries, the regulations, penalties, and enforcements have also failed to rein in the market.[25]

The unintended gender imbalance partially caused by China's One Child Policy has also led to the creation of another extreme market starting in China but extending abroad: brides for all those favored sons wanting to produce their own male heirs. Until the 1940s, marriage by abduction or "seizing the bride" (*qiangqin*) was common in parts of China. The buying and selling of women in pre-Communist China was sometimes a socially accepted way for the rural poor to sidestep the expensive dowry/bride-price system, often after secret negotiations with the girl's parents.[26] Likewise, sophisticated kidnapping gangs would also steal girls from impoverished families and sell them as concubines and slaves in other provinces.[27] And desperate families might sell their own daughters and even wives as brides or maids.[28]

While it is difficult to assess the size of this reemerging market, according to Chinese police statistics, between 2009 and early 2012, there were over 36,000 *reported* cases of women, girls, and babies sold.[29] They report that in 1990–91 Chinese police apprehended 65,236 persons for participating in female trafficking. The scale of this practice continues to rise, even as the average age of the trafficked girls has fallen into the teens.[30] Periodic high-profile cases confirm that the problem remains acute. In 2002, for instance, a Guangxi farmer was executed for abducting and selling more than 100 women for $120 to $360 each.[31] And in the province of Inner Mongolia, another sold 112 women for prices ranging from RMB3,000 to 8,000.[32] In the most gruesome manifestation of this market, in 2007 three men were arrested for murdering two women they intended to sell as "ghost brides" to accompany deceased bachelors in their afterlives. Apparently, the prettier of the two murdered women commanded twice the price ($2,000 rather than $1,000). Officials admitted these were not isolated cases.[33]

The market in brides, like so many other markets suppressed under Mao, has now reached new extremes with international and regional dimensions and includes women from surrounding less-prosperous countries such as North Korea and Vietnam.[34] Other Asian countries are facing similar demographic problems, creating similar demand for brides. For every 100 girls, Taiwanese give birth to 119 boys, Singaporeans 118 boys, and South Koreans 112 boys. Consequently, the traffic is two-way. Wealthier countries such as Japan have turned to China to resolve their bride shortage, buying Chinese wives and creating entire industries. *New York Times* reporter Seth Faison found dozens of agencies brokering marriages between Japanese men and Chinese wives. Such marriages are overtly commercial transactions, such as the case of one Osaka-based Japanese customer, Hitoro, who selected his wife from photo albums and paid $20,000. When he arrived in Shanghai, the potential bride demanded an extra $5,000, which Hitoro refused to pay. Within a day, the broker found another woman willing to marry a stranger with whom she could not even converse. Although Hitoro had hoped they might use English as a *lingua franca*, the new bride, a retired prostitute, claimed that she knew only two English phrases: "I love you" and "I am a virgin."[35]

As poor Chinese women are sold as brides to wealthier coastal provinces, residents of poorer interior provinces who are unable to find brides also are importing less expensive impoverished women from outside China, with prices dropping still further when multiple women are bought as part of a group purchase.[36] In the Tongwei county of Gansu province, one of

China's poorest regions, nine of the ten women police rescued at the end of 2011 were Burmese. One of the women told the police that she had come to China several years earlier after a fellow Burmese woman promised to find her a job in China with a 1,000 yuan monthly salary. But as soon as she arrived in China, she was sold to a Chinese farmer in Tongwei County, who paid 45,000 yuan.[37] The number of trafficked women and girls is much greater along the Chinese–Burma border itself, with an estimated 10,000 Burmese females working in and around Ruili, the notorious trafficking hub on the Chinese border, where the going price for a young bride in "top condition" is $7,500.[38]

The sad irony is that cultural preferences and, indirectly, state policies have created a shortage of brides to make the next generation of baby boys. There are at least some initial indications that this shortage may provide its own solution by raising the market value—and correspondingly the social value—of baby girls. One wonders, however, about the fate of the tens of millions of frustrated bachelors who will not benefit in time from any "market correction" or, worse, of the abducted and even murdered women and girls sold as brides.

SEX TRAFFICKING IN YOUNG WOMEN AT HOME AND ABROAD

Unsurprisingly, the lack of brides, combined with China's hundreds of millions of men of all ages with increased disposable income, also has created a major market incentive for organized criminal networks with transnational ties to build a massive brothel industry. Impersonal market forces can create new opportunities for some consumers, but they can also lead to sharpened inequalities. In China and throughout the region, these inequalities have both class and regional dimensions, as men in rich coastal regions, where the gender imbalance is often the worst, are more likely to be able to afford to pay for sex, wives, children, and mistresses. Nonetheless, markets can also provide opportunities for those elsewhere on the socioeconomic ladder: while migrant male laborers in cities may not be able to afford girlfriends, much less wives, the market allows them to buy sex. Nevertheless, the inability of China's market economy to supply wives and progeny to this new underclass of bachelors, which Beijing estimates will reach 30 million by 2020, may come to pose a serious political threat to its leaders.[39]

The shortage of women and the demand for paid sex underscores the difficulty China's government faces when cracking down on socially dubious markets. After all, how willing (or even able) would the Chinese government be to restrict male access to sex by enforcing a ban on prostitution within China or on sex tours to countries where it is legal? Indeed, one convicted trafficker of women claimed that he was doing the Chinese government a favor by balancing "the yin and yang" (feminine and masculine) by moving women from south-central Sichuan province to points north, where there are too many bachelors and not enough brides. He argued that he was "just trying to supply what the market needs" with an activity that "helps dissolve young guys' sexual tension."[40]

Not only is the possibility of paid sex aided by the transnational trafficking noted earlier, but the sexual revolution underlying the market is itself partially a consequence of China's "opening" to capitalist countries over the past couple of decades and new transnational linkages. In a sense, China is catching up with the sexual norms and practices, including prostitution, of its primary trading partners. With the shift in young urban Chinese women's clothing since 1978 from baggy Mao suits to revealing designer dresses, sex has gone from being invisible to being ubiquitous. Before the reform era, there were few private, unmonitored spaces such as hotels or bars with private rooms for couples to meet, and public spaces were open and crowded, making it difficult to have sex outside marriage. As with so many other changes during the reform era, the shift from suppressed to widespread sexual activity has been rapid. In the 1980s, the vast majority of Beijing residents who got married were virgins, but twenty years later researchers found that 70 percent reported having sex before tying the knot, often with more than one partner. Over the same period, the average age of the first sexual experience of people in China's seven largest cities dropped from 24 to 17. Popular attitudes affirm these changes: one Chinese magazine poll found that one-third of Chinese under the age of 26 did not object to extramarital affairs, and the vast majority did not consider premarital sex immoral.[41]

Along with capital and technology, China has also imported the "best practices" of international advertising, and the sexual references central to the marketing of products, rare in the Maoist era, are omnipresent on Chinese billboards, magazines, and movies and in women's fashion, especially in urban settings. Indeed, such references have become iconic of what it means to live in modern, cosmopolitan times in capitalist countries, a way of contrasting up-to-date urban life with a sexually puritanical, old-fashioned, and inward-looking countryside. After decades of supplying the globe's adult sex toys, China now has its own domestic market, including Guangzhou's hugely popular annual Sex Culture Festival, launched in 2003. Sixty thousand mostly middle-aged men attended the opening day of the 2009 festival, which included guest appearances by Japanese porn stars.[42] Likewise, the southwest city of Chongqing is home to Love Land, the country's first theme park devoted to sex (inspired by a similar park in South Korea) that includes displays of giant genitalia and naked humans.

In addition to making representations of sex ubiquitous in Chinese cities, markets have also created opportunities for paid sex in all manner of locations, both inside and outside China with Chinese and foreign sex workers. Buyers can buy sexual services at hostess bars, from escort services, in massage parlors, in "barber shops," in karaoke clubs, in hotels, and on sex tours to locations such as Thailand and, more recently, Vietnam.[43] Indeed, China now has the largest commercial sex workforce in the world. It is estimated that some 10 million women and men work in the industry—300,000 of these in Beijing alone. Rather than trying to shut it down, some local governments have moved to regulate it.[44] When the northeastern city of Shenyang began laying off tens of thousands of workers from state-owned enterprises in the late 1990s, for instance, the city legalized prostitution to offset some of the layoffs and levied a 30 percent tax on the sex trade's 5,000 "places of entertainment." The policy was so successful that other cities soon followed suit.[45] And like so many reform-era markets that spread and evolve in unpredictable ways, it is hard to eliminate once consumer demands and the state's endless need for new revenue sources both are met and legitimated.

As with other extreme markets, the sex trade within China has also expanded beyond domestic consumption and supply and become part of an international market.[46] While China now exports women and girls to work as sex slaves elsewhere, the country also imports females from North Korea, Vietnam, Mongolia, and Nepal.[47] Indeed, China appears to be on the verge of replacing Thailand as the regional human trafficking hub. According to the U.S. State Department's Office to Monitor and Combat Trafficking in Persons, hundreds of thousands of North Korean refugees fleeing famine are ending up in China, sold either as prostitutes or brides to poor farmers.[48]

Girls are trafficked out of China primarily to Thailand, Malaysia, Singapore, and Taiwan but also to Australia, the United States, and even Africa.[49] In Malaysia, rich married businessmen, as individuals or members of clubs, visit Chinese women, often held against their will, in luxury condominiums in the afternoon to drink, eat, and have sex; in other cases, these women are escorted to homes. Known as "noon brides," these Chinese women are lured from the countryside with promises of office work. In Malaysia, the male consumers' shift in preference from Thai to Chinese girls is partially the result of changing consumer preferences and the mistaken assumption that Chinese women are less likely to carry HIV. The market is also facilitated by a growing Malaysian interest in all things

Chinese and the massive increase in other forms of contact between the two countries, including business, education, and tourism. Crime syndicates import thousands of young Chinese women on student visas, register them at schools, and then farm them out to work in the sex and service industries.[50]

TRANSNATIONAL TRADE IN ORGANS

The extreme market most often decried in the West is that for body parts, such as kidneys, livers, corneas, and pancreases. Although an estimated 2 million Chinese patients are in need of organ transplants, the majority of the 20,000 or so performed each year in China involve foreign patients seeking, once again, something less expensive and more easily purchased in Chinese markets. Over the past decade, China has become a popular destination for medical tourists seeking treatments unavailable or unaffordable in their own countries. While Koreans, Japanese, and Taiwanese flock to China for such treatments, customers also come from Europe and the United States. A salesperson for Citnac, a Shenyang-based subsidiary of a Japanese firm that matches Japanese customers with Chinese organs, acknowledged, "there are so many Japanese people coming to China to get transplants we cannot keep up. Please do not encourage the French to come here!" Such transplants are pricey: $30,000 for a cornea; $62,000 for a kidney; $100,000 for a liver; between $150,000 and $160,000 for a heart; and $170,000 for a pancreas.[51] Foreigners are not the only customers: high demand within China and a shortage of donors has also created a black market that allows wealthy Chinese to buy organs. For instance, the popular comedian Fu Biao bought an executed prisoner's liver for RMB300,000.[52]

After the United States, China has become the world's second largest provider of organ transplants. This raises the question of how a country that did not introduce a system of voluntary donor cards until 2009 and in which many Chinese hold traditional religious beliefs that require an intact body in the afterlife manages to find sufficient organs to offer them to foreign buyers. One source long rumored and finally confirmed by the government was executed prisoners, who account for as many as 95 percent of organ donors.[53] China does not disclose the number of executions, but estimates by international observers range from a few thousand to 10,000 yearly.[54] Whatever the number, China harvests an estimated 3,200 organs annually from executed prisoners.[55]

As China became more sensitive to its international image in the several years preceding the 2008 Beijing Olympics, the Chinese government changed its official line about prisoner donors and tried to better regulate the market. When it finally acknowledged the use of prisoner donors and cracked down on organ trafficking, it also issued new rules ensuring that written consent was obtained from donors and requiring the licensing of hospitals permitted to perform transplants. Authorities also banned the sale of organs from corpses donated for medical research, limited the types of institutions allowed to accept corpses, and regulated the international transport of corpses.[56] That year they also banned exports and stopped giving preference to foreigners on organ lists.[57] China also made it illegal to sell organs, though it remained legal to donate them to relatives, a restriction easily circumvented by criminals who supplied fake identification cards to represent the person selling the organ as a relative.[58]

Since then, fewer executions and the new regulations on harvesting organs from executed prisoners have created acute market shortages for organs inside China and abroad. Consequently, demand has pushed up prices everywhere. The price for a kidney in South Korea, where more than 10,000 people are waiting for transplants, shot up from $27,000 to $37,000 immediately after the Chinese ban.[59] In wealthy countries, there is only one kidney for every ten people on the waiting list, which fuels international demand.[60]

With prices high and supplies increasingly regulated, the black market of individuals willing to sell a kidney continues to develop. In a case that made international headlines, a 17-year-old boy from a poor province who wanted an iPad2 but did not have any money found an organ broker on the internet and sold his kidney for RMB22,000. Unbeknown to his parents, the young man went with the agent to the Number One People's Hospital in Zhengzhou where the operation was performed, and only when the teenager returned home with a new iPad2 and iPhone did his mother discover the truth.[61] There is no shortage of similar stories. A poor farmer from Shaanxi, wanting to help his sick mother, came across an advertisement near a hospital offering cash for kidneys and decided to sell one of his. Once again, he used the internet to find an agent, who in turn found a buyer in Tianjin. The farmer was taken to Tianjin, where he was housed in a flat with twenty others similarly waiting to sell their kidneys and then relocated to Shandong province for the operation.[62] Nor are such stories only about the desperately poor. A 30-year-old single woman who works in the media and makes RMB3,800 a month caused a stir when she posted on her blog site that she was willing to sell one of her organs for around RMB20,000 to raise money to buy a car.[63]

Areas in and around hospitals in China openly advertise organ purchases and sales.[64] Those advertising this controversial service have to strike a delicate balance, claiming to sell fresh organs free of communicable diseases such as HIV while simultaneously reassuring consumers that such organs were ethically obtained, especially with cases of organ theft on the rise, to make such consumption palatable.[65] So, while one 2005 website reassured potential clients that organs came from prisoners awaiting execution, it simultaneously assured them that prisoners' families received a donation and that advanced screening and blood tests would be used to avoid communicable diseases and ensure excellent matches.[66] As with traded commodities in most extreme markets, however, consumers of organs tend not to be overly concerned about where they originated. Perhaps reflecting a widespread attitude among such buyers, an American who paid $40,000 for a Chinese kidney although she suspected it came from a prisoner admitted to a *Los Angeles Times* reporter that she "didn't want to know."[67]

CONSUMING THE WORLD'S LAST

China is now the world's largest consumer of wild plants and animals, many of which are endangered species. Once again, the growth of such markets has been an unintended result of China's economic reforms and related policies. The end of the central provisioning of health care, for instance, has led to renewed interest in traditional Chinese medicine (and heterodox religious organizations claiming to have the secret to good health). The mass media have also contributed to the demand for such products by popularizing interest in folk medicine. Likewise, consumers expect high-end pharmacies and restaurants to sell popular treatments such as golden turtle's blood to cure cancer; sea horse for asthma, heart disease, and impotence; pickled turtle flippers to promote longer life; and owl meat for improved eyesight.[68]

Rising incomes and international trade networks have made consuming rare wildlife more available and affordable at the same time that popular culture, particularly but not exclusively in southern China, holds that eating rare meat can bestow bravery or sexual prowess. Wildlife delicacies are often featured in lavish banquets intended for conspicuous consumption. Although the government has made efforts to limit consumption—in 1989, the Wildlife Protection Law banned the consumption of internationally protected species—once again the law remains difficult to enforce. Media reports of police seizures reveal the extent of the problem. One smuggling ring in the southwestern province of Yunnan, for example, was caught red-handed with 278 bear paws and 416 dead pangolins (anteaters that resemble armadillos). But the biggest bust occurred in 2004, when Chinese customs officials seized the skins of 31 Bengal tigers, 581 Asian leopards, 778 otters, and 2 lynx—a haul worth well over $1 million.[69]

Chinese consumers have used their newfound purchasing power to buy both items long cherished in Chinese culture and items not previously available. Bear's paw, pangolin meat, camel's hump, monkey's brain, tiger bones dipped in liquor, and tiger penis, though long sought-after, were usually expensive because of short supply and thus beyond the means of most Chinese. That market has grown with the means of Chinese consumers, even though many of these items are derived from animals in short supply nationally or internationally, further endangering already endangered species. And Chinese consumers are eating not only their own rare wildlife but the world's, creating smuggling networks that stretch from China to the jungles of Southeast Asia and the coasts of Latin America. The range of exotic animals bought and consumed in China is illustrated by the story of 5,000 rare animals found drifting in an abandoned smuggler's boat off the South China coast. The 200 crates on board included 31 pangolins, 44 leatherback turtles, 2,720 monitor lizards, 1,130 Brazilian turtles, and 21 bear paws—all endangered species banned from international trade but openly sold in Guangdong.[70]

Among these products, practitioners of traditional Chinese medicine, including those in Korea and Japan, consider bear bile an extraordinary health elixir and a key ingredient in over 100 medicines.[71] The bile, which is abundant in ursodeoxycholic acid, is converted into powder as remedies for arthritis, impotence, kidney and liver ailments, and fevers and even to rejuvenate brain cells. Demand has led to the creation of a "bear farming" industry, where caged bears are milked for their bile with catheters. Just as factory-farmed dairy cows in the United States are worked to premature deaths, since the 1980s these Chinese farms have subjected the bears to nightmarish conditions and have shortened their life expectancy from twenty-five to four years. By 2005, China had nearly 500 such "farms," but international pressure from animal rights organizations and the European Parliament has forced them to crack down, reducing the number to 68. The consolidated farms, though, are massive, each housing up to thousands of bears. That their paws are prized culinary delicacies does not help.[72] As with so many other natural resources, demand in China has led to poaching around the world. In Russia, for instance, endangered Himalayan black bears are illegally hunted and sold to Chinese middlemen.

The Chinese have also consumed tigers to near extinction. Their numbers in the wild are down to 2,500 worldwide, and only a few dozen roam freely in China. In 1993, again under international pressure, the Chinese government outlawed the trade in tiger parts, but demand remains strong and there is a flourishing black market: tiger skin used for clothing; bones used in Chinese medicine for joint ailments such as arthritis; tiger meat and health tonics.[73] Neighboring states like India are big providers of ille- gally poached animals, and entrepreneurs have found legal ways around the ban within China, setting up over 100 private tiger breeding "farms" housing 5,000 tigers. These farms, which are also tourist sites, legally sup- ply parts from tigers that die from natural causes. The World Wildlife Fund, however, says they are merely fronts for illegal traders, who often trans- port their products for open sale in the same towns trafficking in women on China's southwest border.[74] Breeders counter that legalizing the trade would lead to less poaching and the preservation of tigers; preservation- ists answer that breeders have no program for reintroducing tigers into the wild.[75]

Shark fin soup is perhaps the best-known Chinese delicacy, found more often on international Chinese menus than, say, braised bear paws. The soup is favored for its medicinal and aphrodisiac qualities and, above all, as a status symbol at Chinese banquets. It is often the most expensive soup on lengthy Chinese menus and, as soup is served last, considered a nice final touch to a meal. Less widely known is the international impact of the increasing Chinese demand, extending all the way to Latin America, where local fishermen hunt sharks just for their valuable fins, which end up in Chinese soups. In Ecuador, a set of dorsal and pectoral fins fetches $100, then sells for thousands of dollars in East Asia and retails for up to hun- dreds of dollars for the tiny quantities served in soup. Hong Kong was the largest market for shark fins in the 1980s, but by the 1990s that distinction had shifted to mainland China. In cities such as Shanghai and Beijing, it is sold in all the fine restaurants and even by some street vendors. Between the mid-1990s and mid-2000s, Ecuador's exports of shark fins to China and Hong Kong doubled to 279,000 pounds, provided by roughly 300,000 sharks.

The impact of this particular Chinese desire on the world's shark popu- lations has been profound. In only fifteen years, 70 percent of shark spe- cies such as the great white and hammerhead have been killed, and other species have disappeared altogether. Countries such as Ecuador have tried unsuccessfully to ban shark fishing and finning, the practice of slicing off fins at sea and dumping the carcass.[76] But lax enforcement and lucrative demand make the prospects for shark survival grim.

In addition to official attempts to curtail such consumption in China, efforts have been made to reduce demand by changing public perceptions toward wildlife. The international kung-fu movie star Jackie Chan, for instance, made a public service advertisement in Mandarin for the NGO WildAid attacking the consumption of shark fins and other endangered species with graphic images and closed with an appeal to consumers: "When the buying stops, the killing can too."[77] Other prominent Chinese figures such as NBA basketball star Yao Ming, Hong Kong actress Michelle Yeoh, and the Olympic gold gymnast and footwear entrepreneur Li Ning have repeatedly made similar spots calling for the end of consumption of endangered species.[78] International NGOs such as the WWF have called for stepped-up campaigns to dissuade the public from buying products derived from endangered species. And in 2012, when Guizhentang, a manufacturer of traditional medicines specializing in bear tonics, applied for public listing, dozens of Chinese celebrities and hundreds of "netizens" on Weibo (the Chinese Twitter) demanded the government block the company's initial public offering application.[79] Likewise, public pressure and changing perceptions have had some effect. In 2012, for instance, the Shangri-La luxury hotel chain announced it was removing shark fin soup from the menus of its seventy-two hotels and implementing a sustainable seafood policy.[80]

Animal-borne illness, though, has done more than such appeals to change public perception. The consumption of civet cats (which resemble mongooses and otters), another delicacy and traditional medicinal ingredient, was blamed by some scientists for the outbreak of SARS in 2002–03, which killed 774 people. Guangdong province responded by banning their sale, and the United States placed an embargo on them.[81] There is some evidence that the negative association of these delicacies with disease is having an effect: a 2009 survey suggested that the number of restaurants serving some exotic wildlife was dropping.[82]

CONCLUSION

Viewed individually, each of these extreme markets may seem exceptional or just a temporary phenomenon and perhaps even a necessary evil during China's ongoing transition toward a market economy. But looking at the variety and extent of extreme markets as a whole reveals the complexity of the challenges posed by deregulated domestic markets meeting unchecked consumer demand.

First, of course, China is not the only country with extreme markets. Furthermore, as this chapter has shown, all these markets are transnational, relying on the complicity of consumers and producers in other countries. The consequences of China's rapidly expanding domestic market behavior include more Chinese adoptees to meet demand on the Upper East Side of New York, more Chinese prostitutes in Thailand and Burmese brides in Gansu, and more Chinese corneas in the eye sockets of Californians.

Second, extreme markets are neither inherent to Chinese culture nor inevitable. All the markets described in this chapter had in fact been declared unacceptable and were not legally or commonly found in China for at least a quarter-century during the Mao era. That attempts to rein them in by China's current leaders have been only modestly successful reveals just how far China's consumer culture has moved from one in which consumption was highly regulated under the Mao-era state to a freewheeling market society in which it has become extremely difficult to place checks on consumer demand. Although mainstream economists and policy makers want China to rescue the global economy by consuming more, neither they nor the Chinese government has proven capable of controlling either what the Chinese consume or the local domestic and global effects of their consumption. What extreme markets put in a particularly harsh light is the simple truth that it is difficult to have it both ways—to create a consumer culture that celebrates individual choice and also successfully regulate what is desired, bought, and sold even within a single national context, let alone internationally.

Third, the flourishing of these markets is not news to the Chinese. All these topics are heavily debated and discussed in Chinese by the Chinese press—and even more so by the Chinese blogosphere—including extremely sensitive issues covered even by China's official news agency, *Xinhua*.[83] In other words, this is not a case of the Chinese government simply looking the other way but rather the number and complexity of the regulatory issues involved, often as a direct but unintended consequence of the retreat of the Chinese state from its former regulatory role over the Chinese economy and society. That said, suggesting that there are unintended consequences of extreme markets is not the same as suggesting they are unexpected. The collective number of cases suggests one would have to be naïve to expect that markets would not have such consequences, though not even the most cynical would argue that the national government embraced market reforms as a way to allow local government officials to profit from confiscating and reselling "illegal" babies.

Finally, despite the undeniably grim conclusions that can be drawn from the examples in this chapter, it is also worth considering that the very Chinese consumers fueling these developments may themselves lead efforts to reform such extreme markets both in China and elsewhere. Just as Chinese celebrities are leading the fight to end shark fin soup consumption as a way to save endangered shark species, in 2012 Chinese activists successfully undermined Canada's attempt to increase seal meat sales to China by petitioning the Canadian government to cease selling products from baby seals in Chinese markets.[84] Acknowledging and responding to extreme markets thus offers consumers and consumer societies everywhere an opportunity to confront the consequences of both desire and restraint.

NOTES

1. "Starbucks looks to triple China presence," *AP*, December 1, 2010.
2. George J. Church, "China: Old wounds Deng Xiaoping," *Time*, January 6, 1986.
3. Rebecca R. Moore, "Outside Actors and the Pursuit of Civil Society in China," in *Constructing Human Rights in the Age of Globalization*, edited by Mahmood Monshipouri, Neil Englehart, Andrew J. Nathan, and Kavita Philip (Armonk, NY: M.E. Sharpe, 2003), p. 146.
4. Daniel H. Rosen and Thilo Hanemann, "An American open door? Maximizing the benefits of Chinese foreign direct investment," *Asia Society*, May 2011. Available: http://asiasociety.org/files/pdf/AnAmericanOpenDoor_FINAL.pdf.
5. Xinhua, "Ultrasound gender test gang busted in Hubei," *China Daily*, April 11, 2012; "China busts woman for illegal backseat ultrasounds on moms wanting sons" *AP*, April 10, 2012.
6. Zhou Zhoujiang and Liu Weidan, "The undercurrents of Wuhan's sex imbalance," *Chutian jinbao*, June 26, 2008.
7. "In Hunan, family planning turns to plunder," *Caixin* [Online]. May 10, 2011. Available: http://english.caixin.com/2011-05-10/100257756.html [April 19, 2012].
8. Tan Yingzi, "Adopting a Chinese baby gets tougher," *China Daily*, February 25, 2010; Andy Newman and Rebecca Cathcart, "In an adoption hub, China's new rules stir dismay," *New York Times*, December 24, 2006.
9. Peter S. Goodman, "Stealing babies for adoption," *Washington Post*, March 12, 2006. US$3,000 is only the donation to the orphanage; total expenses range from $10,000 to $20,000, at least a third less than private adoptions in the United States cost.
10. Goodman, "Stealing babies for adoption."
11. Newman and Cathcart, "In an adoption hub, China's new rules stir dismay."
12. See U.S. Department of State, "FY 2011 Annual Report on Intercountry Adoption." Available: http://adoption.state.gov/content/pdf/fy2011_annual_report.pdf, and US Department of State "Intracountry Adoption." Available: http://adoption.state.gov/about_us/statistics.php [April 19, 2012].
13. Goodman, "Stealing babies for adoption."
14. Wang Peng and Liu Kun, "Fan ying wangluo diaocha: 'Yunfu yunshu' chengwei fanmai ying'er xin shouduan" ["An Internet survey of infant trafficking: 'Transporting pregnant women' becomes a new method of trafficking"], *Jinghua zhoukan*, July 5, 2011. Available: http://news.sohu.com/20110705/n312453758.shtml [15 May 2012]. See also the very helpful report "The Finances of Baby Trafficking," posted at http://research-china.blogspot.com/2005/12/finances-of-baby-trafficking.html.

15. "In Hunan, family planning turns to plunder."
16. Wang Tao, Xie Kun, Luan Yunhai, "Qingdao zhenpo teda fanmai ying'er an ying'er tizhi jueding shou jia" ["In Qingdao, large-scale cases of babies sold based on physical appearance solved"] *Qingdao zaobao*, January 6, 2012. Available: http://news.xinhuanet.com/legal/2012-01/06/c_122546035.htm.
17. Wang Wencan, Qian Lizhen, and Han Zhenzhen, "21 ming gang chusheng ying'er bei fanmai, Hefei zaixian" ["Hefei online reports 21 newborns trafficked"], *Jianghuai chenbao*, January 26, 2010.
18. "Sentencing in case of Hunan Hengyang welfare agency selling babies," *Xinhua*, February 24, 2006.
19. "'Babies for sale' on Chinese eBay," BBC News, October 20, 2005.
20. Zhao Yang, " Daguai chengji feiran xingshi reng yanjun duoshu difang daguaiban you pai wu ren" [The accomplishment of crackdowns is still extremely grim, the majority of offices meant to crackdown exist in name only], *Fazhi ribao*, April 4, 2012. Available: http://www.chinanews.com/fz/2012/04-09/3803264.shtml [15 May 2012].
21. Goodman, "Stealing babies for adoption,.
22. Guan Xiaomeng, "Baby-selling orphanage in Hunan cracked down," *China Daily*, November 24, 2005.
23. For a lengthy interview with a police officer active in rescuing abducted babies, see Qi Rui, "Fenghuang wang duihua yixian minjng" ["A Phoenix Web interview with frontline police"], *Fenghuang wang*, February 10, 2011. Available: http://news.ifeng.com/society/special/jiejiuqitaoertong/content2/detail_2011_02/10/4606125_0.shtml.
24. Mark Magnier, "Child-theft racket growing in China," *LA Times*, January 1, 2006.
25. On the attempts to address the regulatory issues within the United States, see Mirah Riben, *The Stork Market: America's Multi-Billion Dollar Unregulated Adoption Industry* (Dayton, NJ: Advocate Publications, 2007).
26. Anne E. McLaren, "Marriage by abduction in twentieth century China," *Modern Asian Studies*, Vol. 35, No. 4 (2001), pp. 953–84; Angela Ki Che Leung, "To chasten society: The development of widow homes in the Qing, 1773–1911," *Late Imperial China*, Vol. 14, No. 2 (1993), pp. 1–32, at pp. 6–7.
27. Susan Mann, *Precious Records: Women in China's Long Eighteenth Century* (Stanford, CA: Stanford University Press, 1997), pp. 42–3.
28. See Ann Waltner, *Getting an Heir: Adoption and the Construction of Kinship in Late Imperial China* (Honolulu: University of Hawaii Press, 1990), ch. 3.
29. Zhao Yang, " Daguai chengji feiran xingshi reng yanjun duoshu difang daguaiban you pai wu ren" [The accomplishment of crackdowns is still extremely grim, the majority of offices meant to crackdown exist in name only], *Fazhi ribao*, April 9, 2012.
30. Jill McGivering, "Vietnam-China trafficking on rise," BBC News, January 24, 2006; "Women, children smuggling cases on rise in SW China region," *Xinhua*, January 23, 2006.
31. "Public sentencing of 104 from major cases of abducting and selling people," *Xinhua*, May 29, 2002.
32. "Mongolian court in session to hear the biggest cases of abductors and sellers of over a hundred women," *Zhongguo xinwen wang*, May 24, 2001.
33. "3 reportedly held in 'ghost bride' sale," *AP*, January 26, 2007.
34. For a comparison of transnational bride trafficking in the United States and China, see Jane Kim, "Trafficked: Domestic violence, exploitation in marriage,

and the foreign-bride industry," *Virginia Journal of International Law*, Vol. 51, No. 2 (2010), pp. 443–506. Available: http://www.vjil.org/assets/pdfs/vol51/issue2/ Kim.pdf. The author reminds us that "extreme markets" exist in countries other than China, finding striking similarities between the import of North Korean brides to China and foreign brides into the United States.

35. Seth Faison, *Beyond the Clouds: Exploring the Hidden Realms of China* (New York: St. Martin's Press, 2004), pp. 184–86.

36. Xia Tilei, " Kunmang yi gongsi cheng ke 'tuangou' Yuenan xinniang" ["A Kunming company announces 'group buying' of Vietnamese brides"], *Yunnan wang*, May 9, 2012. Available: http://news.xinhuanet.com/legal/2012–05/10/c_123108115. htm [May 14, 2012]. There are many newspaper accounts of such marriages. See, for instance, the story of one young migrant laborer's search for a Vietnamese bride: Zhang Yiye and Ran Wen, "Nongmin gong er daiban huzhao yu fu Yuenan qu waiguo xinniang" ["Migrant worker uses agent to process passport, wants to go to Vietnam to marry a foreign bride"], *Chongqing wanbao*, January 25, 2010. Available: http://pic.people.com.cn/GB/159992/159994/10839386.html [May 14, 2012].

37. "8 ming miandian funü bei guaimai zhi Gansu huojiu hou bu yuan huiguo" ["8 Burmese women trafficked and sold in Gansu, after rescue unwilling to return to Burma"], *Zhongguo Gansu wang*, January 13, 2012. Available: http://news.hsw.cn/ system/2012/01/13/051215239.shtml [April 1, 2012]."

38. Kathleen E. McLaughlin, "Borderland: Sex trafficking on the China-Myanmar border" *GlobalPost*, October 26, 2010. Available: http://www.globalpost.com/ dispatch/china/100928/burma-myanmar-trafficking-border.

39. "A report on investigations into the population: by 2020 the number of bachelors will reach 30 million," *Guangzhou ribao*, January 12, 2007. On the political impli-cations, see the provocative article by Martin Walker, "The geopolitics of sexual frustration," *Foreign Policy*, March/April 2006.

40. Qian Guibao interviewed by Liao Yiwu, *The Corpse Walker: Real-Life Stories, China from the Bottom Up* (New York: Anchor, 2008), pp. 16–7.

41. Hannah Beech, "Sex and the single Chinese," *Time*, December 5, 2005; "An inves-tigation into the condition of morality in the Chinese family," *Beijing ribao*, June 11, 2007.

42. "Guangzhou Sex Culture Festival invites Japanese porn stars," *Guangzhou ribao*, November 1, 2009.

43. On Chinese men crossing the Vietnamese border for sex, see Yuk Wah Chan, "Cultural and Gender Politics in China–Vietnam Border Tourism," in *Tourism in Southeast Asia: Challenges and New Directions*, edited by M. Hitchcock, V. T. King, and M. Parnwell (Copenhagen: Nias Press, 2009), ch. 10.

44. And, indeed, the UN-sponsored Committee on the Elimination of Discrimination Against Women also pushes for decriminalization and tight regulation. See Jason Chan, "Current development: Decriminalization of prostitution in China," *New England Journal of International and Comparative Law*, Vol. 13 (Spring 2007) pp. 329–64.

45. LionelM.JensenandTimothyB.Weston,"Introduction,"in*China'sTransformations*, edited by Jensen and Weston (Lanham, MD: Rowman & Littlefield, 2007), pp. 1–32.

46. For an overview, see U.S. Department of State, "Trafficking in Persons Report" (June 2011). Available: http://www.state.gov/j/tip/rls/tiprpt/2011/164231.htm [January 10, 2012].

47. Wu Yadong and Liu Baijun, "Neidi kuaguo guaimai xin dongxiang: Funü bei guai chujing qiangpo maiyin" ["A new trend in the transnational trafficking: Women trafficked abroad and forced into prostitution"], *Fazhi ribao*, April 15, 2011. Available: http://news.ifeng.com/society/1/detail_2011_04/15/5764285_0. shtml?_from_ralated; and "Yuenan funü bei guai mai Zhongguo" ["Vietnamese women sold in China"], *Huanqiu shibao*, January 26, 2006. Available: http://www .people.com.cn/GB/paper68/16744/1473218.html [May 4, 2012].
48. "China taking in North Korean sex slaves, says US," *Reuters*, December 9, 2005.
49. There is no shortage of such stories in the Chinese media. See, for instance, "Shenqing liuxue lun wei xing nu" ["Apply to study abroad only to become sex slaves"], *Zhongguo xinwen wang*, October 13, 2011. Available: http://edu.sina .com.cn/a/2011-10-13/1708207695.shtml [May 15, 2012]. On Chinese women forced to work as prostitutes in Angola, see " Gong'anbu zhenpo kuaguo qiangpo maiyin an" ["The Ministry of Public Security cracks transnational forced prostitu- tion case"], *Zhongguo wangluo dianshi tai*, November 17, 2011. Available: http:// news.cntv.cn/china/20111117/101698.shtml [May 15, 2012].
50. Baradan Kuppusamy, "Malaysia's hot new import: Chinese sex slaves," *Asia Times*, July 16, 2003.
51. Bruno Philip, "At the heart of China's organ trade," *Guardian Weekly*, May 10, 2006.
52. "Fu Biao's complicated medical procedure, organs come from an executed pris- oner," *Nanjing ribao*, September 17, 2004.
53. Ji Minhua, "Zhongguo qiguan yizhi ye de mimi: Zhongguo 95% gong ti laizi siqiu" ["The secret of China's organ transplant industry: 95% of donors from death row"], *Caijing*, December 9, 2011. Available: http://www.gcpnews.com/ articles/2011–12–09/C1422_75723.html [May 15, 2012].
54. Mark Magnier and Alan Zarembo, "China Admits Taking Executed Prisoners' Organs," *LA Times*, November 18, 2006.
55. Thomas Diflo, "Use of organs from executed Chinese prisoners," *The Lancet*, Vol. 364, Supplement 1 (December 18, 2004), pp. 30–31.
56. "China bans corpse trade," *Aljezera*, July 15, 2006.
57. Yao Yijiang and Xu Guoyun, "Zhongguo jiao ting qiguan yizhi lüyou" ["China calls for an end to organ tourism"], *Nanfang zhoumo*, July 19, 2007.
58. Ouyang Xiaofei, "Mai shen xiaohuo lun wei qiguan zhongjie shoushen bei kong feifa daomai shenzang" ["A young man who sold his kidney becomes an interme- diary, on trial for illegally reselling kidneys"], *Jinghua shibao*, February 11, 2011. Available: http://news.qq.com/a/20110211/000024.htm [May 1, 2012].
59. "Drop in executions leads to organ shortage," *Reuters*, March 28, 2007.
60. Moises Naim, *Illicit: How Smugglers, Traffickers, and Copycats are Hijacking the Global Economy* (New York: Doubleday, 2005), p. 160.
61. "17 sui gaozhong nansheng wangshang jiechu mai shen zhongjie" ["17 year- old high school student goes on-line to contact intermediary to sell kidney"], *Zhongguo guangbo wang*, June 3, 2011. Available: http://news.jinghua.cn/351/ c/201106/03/n3364635.shtml [May 6, 2012].
62. Ouyang Xiaofei, "Mai shen xiaohuo lun wei qiguan zhongjie shoushen bei kong feifa daomai shenzang" ["A young man who sold his kidney becomes an interme- diary, on trial for illegally reselling kidneys"], *Jinghua shibao*, February 11, 2011. Available: http://news.qq.com/a/20110211/000024.htm [May 1, 2012].
63. Wang Huan, "Nü bailing yu mai qiguan mai che yong bu wanzheng de shenti huan wanmei rensheng" ["Female white-collar worker wants to sell organ to

buy a car, willing to exchange an imperfect body for a perfect life"], *Dongya jing-mao xinwen*, July 10, 2007. Available: http://www.hsw.cn/news/2007-07/10/content_6408793.htm [April 20, 2012].

64. Bruno Philip, "At the heart of China's organ trade," *Guardian Weekly*, May 10, 2006.

65. See "Xiaohuozi fu Nanjing yingpin mai yiliao haocai shui zhi 'haocai' jing shi ziji de yige shen" ["A young man went to Nanjing to sell 'medical supplies'—who knew the 'medical supplies' was his own kidney"], *Wenzhou dushi bao*, September 19, 2011. Available: http://www.wzrb.com.cn/article300165show.html [May 1, 2012].

66. Jo Revill, "UK kidney patients head for China," *Guardian*, December 11, 2005.

67. Mark Magnier and Alan Zarembo, "China admits taking executed prisoners' organs," *LA Times*, November 18, 2006.

68. Clifford Coonan, "Endangered wildlife moves up wealthy Chinese menus," *The Independent*, April 28, 2006; Deng Shaojun, "Mei you mai mai, jiu mei you shahai!" ["If there is no buying and selling, there is no killing!"], *Jiangmen ribao*, November 30, 2011. Available: http://www.jmnews.com.cn/c/2011/11/30/02/c_1188662.shtml [May 14, 2012].

69. Clifford Coonan, "Endangered wildlife moves up wealthy Chinese menus," *The Independent*, April 28, 2006.

70. Jonathan Watts, "'Noah's Ark' of 5,000 rare animals found floating off the coast of China," *Guardian*, May 26, 2007. On the role of Chinese turtle farms in the black market, see Shi Haitao, James F. Parham, Michael Lau, and Chen Tien-His, "Farming endangered turtles to extinction in China," *Conservation Biology*, Vol. 21 (2007), pp. 1, 5.

71. For an overview of bear farming and bile extraction, see Peter J. Li, "China's bear farming and long-term solutions," *Journal of Applied Animal Welfare Science*, Vol. 7, No. 1 (2004), pp. 71–81.

72. Tim Johnson, "China refuses calls to shut bile farms," *Chicago Tribune*, January 15, 2006.

73. "Beijing hu gu jiu paimai bei jinji jiao ting yue 400 ping bei che pai" ["Beijing tiger bone wine auction halted, 400 bottles removed"], *Diyi caijing wang*, December 5, 2011. Available: http://finance.sina.com.cn/roll/20111205/011010935856.shtml [May 14, 2012].

74. Adam H. Oswell, *The Big Cat Trade in Myanmar and Thailand* (Petaling Jaya, Selangor, Malaysia: TRAFFIC Southeast Asia, 2010).

75. Clifford Coonan, "Chinese bid to lift ban on tiger trade will result in extinction, say conservationists," *The Independent*, May 18, 2007; K. Nowell and Xu Ling, *Taming The Tiger Trade: China's Markets for Wild and Captive Tiger Products Since the 1993 Domestic Trade Ban* (Hong Kong, China: TRAFFIC East Asia, 2007).

76. Juan Forero, "Letter from South America: Asia's love for shark fin comes at a brutal price," *International Herald Tribune*, January 6, 2006.

77. The graphic video for Jackie Chan and the other Chinese stars are posted at the WildAid website: http://wildaid.org/index.asp?CID=7&PID=507. See also Feng Lin, Wang Bei, and Luo Wenwen, "Zhongguo: Yuchi xiaofei jiema" ["China: Shark fin consumption decoded"], *Tianxia meishi* [magazine], March 21, 2011. Available: http://huaxia.com/tslj/cfht/2011/03/2340205_3.html [May 14, 2012].

78. Zhou Rui, "Yao Ming deng mingxing lianhe huyu zhongzhi huo xiongqu dan" ["Yao Ming and other stars jointly call for an end to bear bile"], *Zhongguo wang*,

February 23, 2012. Available: http://news.china.com.cn/txt/2012-02/23/content_24707459.htm.

79. Zhang Ke, "Guizhentang mou shangshi zai zao zuji minjian dongwu baohu zuzhi jianjue dizhi" ["Guizhentang effort to seek listing again blocked by animal protection NGO protests"], *Diyi caijing ribao*, February 6, 2012.

80. Jonathan Watts, "Shangri-La hotels take shark fin soup off the menu," *Guardian*, January 18, 2012.

81. Clifford Coonan, "Endangered wildlife moves up wealthy Chinese menus," *The Independent*, April 28, 2006; "Origins of SARS found," *Nanfang ribao*, January 12, 2009.

82. "China seizes bear paws, dead pangolins," *Reuters*, April 27, 2006; Zhang Qian, "Think fin, save sharks," *Shanghai Daily*, July 28, 2009.

83. In addition to the previously cited examples, see, for instance, the *Xinhua* reporters' coverage of babies stolen from migrant labor communities in major cities. The report, for instance, notes that as victims often have more than one child they are fearful of going to the authorities. Li Shu and Wu Liang, "Xinhua she jizhe jie kua sheng fan ying jituan heimu" ["Xinhua News Agency reporters expose the inside story of cross-provincial trafficking of babies"], *Xinhua News Agency*, February 10, 2011. Available: http://news.ifeng.com/opinion/special/guaimaiertong/detail_2011_02/10/4606551_0.shtml.

84. Song Fuli, "Zuji haibao zhipin jinru Zhongguo" ["Block the entry of seal products into China"], *Jingji guancha wang*, February 23, 2012. Available: http://www.eeo.com.cn/2012/0223/221272.shtml; see also: http://www.humanesociety.org/issues/seal_hunt/timelines/seals_victories.html [May 10, 2012].

PART THREE

Globalization and Domestic Resistance

CHAPTER 6

⌒⌣⌒

Addressing Global Imbalances

Domestic and Global Dynamics

ANDREW WALTER

Since the turn of the new century, "global imbalances" have become a central preoccupation of policy makers, journalists, and academics concerned with problems of global economic governance. China's sudden emergence in 2005 as the largest current account surplus country is commonly interpreted as an indicator both of its extraordinary economic rise and of its disruptive global implications.[1] As in the area of global climate change (discussed in chapter 8 in this volume), the negative externalities of China's rise can be seen in its manufacturing pre-eminence, its apparent insistence on maintaining an undervalued exchange rate, and its steady and unprecedented accumulation of foreign exchange reserves and (mostly) U.S. sovereign debt. In the popular diagnosis that emerged in the wake of the recent and continuing global financial crisis, global payments imbalances—and China's large and growing contribution to them—now threaten the stability of the U.S. dollar-based international monetary system, of global finance, and of the world economy more generally.[2] Chinese "mercantilism," in short, is often taken as a definitive indication that Beijing's stated objective of a "harmonious rise" is hollow and misleading, and its unwillingness or inability to contribute substantively to the resolution of the problem of global imbalances seen as a key obstacle to effective global economic governance.[3]

   In this chapter, I argue that China's contribution to global payments imbalances does pose a significant challenge to claims by the Chinese leadership that its policies are consistent with global economic and political stability, as well as to arguments that China's foreign policy stance has been broadly convergent with global norms, rules, and standards. Since this inconsistency has become increasingly costly for China, it requires explanation. I show that its policy choices are not well explained by several stylized accounts of China's foreign economic policy choices. Instead, I argue that these decisions have been shaped by a complex and evolving dynamic between the leadership and two very different audiences. The first audience, domestic society, as the Introduction to this volume argues, has enhanced its expectations of the government in light of China's economic resurgence to which the leadership feels some compulsion to respond. This constituency has steadily gained greater importance in recent years, as the leadership has tried to address widespread concerns about economic inequality, welfare provision, employment, housing, environmental degradation, and corruption. The second audience is external, consisting mainly of the governments of other major states, China's regional neighbors, and international organizations. This audience has asked China to take greater account of the external implications of its policy choices and to contribute more to regional and global governance. Responding effectively to these growing pressures has been difficult especially when they conflict, as often in the case of global imbalances, and in such cases the leadership has given greater priority to its domestic audience while attempting to limit and deflect external pressure.

My argument could be interpreted narrowly in terms of the two-level games framework,[4] but it puts much greater emphasis on the dynamic evolution of the relationship between audience and leadership expectations and preferences. It could also be seen as consistent with a neoclassical realist model of foreign policy making in its emphasis on the importance of and interaction between domestic and international levels in foreign policy outcomes.[5] However, it gives more weight than neoclassical realism to the role of ideas and perceptions in Chinese policy outcomes—an approach that complements those adopted in Part 1 of this edited collection. These ideas have shaped perceived interests and influenced policy debates in China.

The rest of this chapter is organized as follows. The first section briefly describes the evolution of the debate about China's role in global imbalances and its relationship with the international macroeconomic surveillance regime.[6] The second section addresses the strengths and shortcomings of some standard political economy approaches to understanding Chinese policy outcomes in these areas. The third section illustrates how attention to the Chinese leadership's difficulty in responding to the demands of both its domestic and international audiences can help us to understand the evolution of Chinese policies over the past decade. The conclusion addresses the broader implications of the argument.

CHINA AND THE MACROECONOMIC SURVEILLANCE REGIME

China joined the IMF and World Bank in 1980, after the diplomatic deal between Washington and Beijing that brought the People's Republic of China (PRC) into a variety of Western-dominated international institutions.[7] At the time, China's government almost certainly saw few costs and considerable benefits following from such membership. Its early relations with these two major institutions were generally good. China was a significant consumer of technical advice from both and eventually became the largest client for World Bank loans. It developed a good working relationship with International Monetary Fund (IMF) staff over this period, who were generally supportive of Beijing's reforms.[8] China's senior leadership did not foresee any need for substantive financial dependence upon the IMF. It borrowed only twice from the IMF in 1981 and 1986, but conditionality on these occasions was neither intrusive nor inconsistent with the leadership's own desire to control inflation in the context of rapid growth. In this early period, China's current account was approximately in balance and its limited size meant that it was not deemed to pose significant systemic risks. The IMF's attention was also closely focused on Latin America during this period. All this allowed China's leadership considerable practical policy autonomy. Capital controls were extensive and China's financial system was almost completely separated from global markets. China unified its exchange rate regime in 1994 on a fixed peg against the U.S. dollar. The government devalued the renminbi at this time, but China's high domestic inflation meant that the currency appreciated in real terms.

China's relatively insignificant global economic status in the first decade of its reforms also meant that its macroeconomic policies garnered relatively little attention from other major governments. This only began to change in the early 1990s. The United States, the most important member of the IMF and Asia's largest trading partner, was still far more concerned with Japan at the beginning of this decade. The U.S. Treasury's reporting obligations under the 1988 Trade and Competitiveness Act initially focused on Japan and the more advanced emerging market countries such as South Korea and Taiwan in the first few years. The latter two were cited for "currency manipulation," which as section 304 of the 1988 Act specified was "for purposes of preventing effective balance of payments adjustments or gaining unfair competitive advantage in international trade."[9] It noted for the first time in May 1991 that the U.S. bilateral trade deficit with China had grown rapidly to become the third largest with emerging Asia.[10] For the following three years, the U.S. Treasury cited China as a currency

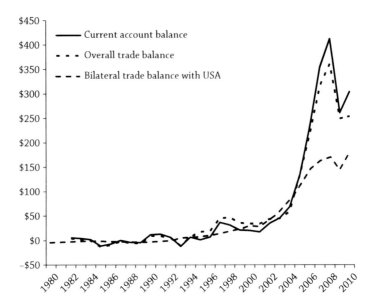

Figure 6.1
China: Current account balance, overall trade balance, and bilateral trade balance with the United States, 1980–2010, US$ billions.
Source: IMF, Direction of Trade Statistics and International Financial Statistics Databases, January 2012.

manipulator. From the American perspective, the United States was acting as the self-enforcer of the IMF's own exchange rate surveillance rules, which since 1977 had proscribed currency manipulation in similar terms to the U.S. act but which proved too politically sensitive to enforce.[11] By late 1994, the U.S. Treasury deemed Chinese currency reform to be sufficient to cease citing China as a currency manipulator.[12]

China's growing regional importance was underlined during the Asian financial crises of the late 1990s, when China maintained a fixed dollar peg despite large currency depreciations among other emerging Asian economies. Its economic growth also remained robust throughout the crisis, serving as an important engine of regional growth during a period in which the larger Japanese economy continued to stagnate. For Beijing, the lesson of the Asian crises was that the growing volatility of capital flows and the detrimental impact of IMF policy conditionality in its lending programs required continued national protection in the form of capital controls and larger foreign exchange reserves.[13]

The real turning point in China's position in global trade and payments, however, took place after 2000. Its trade and current account surpluses rose sharply from 2003, as did its bilateral trade surpluses with the United States (Figure 6.1). It is also notable that until 2004, China's bilateral trade surplus with the United States closely followed its overall trade and current

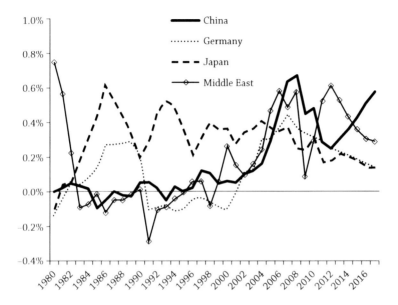

Figure 6.2
Current account balances as a percentage of world GDP, major surplus countries and regions, 1980–2017E (estimates from 2010).
Source: IMF, World Economic Outlook Database, April 2012.

account surpluses—from 2005, these sharply diverged, although the bilateral trade surplus with the United States remained by far the largest element in the overall trade surplus (Figure 6.1). By 2006, China had over-taken Japan and Germany as the world's largest current account surplus country and rivaled the Middle East in importance (Figure 6.2).

This unprecedentedly rapid emergence of China as a large surplus coun-try led to growing external pressure, especially from the United States, for China to revalue the renminbi and to adopt a more flexible exchange rate policy more generally. The George W. Bush administration was itself caught between divergent interests on this issue: between trade-intensive global firms and importers who were benefiting from a cheap renminbi and import-competing firms and labor that were suffering from cheap Chinese imports. By mid-2005, the administration sought a middle way by encour-aging the Chinese in bilateral and multilateral forums to shift its policy stance.[14] Concern over China's currency policy was also growing in Japan and Europe. Supported by this emerging consensus among the G7 coun-tries and under growing pressure from the United States in particular to take action, the IMF adopted an increasingly critical stance toward Chinese currency policy and engaged in robust policy discussions aimed at encour-aging a more flexible exchange rate policy.[15]

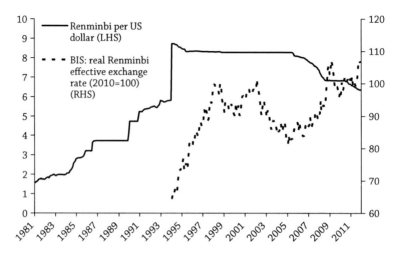

Figure 6.3
Chinese renminbi nominal exchange rate against the U.S. dollar (left scale) and estimated real effective exchange rate index (right scale).
Sources: U.S. Federal Reserve FRED database, and BIS real exchange rate database.

Faced at home with rising inflation and with the growing possibility of a united front externally, the Chinese government agreed in mid-2005 to a policy of managed renminbi appreciation against the U.S. dollar. Although the policy of nominal appreciation did contribute to a rise in China's real effective exchange rate from 2005 (Figure 6.3), the policy shift proved a failure in a variety of ways. The current account surplus continued to grow rapidly over 2005–08, external pressure for accelerated renminbi appreciation increased rather than diminished, and market expectations of continued currency appreciation encouraged large speculative capital inflows that required the People's Bank of China (PBOC) to intervene ever more vigorously in exchange markets and to accumulate dollar reserves. U.S. and IMF criticism intensified rather than diminished and China's relationship with the IMF worsened substantially. In an indication of Beijing's growing frustration with IMF surveillance and its perceived bias in favor of Washington, Beijing voted against the adoption of the 2007 Decision on Bilateral Surveillance (seen as lowering the bar for declaring China in breach of its IMF commitments) and withdrew from bilateral surveillance discussions with the IMF over 2007–08.[16] This reflected a sharp break with what had hitherto been a fairly cooperative and pragmatic working relationship with the IMF.

As the financial crisis in the advanced economies worsened and the prospect of a deep global recession loomed, Beijing chose to cease currency appreciation in mid-2008. Given the domestic preoccupations of most governments, this move attracted only limited international criticism. However, the divergent paths of economic recovery between China and the advanced countries in 2009 generated renewed criticism, and China eventually reverted to a policy of slow appreciation in June 2010. Since then, the nominal and real appreciation of the renminbi has been modest (Figure 6.3), prompting the U.S. government and the IMF to revert to their policy of encouraging China to engage in more rapid currency liberalization.[17]

From Beijing's perspective, this renewed criticism failed to take into account the sharp fall in China's current account surplus from a peak of about 10 percent of national gross domestic product (GDP) in 2006 to 3 percent in 2011. This, Chinese policy makers have argued, is due to the delayed effects of cumulative currency appreciation since 2005, rising wage and other factor costs, and structural reforms aimed at promoting domestic consumption.[18] Some Western analysts agree that the IMF has overestimated the likely size of China's future current surplus, though temporary factors such as slow growth in Europe and the United States have contributed to post-crisis rebalancing.[19] Even if China's surplus remains low in relation to the size of its economy compared to the pre-crisis years, however, under plausible projections the Chinese surplus is still likely to remain one of the largest components of global payments imbalances for the foreseeable future (Figure 6.3).

In other ways, China's position in the debate over global imbalances and multilateral surveillance has worsened since the crisis despite the reduction of its current surplus. Prominent Western economists and policymakers, including many associated with the IMF, have linked global imbalances directly to financial fragility.[20] This analysis has compounded the view that global imbalances are dangerous and that China in particular needs to adopt adjustment policies that produce sustained lower surpluses. From Beijing's perspective, this stigmatizes China and attempts to shift blame for the crisis from Western policies to Beijing. As Premier Wen Jiabao argued in early 2009, "it is completely confusing right and wrong when some countries that have been overspending then blame those that lend them money for their spending."[21] Foreign criticism of Chinese currency policy since 2008 is similarly held to overlook the effects of extraordinarily loose Western fiscal and monetary policies on China's reserve accumulation.[22]

China has been noticeably more robust in its response to such criticisms since the crisis. It has stepped up its criticism of what it sees as the main asymmetries of the macroeconomic surveillance regime, notably the excessive focus on exchange rate policies and the lack of IMF leverage over major advanced economies—a view that is widely shared among the IMF's membership, as is evident from the IMF's own recent independent reviews of surveillance.[23] China also opposed the U.S. Treasury Secretary's proposal to adopt current account indicators as policy targets in order to promote rebalancing.[24] It has also intensified its demands for the reform of the governance of the IMF by enhancing the voice of emerging countries, an issue on which Western governments have dragged their feet.[25] China's leadership also permitted Zhou Xiaochuan, the PBOC governor, to argue that in the longer term the international monetary system should be reformed to promote the Special Drawing Rights as an alternative reserve asset to the U.S. dollar.[26] Finally, Beijing has argued vigorously for more extensive IMF surveillance of the United States and for guarantees from Washington that it would pursue more "responsible" monetary and fiscal policies.[27] A second round of quantitative monetary easing by the Federal Reserve was widely interpreted in the developing world, particularly in China, as an attempt on the part of the U.S. authorities to engineer recovery by a beggar-thy-neighbor strategy of encouraging dollar depreciation.[28]

To summarize, over time as China gained an increasingly prominent role in the global economy and the major institutions and regimes of global economic governance, its relations with the IMF and the macroeconomic surveillance regime became increasingly uncomfortable. In the following section, I discuss how this poses challenges to three standard accounts.

EXPLAINING CHINA'S STANCE ON MACROECONOMIC SURVEILLANCE

The commentary on China's foreign policy choices is diverse. At one end of the spectrum, some authors argue that China has become increasingly convergent with global norms and associated rules and institutions, driven by a mixture of self-interest, mimicking, and normative socialization. At the other end, there are authors who argue that China's leadership is primarily driven by the statist objective of policy autonomy and increased global influence by ensuring export-led growth and financial independence. Others put less emphasis on party-state preferences and instead argue that dominant societal interests have shaped China's economic policy choices and have prevented convergence with the global macroeconomic surveillance regime. I briefly review each of these in turn, assessing their strengths and shortcomings.

Normative convergence?

The trend toward growing divergence between China and the global macroeconomic surveillance regime described previously obviously contradicts the story that others have outlined of gradual convergence with the regime, let alone Chinese "socialization" into its main norms and associated rules, principles, and procedures. It is thus at odds with broad characterizations of China as increasingly convergent with global norms and institutions,[29] or of an international liberal order that is "hard to overturn and easy to join."[30] This is not to deny a general tendency in Chinese policy toward a higher level of behavioral consistency with norms in a number of important areas of global politics and economics.[31] However, it is also clear that in some areas, including macroeconomic surveillance and in the global climate protection regime (see chapter 8), China has found it difficult to accept existing norms. China's leadership may even see its generally convergent portfolio of foreign policies as buying it the right to diverge in those areas where it believes its vital interests would be threatened by convergence and where, as in the case of macroeconomic surveillance, existing rules are perceived as highly biased.

To be sure, China has not objected to the basic principle of the IMF's right to undertake macroeconomic surveillance of its members, with a particular focus on the most systemically important economies. Since the crisis, China has also signed up to G20 agreements to strengthen peer surveillance, with the IMF playing a key advisory and analytical role, and as noted earlier it is especially keen to see surveillance over Western countries strengthened. However, China has found itself increasingly at odds with the rules on exchange rate policy, which have long been the part of the macroeconomic surveillance framework with greatest specificity. In China's view, the proscription of currency manipulation disadvantages relatively poor countries that choose to manage their exchange rate for purposes of economic development, a policy associated in China and in other parts of East Asia with rapid growth in trade and output.[32] In combination with the very limited constraint placed by the surveillance framework on the United States and other major developed countries, this has served to place most of the burden of adjustment to global imbalances on China and other developing countries.[33] This lack of perceived procedural and substantive fairness at the heart of the international macroeconomic surveillance regime has thus encouraged Chinese divergence as China's importance within the global economy has grown—though I argue later in the section on domestic and external audience dynamics that this is probably not the most important reason for nonconvergence in this area.

It is also worth noting that there are closely related areas of macroeconomic policy in which China has been more than willing to depart from what might be described as consensual international policy norms. Despite the growing acceptance of the norm favoring capital account liberalization since the 1970s, China has exhibited a conspicuously gradualist approach to currency liberalization and retains a variety of capital controls—much more so than India or Brazil, for example. Domestically, it also persists with policies promoting financial repression, in which real interest rates are controlled and suppressed for savers and corporate borrowers, which has transferred wealth from households to the corporate and government sectors.[34] In short, in various areas of macroeconomic policy China has been at odds with the international policy consensus favoring more market-oriented solutions and it has been willing to defend its right to diverge when this consensus is deemed to be at odds with domestic priorities.

Leadership preferences?

The literature on foreign economic policy making has often contrasted "statist" with "society-oriented" explanations.[35] Statist approaches, often associated with Realism, view foreign economic policy as a function of perceived state interests, though it allows for conflicting conceptions of national interests among different agencies of the state. As noted earlier, some contributors to the debate over global imbalances have seen Chinese policies as reflecting a state-led mercantilist strategy in which the objective of rapid national economic development is a means of consolidating political power at home and obtaining both autonomy and greater influence abroad.[36] In this view, China's emergence as a major economic and political power represents a challenge to the extant liberal economic order.

It is difficult to argue with the proposition that the Chinese leadership has prioritized rapid economic development as a means of retaining its power at home and, at a minimum, the maintenance of its autonomy vis-à-vis a variety of external actors and pressures. How much the leadership wishes to enhance its power over regional and global outcomes is of course hotly disputed. Leaving this aspect of the debate aside, is the argument that global imbalances are in part a product of state-led Chinese mercantilism compelling?

In the early reform period a key priority of the leadership's development strategy was the promotion of low-value-added manufacturing in order to produce rapid growth in output and employment. This drew heavily on the prior successful experiences of Japan and other Asian developing economies.[37] But in contrast to the mercantilist interpretation, this strategy entailed a rapidly rising level of dependence on foreign markets, particularly the United States, on imported components from factories elsewhere in Asia, and on multinational firms, which played a crucial role in the development of manufacturing in China, particularly in the very

Figure 6.4
Chinese foreign exchange reserves, US$ billions, 1980–2010.
Source: International Monetary Fund, *International Financial Statistics*, December 2011.

trade-intensive consumer electronics sector that boomed from the 1990s. The leadership has therefore accepted substantially *reduced* autonomy as one of the prices of rapid economic development—reflecting a sharp break from the Maoist strategy of self-reliance. Dependence has also intensified over time: IMF economists estimate that net exports and fixed investment linked to the traded sector accounted for nearly two-thirds of China's total output growth over 2001–08, compared to 40 percent in the 1990s.[38] The extraordinary success of this growth strategy over the past three decades has understandably made the leadership reluctant to endanger the competitiveness of China as a manufacturing base for domestic and multinational firms. Many Chinese analysts have also drawn lessons from the negative experience of Japan since the early 1990s: that an unreformed financial sector can jeopardize the sustainability of growth, and that overly rapid currency appreciation can undermine growth and manufacturing competitiveness.[39] This interpretation has particular resonance in China because it fits another popular narrative in which the United States systematically tries to prevent the emergence of viable challengers to its predominance.

An important aspect of the mercantilist interpretation of Chinese strategy is that China's extraordinary accumulation of foreign exchange reserves reflects a revealed preference for both monetary and financial autonomy as well as a means of potential leverage over other countries, including China's major debtor, the U.S. government. There was certainly a period after the Asian crises of the late 1990s where the leadership wanted to build its reserves of convertible currencies as self-insurance against a sudden end to the private capital inflows that had helped to fuel China's boom and against any prospect of having to submit to a U.S.-dominated IMF. The demonstration effect of the fate of the Suharto regime in Indonesia in 1998 would by itself probably have been sufficient to instill this determination, but the general humiliation of East Asia at this time was no doubt felt keenly in Beijing. As Figure 6.4 shows, China's foreign exchange reserves were then minuscule by current standards and almost certainly deemed insufficient by the leadership when the Asian crises broke. But this relatively recent strategy has also had costs, including a new form of external financial dependence. By the mid-2000s, China's foreign exchange reserves far exceeded the minimum required for effective self-insurance, and had substantially increased China's dependence on economic policy decisions in the United States as well as in the Eurozone (it is estimated that about two-thirds of Chinese reserves are held in the form of U.S. dollar debt, with Euro-denominated debt making up most of the rest). This new dependence comes in the form of the credit and market (i.e., price) risk involved in holding a large proportion of the Chinese state's own savings in foreign currency debt instruments. Most analysts have focused on China's so-called dollar trap, but in fact a dual "Euro-dollar trap" has emerged with the recent European debt crisis, raising the question of whether China should contribute even more financial resources to rescue the relatively prosperous Eurozone. Fears about the possible demise of the Euro have only exacerbated longer-standing concerns in Beijing about overdependence on the U.S. dollar and on Western export markets generally. Nor has China found it possible to convert its savings into foreign policy leverage.[40] This has been conspicuously true in the area of U.S. and Eurozone monetary and fiscal policies, which the Chinese leadership fears are sharply increasing both currency and default risk for China. As Luo Ping, a senior Chinese bank regulator, memorably explained in 2009, "We know the dollar is going to depreciate, so we hate you guys, but there is nothing much we can do."[41]

To be sure, China's rise and its large foreign reserves have given it some increased voice and leverage in international institutions, including over the long overdue reforms to the governance of the international financial institutions (IFIs) and a variety of international standard-setting bodies. At the same time, however, they have also substantially increased the external pressure on Beijing to allocate more of its reserves to global economic stabilization.

For all these reasons, the interpretation of China's developmental strategy as unambiguously mercantilist is problematic. But there is another problem for the mercantilist interpretation: there are clear signs that leadership preferences are increasingly divided over key policy questions and their consequences.

Support for the model of export-led growth has not gone unchallenged in China. In recent years the leadership has explicitly recognized its drawbacks, pledging to rebalance the economy toward domestic consumption, which has steadily fallen to the exceptionally low level of about a third of GDP today. In a blunt recognition of these concerns, Premier Wen Jiabao famously stated after the National People's Congress of March 2007 that "China's economic growth is unsteady, unbalanced, uncoordinated, and unsustainable."[42] The goal of rebalancing and reshaping the Chinese growth model has been conceptualized under the slogan of "Scientific Developmentalism."[43] These "rebalancing" objectives received even more prominent emphasis in the 12th Five Year Plan. As Wen Jiabao stated in his speech to the National People's Congress in March 2011, "Expanding domestic demand is a long-term strategic principle and basic standpoint of China's economic development as well as a fundamental means and an internal requirement for promoting balanced economic development."[44] Much more than external trade dependence is at stake. A low exchange rate has been associated with exceptionally high levels of investment in capital-intensive manufacturing, very low employment growth, rising dependence on commodity imports, and rapidly increasing pollution and greenhouse gas emissions. The PBOC has also openly voiced its concerns with the erosion of monetary control and the financial instability that a highly controlled exchange rate entails.

Although the leadership has found it very difficult to achieve its rebalancing objectives over the past decade, this has only sharpened the large differences of opinion in its senior ranks. The increasingly open disagreement between the powerful Commerce Ministry and the PBOC over exchange rate policy reflects this split.[45] Currency appreciation has been resisted by the Commerce Ministry. Chen Deming, Minister of Commerce, argued in November 2009 for "maintaining the stability of the RMB exchange rate ... [so that] export companies could have a stable expectation of the future."[46] In contrast, prominent economists associated with the PBOC have argued that currency flexibility and appreciation are the only effective means by which the Chinese government can achieve domestic monetary and financial stability and reduce the need to continue to accumulate excessive foreign exchange reserves. Yu Yongding, notably, has argued that:

> Given that many large developed countries are simply printing money ... China must realise that it can no longer invest in the paper assets of the developed world. The People's Bank of China must stop buying US dollars and allow the renminbi exchange rate to be decided by market forces as soon as possible.[47]

China's response to the global economic crisis in 2008 was also revealing of the policy inconsistencies produced by conflicting leadership objectives.

Beijing did not choose to reduce its trade and financial dependence on the United States and European Union (EU) by allowing the renminbi to appreciate and the PBOC to cease accumulating foreign currency debt. Instead, it ceased the gradual appreciation of the renminbi it had allowed since mid-2005 to support the rapidly weakening export sector, while at the same time unleashing a massive stimulus to domestic demand. This policy stance was barely consistent with the stated policy of boosting domestic consumption: the largest boost was to domestic investment, particularly infrastructure.[48] There were some new measures to boost domestic consumption, including increased public spending on health and education, but there was no decisive use of the crisis to accelerate the transition toward the new growth model previously announced by the leadership as a primary objective. This does not mean that leadership declarations of this kind are wholly insincere, but the policies aimed at achieving them often lack clear targets and contain crucial inconsistencies.[49] These splits cast further doubt upon a purely statist explanation of China's attitude toward international macroeconomic surveillance.

Interest group pressures?

The shortcomings of a statist explanation of Chinese policy choices could be interpreted as good news for a society-centered account of China's difficulties with the international macroeconomic surveillance framework. From the latter perspective, rather than being a product of state-led mercantilism, Chinese policy has been seen as the product of a weak and divided central leadership that recognizes the need for change but which has been increasingly constrained by the dominant preferences of a powerful private domestic and multinational firm coalition.[50] Standard political economy models also lead us to expect interests in the export sector to favor an undervalued, stable exchange rate with the currencies of major trading partners and to organize to influence policy outcomes.[51]

To some extent, this has been borne out in China over the past decade, with the Commerce Ministry acting as an important institutional voice for the export lobby, which also has allies in other key bodies such as the National Development and Reform Commission (NDRC) and on the State Council itself.[52] Indeed, the often close relationship between Chinese domestic firms and the party-state apparatus indicates that the Chinese political economy does not fit comfortably into the standard interest politics model, implicitly based as it is upon the relatively pluralistic American political system. In the Chinese system, party bosses in the rapidly developing Eastern provinces have also acquired a powerful political and often personal inter-est in the continuation of the export boom and associated inward foreign investment. The Chinese firms in the export sector are often closely con-nected with the party-state, including those enterprises that are explicitly state-owned and the state-owned banks that lend to them. More generally, all firms in China still operate within the policy and political boundaries established by the party-state.[53] To a much greater extent than in more advanced democratic countries, this is also true of foreign firms operating in China, including those utilizing abundant Chinese labor in the manufac-turing export sector.

The often close relationship between party-state and societal forces in the political economy of Chinese policy making could be seen as reinforcing the claim that export and related interests are privileged in the policy-making process. But this would be to ignore the significant interests that are either relatively indifferent or that lose from a range of policies connected with China's growing current account surplus. For example, many of the firms in the assembly-for-export sector import a large proportion of their produc-tion inputs from abroad and thus would not be greatly affected by renminbi appreciation.[54] Firms that primarily serve the domestic market would gain from currency appreciation if this permitted them to reduce their input costs, as would the banks that lend to such firms. To the extent that appre-ciation shifted investment away from capital-intensive manufacturing toward labor-intensive projects in the medium term, it would also have a positive effect on employment and on a variety of domestic businesses.[55] Furthermore, a more flexible exchange rate policy would permit the PBOC a greater degree of domestic monetary control and thereby facilitate a more effective anti-inflationary policy. The leadership has also consistently indicated over the past decade that it is sensitive to societal concerns about rising consumer and asset price inflation and the growing inequality asso-ciated with the existing growth model. As Wen Jiabao characteristically noted in his speech to the People's Congress in March 2011:

> We are keenly aware that we still have a serious problem in that our develop-ment is not yet well balanced, coordinated or sustainable...Moreover, we have not yet fundamentally solved a number of issues that the masses feel strongly about, namely the lack of high-quality educational and medical resources, and their uneven distribution; increasing upward pressure on prices, and exorbitant housing price increases in some cities; increasing social problems resulting from illegal land expropriations and housing demolitions; significant problems con-cerning food safety; and rampant corruption in some areas. We must therefore have a strong sense of responsibility toward the country and the people and work

tirelessly and painstakingly to solve these problems more quickly to the satisfaction of the people.[56]

Firms in the export sector are hardly immune from such social pressures,
having faced growing labor demands for significant wage rises to compensate for rising living costs in recent years.[57]

Thus, since mid-2005 the leadership has evidently tried to steer a course
between the apparent interests of the export and related sectors on the one
hand and those interests that would benefit from renminbi appreciation on
the other. The policy of gradual appreciation since then has attempted to
avoid extensive disruption of the export sector while facilitating adjustment
to a higher level of the exchange rate as part of a broader policy strategy of
moving to a different growth model. As the leadership is well aware, a lower
trade and current account surplus requires complementary policy action in
a range of other areas, including the development of a more effective social
security system, the reduction in corporate subsidies for a variety of important inputs into production, including finance, and the reform of corporate
governance to tackle the problem of growing net corporate savings. Many
reforms have been announced and will take time, but the leadership's tentative approach to date reflects both the perceived need for rebalancing as
well as the many conflicts of interest that reform confronts.

DOMESTIC AND EXTERNAL AUDIENCE DYNAMICS

All the explanations discussed previously have strengths but also significant shortcomings in explaining China's stance in the global imbalances
debate. The statist and societal approaches, which underlie much of the
commentary regarding China's policy choices, are both partial and usually
far too static in orientation. The argument that China has become increasingly enmeshed within a liberal international order and its institutions and
rules is more dynamic in nature and better able to account for the considerable evolution of Chinese foreign policy in recent years. However, it cannot easily explain why China has moved to the center of the debate about
global imbalances and macroeconomic surveillance and why the Chinese
leadership has been increasingly willing to signal its displeasure with the
surveillance regime.

In this final section I argue that understanding China's changing stance
requires greater attention to the evolving dynamic between the leadership
and two different audiences, domestic and external. Responding effectively
to the growing pressures from both audiences has proven very difficult.

Part of the frustration of China's leadership with the demands made by the IMF and the United States for more rapid rebalancing is its perception that foreign demandeurs underappreciate both the efforts the leadership is making to rebalance the economy and how external pressure could be counterproductive and domestically destabilizing.[58]

The domestic audience

If one takes the view that China's political system remains fundamentally authoritarian and that this permits the Chinese Communist Party (CCP) leadership to make policy choices in a largely unconstrained manner, emphasizing the rising importance of the domestic political audience will make little sense. However, while it would be wrong to argue that China's political system has become quasi-democratic, the leadership has signaled a much greater concern over the past decade to address a growing number of widely held societal concerns about a large number of issues. As indicated in the speech by Wen Jiabao cited earlier, these concerns include inflation, economic inequality, welfare provision, employment, the availability of affordable housing, environmental degradation, and corruption. The leadership's evident desire to be seen to address these and other issues directly is no doubt driven by its concerns about the potential for social instability and the erosion of the legitimacy of the CCP's monopoly of power. But there is also little doubt that these problems have become more widely discussed in recent years, that the government has often signaled its intention to tackle them, and that over time it has also permitted a greater degree of openness in the debate about how to do so.

Nevertheless, the complexity of the issues involved in rebalancing the economy make it difficult for the leadership to mobilize public support for a policy framework that would effectively promote a transition toward a political economy more oriented toward domestic demand. For example, additional currency appreciation would favor domestic consumption, but it would also risk higher levels of unemployment among workers in the export and related sectors. A reduction in financial repression (low or negative real interest rates on retail saving deposits) and in the many other subsidies to domestic firms would also favor consumers, but this would require the leadership to distance itself from its strategy of maintaining control over the commanding heights of the Chinese economy.

Furthermore, promoting more rapid currency appreciation could easily be interpreted by domestic nationalists as submitting to the demands of external powers, in particular the United States. Hu Jintao and Wen Jiabao have both referred to the need for external actors to understand that making increased demands of China can make it more rather than less difficult for the government to respond positively. This could be seen as a useful excuse for inaction, but it does reflect the sensitivity of the leadership to be seen as deferential to foreign powers—a phenomenon explored in detail in chapter 3. As noted earlier in this chapter, the perceived precedent of Japan resonates with a nationalist narrative that U.S. pressure on other countries to rebalance is a standard tactic to deal with rising powers.[59] Choosing currency appreciation has been easier for the Chinese leadership when it can be justified as a means of addressing the widespread concerns of ordinary Chinese with inflation. But the domestic audience is itself split on the issue, with those concerned about export competitiveness wary of anything more than very modest appreciation.

The external audience

At the same that the leadership has signaled its desire to respond more effectively and directly to its domestic audience, China's dramatic economic rise has led to growing demands from its external audience that it take greater account of the external implications of its policy choices and contribute more to regional and global governance. To be sure, there are important divisions of opinion within this external audience, as in the leadership's domestic audience, with most of Europe and China's near neighbors favoring a less robust stance compared to the United States. Nevertheless, at important junctures, such as in mid-2005 and again in 2010, the United States has received considerable support from other major countries in its demands for Chinese rebalancing measures.

Caught between rising demands at home and abroad, the leadership has not always opted (or been able) to satisfy its domestic audience at the expense of external demands. As noted earlier, across a broad portfolio of external policies China has become more rather than less convergent with global norms and rules. Where the conflicts between domestic and external demands are limited, the leadership has been able to provide some satisfaction to both sides. But in cases in which domestic and external demands have been more in conflict, as in the area of macroeconomic surveillance, China tends more often to diverge from these external demands.

However, even in this policy area, China's leadership has not been completely unconstrained by the global regime and by the demands of other external actors. China's leadership has accepted in principle the need for economic rebalancing over the medium term, within the IMF since the

early 2000s and more recently in the context of the G20. But the leaders have contested claims by foreign governments and the IMF that they
should accept more rapid currency appreciation in the short term.[60] When
domestic audience concerns about rising inflation and external demands
for rebalancing have pushed in the same direction, as in mid-2005 and
again in mid-2010, the leadership accepted the need for gradual appreciation. China has also agreed since 2008 to significant modifications to the
macroeconomic surveillance regime, which in turn makes it more difficult
to avoid future constraint on itself. This greater potential for intrusiveness
is evident in the G20's Mutual Assessment Process (MAP), with its more
extensive focus on and analysis of the external effects of economic policy decisions by major countries ("economic spillovers") compared to the
G8.[61] By November 2011, the IMF had produced reports on seven countries identified under these criteria: China, France, Germany, India, Japan,
the United Kingdom, and the United States. The report on China argued
straightforwardly that:

> ...rebalancing the [Chinese] economy...requires wide-ranging reforms, includ-
> ing strengthening social insurance, appreciating the exchange rate, and raising
> domestic interest rates. Such steps would improve welfare, both in China and the
> rest of the world. That is why the Chinese authorities have made these measures
> the crux of the nation's new Five-Year Plan.[62]

As is evident from this statement, the IMF understands the need to justify
these reforms in terms of Beijing's own policy agenda and in ways that
take the latter's domestic audience into account. The hope of those favoring persuasion over a more aggressive stance toward China, which includes
most of the Obama Administration, Europe, Japan, as well as the IMF, is
that a combination of gentle pressure within the G20 and appealing to
Beijing's domestic policy agenda will be sufficient to produce the necessary reforms. The international coalition favoring Chinese rebalancing has
certainly increased since the crisis: in 2010, for example, Brazil, India and
other developing countries began to take a more critical stance on China's
exchange rate policy.[63] This may have helped to nudge China toward the
resumption of its policy of gradual renminbi appreciation in June 2010,
just before the Toronto G20 summit.

Nevertheless, as the IMF report recognizes, "the roots of China's imbalances lie deep in the economy's structure."[64] It might have added that they
lie deep in the political structure as well and in the leadership's increasingly
complicated relationship with domestic society. The Chinese leadership's
rebalancing objectives have been at the top of its stated policy agenda for

nearly a decade, but the results have been very disappointing. There has been a considerable reduction in the relative size of China's current surplus since 2008, but it is difficult to know how much of this is due to economic stagnation in the advanced countries that may not persist. Certainly, international agencies including the IMF project global imbalances to remain large over the medium term and point to associated internal imbalances in China (e.g., between investment and consumption, and between growth and environmental sustainability) that require a wide range of very difficult reforms.[65] China's own transition to a different growth model will also be difficult as long as the United States fails to make its own transition away from consumption-driven growth. As yet, there are few signs of such a transition occurring on the other side of the Pacific, adding to Chinese skepticism regarding the macroeconomic surveillance regime.

CONCLUSION

China's relationship with the global macroeconomic surveillance regime and its problematic stance on the issue of global imbalances is not well explained by some of the standard accounts of its foreign economic policies. This relationship has become more complicated over time and, for all sides in the dispute, more uncomfortable. It reflects a complex and very incomplete process of (at least) three related transitions: from a highly closed and authoritarian polity toward one in which Chinese citizens have greater influence over and expectations of government, from an export-oriented manufacturing economy toward a more consumption-oriented and technology intensive economy, and from a relatively small developing country economy to an increasingly pivotal emerging market economy with a crucial role in global economic governance. The complexity of these multiple transitions produces a variety of challenges for the leadership in Beijing, and, unsurprisingly, many tensions and contradictions in its policy choices. As pointed out in chapter 1 in this volume, the policy slogans of "harmonious world" and "harmonious society" neither capture nor resolve these contradictions. Balancing the need to prevent external isolation against the desire not to be seen as bowing to external pressure to take costly adjustment measures—not least by an ever more critical domestic audience—has become increasingly challenging for China's leadership as Robert S. Ross argues in chapter 3. The increasingly public differences among key economic policy makers within China reflect these difficulties.

The problems that the leadership has in responding effectively to the growing demands of domestic and external audiences have had another effect. China has become more assertive in recent years regarding the reform of global economic governance. Since Beijing has been unable fully to meet the demands of its external audience it has become more vocal in demanding a more symmetric global macroeconomic surveillance regime and the reform of the international monetary system to reduce the role of the dollar. If the configuration of Chinese policies effectively condemn it to continue running large payments surpluses and the steady accumulation of financial claims on developed countries for years to come, the need for reassurance from the United States and EU about the value of its foreign assets increases. The dilemma for China's leadership is that if it is able, with other partners, to promote a more symmetric and effective system of macroeconomic surveillance it may also increase the level of external constraint for China itself. Reconciling a more intrusive system of this kind with the growing demands of many Chinese citizens for reform will be a major challenge for any future Chinese government. Whether or not it can meet this challenge will be of great importance for us all.

NOTES

1. Martin Wolf, *Fixing Global Finance* (Baltimore: Johns Hopkins University Press, 2008).
2. Anton Brender and Florence Pisani, *Global Imbalances and the Collapse of Globalised Finance* (Brussels: Centre for European Policy Studies, 2010); Maurice Obstfeld and Kenneth Rogoff, "Global Imbalances and the Financial Crisis: Products of Common Causes," CEPR Working Paper No. 7606 (December 2009).
3. C. Fred. Bergsten, "A partnership of equals: How Washington should respond to China's economic challenge," *Foreign Affairs*, Vol. 87, No. 4, July–August 2008, pp. 57–69; Arvind Subramanian, "New PPP-Based Estimates of Renminbi Undervaluation and Policy Implications," *Policy Brief* 10–8, Peterson Institute for International Economics, April 2010.
4. Robert D. Putnam, "Diplomacy and domestic politics: The logic of two-level games," *International Organization,* Vol. 42, No. 3 (1988), pp. 427–60; Helen V. Milner, *Interests, Institutions, and Information* (Princeton, NJ: Princeton University Press, 1997).
5. Gideon Rose, "Neoclassical realism and theories of foreign policy," *World Politics,* Vol. 51, No. 3 (1998), pp. 144–72.
6. For an overview of the macroeconomic surveillance regime, see Rosemary Foot and Andrew Walter, *China, the United States, and Global Order* (Cambridge: Cambridge University Press, 2011), pp. 82–95.
7. Harold J. Jacobson and Michel Oksenberg, *China's Participation in the IMF, the World Bank, and GATT: Toward a Global Economic Order* (Ann Arbor: University of Michigan Press, 1990).
8. Author interview with IMF staff in Beijing, November 2008.
9. See U.S. Treasury, *Report to the Congress on International Economic and Exchange Rate Policy* (Washington, DC: U.S. Department of the Treasury, April 1990).

10. US Treasury, *Report to the Congress on International Economic and Exchange Rate Policy, May 1991* (Washington, D.C.: US Department of the Treasury, May 1991), pp. 13, 23–28.
11. IMF, "Surveillance Over Exchange Rate Policies," Decision No. 5392-(77/63), April 29, 1977.
12. U.S. Treasury, *Seventh Annual Report to the Congress on International Economic and Exchange Rate Policy, December 1994* (Washington, DC: U.S. Department of the Treasury, December 1994), p. 26.
13. Zhou Xiaochuan, "On savings ratio," *Banque de France Financial Stability Review,* special issue on "Global imbalances and financial stability," No. 15 (February 2011), p. 167.
14. John B. Taylor, *Global Financial Warriors: The Untold Story of International Finance in the Post-9/11 World* (New York: W.W. Norton, 2007), pp. 291–300.
15. IMF, "People's Republic of China: 2005 Article IV Consultation—Staff Report; Staff Statement; and Public Information Notice on the Executive Board Discussion," Country Report No. 05/411 (November 17), 2005, pp. 15–17; IMF, *"People's Republic of China: 2006 Article IV Consultation—Staff Report; Staff Statement; and Public Information Notice on the Executive Board Discussion"* (Washington, DC: IMF, October 2006), pp. 17–20.
16. Foot and Walter, *China, the United States, and Global Order*, pp. 113–16.
17. IMF, "People's Republic of China: 2011 Article IV Consultation," Country Report No. 11/192 (July 2011), pp. 18–9.
18. Statement by Jianxiong He, Executive Director for People's Republic of China and Zhengxin Zhang, Senior Advisor to the Executive Director, July 15, 2011, appendix to IMF, "People's Republic of China: 2011 Article IV Consultation," p. 4.
19. William R. Cline, "Projecting China's Current Account Surplus," *Peterson Institute Policy Brief* 12–7, April 2012.
20. Steven Dunaway, *Global Imbalances and the Financial Crisis* (New York: Council on Foreign Relations, 2009); Obstfeld and Rogoff, "Global Imbalances and the Financial Crisis"; Raghuram G. Rajan, *Fault Lines: How Hidden Fractures Still Threaten the World Economy* (Princeton, NJ: Princeton University Press, 2010).
21. "Interview with Wen," *FT.com*, February 1, 2009.
22. Statement by Jianxiong He and Zhengxin Zhang, July 15, 2011, p. 4.
23. E.g., Independent Evaluation Office of the IMF, *IMF Performance in the Run-Up to the Financial and Economic Crisis: IMF Surveillance in 2004–07* (Washington, DC: IEO/IMF, 2011), pp. 20, 35, and Jack Boorman and Teresa Ter-Minassian, *"TSR External Report on Interviews with Country Authorities,"* Washington, DC, IMF, May 15, 2011.
24. "Rift lowers hopes of G20 breakthrough," *FT.com*, February 18, 2011.
25. "Interview with Wen," *FT.com*, February 1, 2009.
26. Zhou Xiaochuan, "Reform the International Monetary System," statement issued on the PBOC website, March 23, 2009.
27. "China rules out 'nuclear option' on T-bills," *FT.com*, July 7, 2010.
28. E.g., "Currency war: Overflowing dollar against other currencies," *China Daily*, October 26, 2010.
29. Ann Kent, *Beyond Compliance: China, International Organizations, and Global Security* (Stanford, CA: Stanford University Press, 2007); Alastair Iain Johnston, *Social States: China in International Institutions, 1980–2000* (Princeton, NJ: Princeton University Press, 2008).

30. G. John. Ikenberry, "The rise of China and the future of the West: Can the liberal system survive?" *Foreign Affairs*, Vol. 87, No. 1, January/February 2008, pp. 23–37.
31. Foot and Walter, *China, the United States, and Global Order*.
32. Commission on Growth and Development, *The Growth Report: Strategies for Sustained Growth and Inclusive Development* (Washington, DC: The World Bank, 2008), pp. 49–50, and Independent Evaluation Office, *IMF Performance in the Run-Up to the Financial and Economic Crisis*, pp. 20, 35.
33. "Interview with Wen," *FT.com*, February 1, 2009.
34. Nicholas Lardy, "Financial Repression in China," *Peterson Institute Policy Brief* 08–8, 2008.
35. G. John Ikenberry, Michael Mastanduno, and David Lake, eds, *The State and American Foreign Economic Policy* (Ithaca, NY: Cornell University Press, 1988).
36. Bergsten, "A partnership of equals"; Subramanian, "New PPP-Based Estimates."
37. Michael P. Dooley, David Folkerts-Landau, and Peter Garber, "An Essay on the Revived Bretton Woods System," NBER Working Paper No. 9971 (September 2003); Commission on Growth and Development, *The Growth Report*.
38. Kai Guo and Papa N'Diaye, "Is China's Export-Oriented Growth Sustainable?" IMF Working Paper WP/09/172 (Washington, DC: IMF, October 2009).
39. Yu Yongding, "Global Imbalances: China's Perspective," Paper prepared for conference on European and Asian Perspectives on Global Imbalances, Beijing, July 12–14, 2006.
40. Daniel W. Drezner, "Bad Debts: Assessing China's Financial Influence in Great Power Politics," *International Security*, Vol. 34, No. 2 (5) 2009, pp. 7–45.
41. "China to stick with U.S. bonds," *FT.com*, February 11, 2009.
42. Quoted in Lardy, "Financial Repression in China," p. 5.
43. Barry Naughton, "What price continuity?" *China Leadership Monitor*, No. 34 (February 2011), p. 3.
44. Wen Jiabao, "Report on the Work of the Government," speech delivered at the Fourth Session of the Eleventh National People's Congress, March 5, 2011. Available: http://www.china.org.cn/china/NPC_CPPCC_2011/2011–03/15/content_22143099.htm [May 7, 2012].
45. "China officials wrestle publicly over currency," *New York Times*, March 25, 2010; Charles W. Freeman III and Wen Jin Yuan, "China's Exchange Rate Politics: Decoding the Cleavage Between the Chinese Ministry of Commerce and the People's Bank of China," Center for Strategic and International Studies, June 2011.
46. Cited in Freeman and Wen, "China's Exchange Rate Politics," p. 7.
47. Yu Yongding, "China can break free of the dollar trap," *FT.com*, August 4, 2011.
48. Wen Jiabao, "How China plans to reinforce the global recovery," *FT.com*, June 23, 2011.
49. Naughton, "What price continuity?"
50. For accounts that emphasize the role of at least some parts of China's export sector, see Barry J. Eichengreen, "Is a change in the renminbi exchange rate in China's interest?" *Asian Economic Papers* Vol. 4, No. 1 (2005), pp. 40–75; He Xingqiang, "The RMB exchange rate: Interest groups in China's economic policymaking," *China Security*, No. 19, pp. 23–36.
51. Jeffry Frieden, "Exchange rate politics: Contemporary lessons from Latin America," *Review of International Political Economy*, Vol. 1, No. 1 (1994), pp. 81–103.
52. Barry Naughton, "China's economic leadership after the 17th Party Congress," *China Leadership Monitor*, No. 23, 2008.

53. Shaun Breslin, "Government-Industry Relations in China: A Review of the Art of the State," in *East Asian Capitalism: Continuity, Diversity and Change*, edited *by* Andrew Walter and Xiaoke Zhang (Cambridge: Cambridge University Press, 2012), pp. 29–45.
54. Eichengreen, "Is a change in the renminbi exchange rate in China's interest?"
55. C. Fred Bergsten, Charles Freeman, Nicholas R. Lardy, and Derek J. Mitchell, *China's Rise: Challenges and Opportunities* (Washington, DC: Peterson Institute for International Economics/Center for Strategic and International Studies, 2007), pp. 110–11.
56. Wen Jiabao, "Report on the Work of the Government."
57. On the politics of domestic inflation, see Victor Shih, *Factions and Finance in China: Elite Conflict and Inflation* (New York: Cambridge University Press, 2008).
58. "Wen warns against Renminbi pressure," *FT.com*, October 6, 2010.
59. "Time for RMB appreciation?" *People's Daily Online*, June 9, 2010.
60. IMF, "People's Republic of China: 2011 Article IV Consultation," p. 19.
61. See "Communiqué," Finance Ministers and Central bank Governors Meeting, Washington DC, April 14–15, 2011.
62. IMF, *People's Republic of China Sustainability Report* (Washington, DC: IMF, November 2011), p. 2.
63. "Renminbi's rise fuels talk of China policy shift," *FT.com*, August 11, 2011.
64. IMF, *People's Republic of China Sustainability Report*, p. 2.
65. IMF, *G20 Mutual Assessment Process: From Pittsburgh to Cannes—IMF Umbrella Report* (Washington, DC: IMF, November 2011), pp. 2, 19; Bank for International Settlements, *Annual Report 2010/11* (Basel: Bank for International Settlements, 2011), pp. 33–49; World Bank, *China 2030: Building a Modern, Harmonious, and Creative High-Income Society* (Washington, DC: World Bank, 2012).

CHAPTER 7

ᴄᐱᴐ

Norms Without Borders?
Human Rights in China

GUDRUN WACKER

Human rights have been the subject of contestation between the People's Republic of China (PRC) and the outside world, mainly Western democracies, over the last several decades. Ever since the Chinese leadership deployed military force against demonstrators in and around Tian'anmen Square in June 1989, China's human rights situation has been under close scrutiny from the outside and the object of regular criticism. As with the other chapters in part 3 of this volume, the topic represents a clear case where global processes work in a variety of ways to influence a state's development, official policies, and society.

The majority of the many publications on this issue focus either on the domestic human rights situation in China and its development[1] or on Western[2] efforts to improve this situation and the instruments used for this purpose.[3] This division is unhelpful, however, if it comes to understanding the complex relationship between Chinese society, the government and overseas actors, and the more intense Chinese involvement with an issue that has come to provide the "dominant moral vocabulary in foreign affairs"[4] over this period. This chapter examines these interactions involving China, global normative change, and overseas actors mainly in the period since the end of the twentieth century.

Two clusters of factors can be identified that have become relevant for the development of human rights in China over the last decade or so. The first set relates to the diffusion of power on the global level and within

China itself. China's economic, political, and military weight has increased substantially over the last ten years, but other countries, like India or Brazil, have also emerged as important actors on the international stage. Within China, various civil society actors play a bigger role and the rapid spread of new communication technologies has resulted in a diffusion of power away from the official media. Access to outside information has become easier thanks to China's growing global integration.

The second bundle of factors coming into play is the Chinese leadership's preoccupation with stability and the fear that events outside China, such as the so-called color revolutions or, more recently, the Arab Spring, could infect China and lead to more widespread unrest, ultimately challenging social and political stability at home.

None of these factors is entirely new—most elements existed in the 1990s as well—but they have become stronger and more pronounced over the last decade, thus acquiring a new quality. The analysis that follows shows what their effects on the development of human rights in China and on China's human rights diplomacy have been and how they are interconnected.

As a first step, the chapter briefly reviews the domestic and international causes for China's deepening involvement with the human rights issue in the period since Reform and Opening to the end of the twentieth century. The second part examines continuities and changes discernible in the development of human rights in China over the last decade. The third section investigates both the global and domestic diffusion of power in the years after 2000 when Beijing became a more influential actor in world politics and when its citizens came to expect more of their government in terms of protection both at home and overseas. The fourth part addresses potentially contagious and stability-challenging international events and the reaction of China's decision makers. These international events notably include the run-up to the 2008 Summer Olympic Games held in Beijing. Hosting the Games made China susceptible to many kinds of external pressure on the human rights front. The conclusion highlights the interplay between the domestic and external realms. It shows that while China has become more open and globally integrated over the past decade, pressure on human rights has remained prominent from both the outside as well as the inside. The leadership's ability to handle or to deflect such criticism has become more refined, and it also has become normal to discuss the topic of human rights in China and with Chinese. However, when the stability of the system seems at stake from the perspective of China's leaders, human rights and the rule of law clearly have to take a backseat.

STAGES, ACTORS, AND STRATEGIES: LATE 1970S
TO EARLY 2000S

In the 1970s and 1980s China was welcomed back into international society after decades of largely self-imposed isolation. The break of China's leaders with the ideological past and the proclamation of a new identity for China as a modernizing state[5] found a positive echo in the Western industrialized countries. The leadership's distancing itself from the Cultural Revolution included also the admission of shortcomings in human rights during that upheaval. Western democracies granted China a "grace period" in terms of this new beginning, and the country widely became considered as the frontrunner of socialist reform, in positive contrast to the Soviet Union and other Eastern European countries. While China had previously refused any dialogue on human rights as a matter of principle, it cautiously opened up for such a debate during the 1980s.[6]

The year 1989 marked a turning point from which China's image has never totally recovered—at least in the opinion of many people in Western democracies. With the transformations in Eastern Europe and the Soviet Union under way, China mutated practically overnight from the spearhead of socialist reform into the taillight of history. China's greater openness to the media, and the visit of Soviet leader Mikhail Gorbachev to China in May 1989 ensured widespread coverage of the dramatic developments in Tian'anmen Square that led to the military crackdown on the night of June 3–4. The West reacted with strong criticism and with economic and political sanctions. Even though these sanctions were—with the notable exception of export restrictions for military goods—quietly lifted soon after the events, the image of China's leaders in the international media and publics was tarnished. For international human rights groups like *Amnesty International*, which had been following the human rights situation in China for several years, this provided an opportunity to make themselves heard among a wider audience and to draw attention to human rights violations in China more generally.

China's response to the international condemnation immediately after Tian'anmen consisted primarily in damage control. On the one hand, a stronger debate in China on human rights was initiated top-down and government-organized nongovernmental organizations (GONGOs) focusing on human rights were founded, several domestic and international conferences were held, and the Chinese government published its first White Paper on Human Rights in 1991. In sum, there was a more proactive human rights policy in the early 1990s largely in response to international criticism.

Beyond these direct and immediate actions post 1989, China also explored ways of escaping from the international sanctions and international criticism. For example, by abstaining in the UN Security Council on resolution 678 (November 29, 1990) authorizing the use of force against Iraq, China was able to restart high-level meetings with the United States. Beijing next regained access to credits from the World Bank, without, however, alienating Arab and Islamic countries.[7] At the UN level, it became an important goal for China in the 1990s to prevent the United Nations Commission on Human Rights (UNCHR) from passing a China-critical resolution. This was successfully managed by mobilizing allies like Pakistan to table a no-action resolution.[8] As for the Western countries, China successfully convinced them in the second half of the 1990s to refrain from publicly denouncing China's human rights violations at the UN level by offering to hold regular human rights dialogues bilaterally behind closed doors. The European Union (EU), some European member states, the United States, and Canada all switched to this form of "quiet diplomacy." Helpful to the Chinese negotiations with the Western states was its decision to sign the two core human rights covenants: in 1997 Beijing signed the International Covenant on Economic, Social and Cultural Rights; one year later the International Covenant on Civil and Political Rights.

However, at the end of the 1990s, China's approach to human rights diplomacy seemed to harden again. Domestically, two developments demonstrated China's determination to ignore and suspend specific civil rights if the stability of the political system and the power monopoly of the Chinese Communist Party (CCP) seemed to be under threat. When some activists associated with the student demonstrations in 1989 used the opportunity of U.S. President Bill Clinton's visit to China in 1998 to register the Democracy Party of China,[9] they were accused of subversion and sentenced to long prison terms. And when in April 1999 thousands of Falungong followers gathered quietly in front of Zhongnanhai, the very center of political power in China, the spiritual group was banned and its followers persecuted. On the international stage, the military campaign against Serbia without a UN mandate and the "accidental" bombing of the Chinese embassy in Belgrade in 1999 (Chinese leaders and media called into question that this was unintended) heightened Chinese suspicions of the West. China reacted by suspending not only high-level military contacts and cooperation on nonproliferation with the United States but also the human rights dialogue.[10]

In sum, over the course of these decades, China became more deeply involved both internationally and domestically with the human rights idea. Internationally, the end of the Cold War reduced the strategic significance of China to the West and led to a sharper focus on domestic conditions in China, particularly after the tragedy of Tian'anmen. Over the course of this period, global attention to human rights also increased, not just at the governmental level but also as a result of the growth in power and number of non-state human rights organizations. China's open door and its changing strategic circumstances coincided with the consolidation of the global norm.

On the national level, the late 1970s break with the ideological past, the new identity as a modernizing state, the gradual reintegration into the international community, and the desire to be accepted as a responsible global power provided the ground for China's greater openness to the international human rights debate. Promoting a discourse on human rights within China contributed to formulating an official Chinese conception of human rights to counter the Western position, but the involvement in the international discourse on human rights also created space for groups within China to explore the issue of human rights. However, this openness had its limitations, when considerations of national stability or, to be more precise, regime stability and the power monopoly of the CCP took priority, as was the case with Tian'anmen or the founding of a democratic party.

CONTINUITIES AND NEW DEVELOPMENTS SINCE 2000

The dominant official and publicized position of China on human rights has not fundamentally changed over the last decade. The repertoire of arguments to deflect external criticism of human rights violations that China has developed in the course of the 1990s is still used (albeit somewhat refined) today. One approach is denial: reports on human rights violations are simply false, the sources doubtful or unreliable. Another is to reinterpret the issue in dispute: it is not a human rights issue but a matter of national sovereignty or territorial integrity as has often been claimed in reference to matters that affected either Tibet or Xinjiang. A further tactic is to make the argument that China (or all of Asia as claimed in the "Asian values" debate in the mid-1990s) was different due to its specific historical and cultural background and therefore interpreted human rights on the basis of different values and norms. And still another approach involves conceding that there are shortcomings in China's level of protection, but this was due to China's development stage and would be improved in the future.[11] Finally, China can turn the tables and point out human rights deficiencies in Western countries, especially the United States, and accuse the West of applying double standards.

Chinese debates on human rights among academics and on the official level have continued and have not led to consensus on the most contested

points. A few years ago the term "universal values" *(pushi jiazhi)* was introduced into the domestic dispute over the question of universality versus
cultural relativity *(Zhongguo tese,* "Chinese characteristics"), and this has
become a hotly debated topic.[12] In official statements, universality is sometimes conceded, at least as a joint goal of humankind.[13] However, China still
argues that countries have different priorities and make specific choices
when it comes to these universal human rights, and that these differences
can be explained by different stages in the development of a country or by
its cultural and historical background.

Ambivalence on the question whether or not human rights are a legitimate issue in international politics or a purely domestic affair has persisted
as well: China's growing involvement in the international human rights
mechanisms demonstrates the first line, the insistence on the principles
of state sovereignty and noninterference the second point. On this fundamental question, the official Chinese position seems to fluctuate, as it
does on the universality and indivisibility of human rights. A degree of
inconsistency can also be identified at the official level when it comes to
the admission of deficiencies in China's human rights situation and efforts
to improve it on the one hand and active defense of China's own levels of
protection on the other hand.

Judging from its positions and voting behavior in the United Nations and
the Security Council, China has been practicing a pragmatic and case-by-
case approach and has even made some concessions on the principle of
noninterference. Most relevant in the context of the international human
rights regime, the new norm "Responsibility to Protect" (R2P), which was
introduced at the United Nations World Summit in 2005, endorsed by the
UN Security Council in 2006 and adopted by the UN General Assembly
in 2009, has been accepted by China, albeit with some reservations that
emphasize the role of the state in preventing abuses.[14] These were formulated in a Chinese Position Paper at the UN General Assembly in September
2008:

> The responsibility to protect civilians rests first with the government of the
> country involved in accordance with the Charter of the United Nations and the
> International Humanitarian Law. Humanitarian assistance should respect the
> principles of impartiality, neutrality, objectiveness and independence, respect
> the sovereignty and territorial integrity of the countries concerned and refrain
> from interfering in local political disputes or impeding the peace process.[15]

On the domestic level, China's National People's Congress (the parliament)
ratified the UN Covenant on Economic, Social, and Cultural Rights in

March 2001, four years after the country's signature of this treaty—with a reservation on the key Article 8 concerning labor rights (forming and joining trade unions). In 2004, China enshrined human rights in the Chinese Constitution, but only in the most general terms: "The State respects and preserves human rights."[16]

In terms of producing documents on human rights, China also remained quite active: In addition to several more White Papers,[17] a Human Rights Action Plan[18] was published in 2009. China also fulfilled its obligation to report to the UN Human Rights Council, which had replaced the UNCHR in 2006, by handing in a report in 2008.[19] Most of the human rights dialogues with Western countries, which had been started in the late 1990s, took place regularly after 2000. Thus, references to human rights, White Papers, and dialogues have become routine in and with China.[20]

One consequence of the reference to rights in the Constitution as well as signature of core international treaties has been to encourage those inside China to test the boundaries of this claimed adherence to human rights protections. In December 2008, the document "Charter 08" (*Ling-ba xianzhang*)[21] was circulated on the occasion of the sixtieth anniversary of the Universal Declaration of Human Rights. It was modeled after Charter 77, which had been initiated by dissidents in former Czechoslovakia. Charter 08 was originally signed by more than 300 Chinese academics, journalists, writers, lawyers, teachers, retired officials, and peasants. Among the signatories was Liu Xiaobo, who was shortly afterwards detained and in December 2009 sentenced to eleven years in prison. Much to China's indignation, Liu was awarded the Nobel Peace Prize in 2010 (see the next section).

This domestic–global nexus, manifest in the case of Charter 08, was evident in several other areas of rights-related policy in the 2000s, demonstrating vividly how weaker societal actors can use international measures against a resistant state. As noted earlier, there were many similarities in the way that the Chinese government approached the human rights issue compared with the 1990s. Nevertheless, by the early 2000s, there was strong evidence that power was diffusing both at the global level but also within China itself. The PRC had clearly emerged as a more prominent actor in global politics, both more integrated into international society and more powerful economically. It became a key member of the G20 and was recognized as the most powerful state among the so-called BRICS.[22] Other important developments affected the influence of civil society groups, through the power of technology and social networking, not only at the international level but also within China. Alongside these developments, the West itself lost some of its authority and legitimacy on the human

rights question: it stood accused of serious human rights violations in relation to the so-called Global War on Terror.

The question is what difference, if any, did these changes make to China's
positions on human rights at home and in terms of its global diplomacy?
While China's leaders could feel more self-confident as a result of the country's economic and political rise and the emergence of a group of similarly
positioned countries on the global stage, the growing openness at the same
time made them concerned that the stability of the system could be challenged from within the Chinese society and that such a development could
also be triggered or inspired by political and social upheavals elsewhere. I
tackle these two distinctive developments—the change in China's relative
power, as well as the development of social networking inside China—to
show how they were manifest in terms of official policies.

THE DIFFUSION OF POWER AND CHINA'S HUMAN RIGHTS

China's growing power and growing interdependence

Since the start of the twenty-first century, China has become more powerful economically, politically, and militarily on the regional as well as the
global stage, but at the same time more integrated internationally, especially since joining the World Trade Organization (WTO) in 2001. Its economy has also become more interdependent with neighboring countries as
well as U.S. and European markets. China's neighbors' perceptions of the
PRC as a growing market of key importance to them, as well as Western
realization of the country's economic significance as the fastest growing
economy in the world, should make it easier for China to create unwelcome
choices for countries that criticize Beijing on human rights grounds. There
is more at stake now for these countries than there was in the 1990s, when
China was not yet the second biggest economy in the world, one of the
biggest trading nations or the biggest holder of U.S. treasuries. From the
perspective of the Western countries, China has become a crucial actor on
most global issues, including in the area of climate change, or in rebalancing the global economy at a time of recession (both issues that are treated
elsewhere in this section of the book). China can either act as a cooperative partner or a spoiler or it can show disinterest. Its bargaining position
potentially could have increased enormously over the last decade.

However, the outcomes are in fact more mixed than this. Pressure on
China concerning human rights has continued to exist. While Western
governments have mostly agreed to raise human rights issues with their

Chinese counterparts behind closed doors and in human rights dialogues, pressure from international nongovernmental organizations (NGOs), media, parliaments, and the broader public has made sure that the topic does not disappear entirely from political agendas.

The events around the Nobel Peace Prize for Liu Xiaobo have demonstrated that China's ability to silence external criticism of its human rights situation is in fact limited despite its increased economic and political clout. The fact that Liu Xiaobo was nominated by the committee as a candidate for receiving the prize was in itself a signal to China that Liu's eleven-year prison sentence for "subversion" had not gone unnoticed internationally. When rumor spread that he was a nominee for the award, China first tried to exert pressure on the Committee responsible for selecting the winner. When this proved unsuccessful, governments around the world were warned not to attend the award-giving ceremony, but this did not lead to the desired result either: only eighteen countries declined the invitation to attend the ceremony, while forty-four accepted.[23] Finally, China froze political relations with Norway and some goods were subject to boycott; but the effect of these measures has been limited.[24]

Another case in which China has warned governments and exerted pressure by threatening sanctions is foreign officials' reception of the Dalai Lama. China reacted to meetings between heads of states and the Dalai Lama in the last years not only with strong verbal protest but also with sanctions. In the case of Germany in 2007, some prescheduled visits were canceled and the atmosphere remained frosty for several months. Less clear is whether trade or investment contracts were also negatively affected. When more than a year later French President Sarkozy announced that he would meet the Dalai Lama in Poland, the entire European Union was taken hostage: China "postponed" the EU–China summit scheduled for December 2008, stating that the atmosphere was not good and the expected goals could not be achieved.[25]

Both cases presented above generated a lot of international attention, not least because of the strength of China's reaction. However, this Chinese strategy of warning of consequences produced mixed results at best, since most countries—just like China itself—react negatively to this kind of pressure. In addition, domestic groups were able to exert pressure on their respective governments, urging them to attend the Nobel ceremony and to meet the Dalai Lama. In some respects, this showed that it was politically more costly for Western leaders to cave in to Chinese pressure than to bear Chinese sanctions for a certain period and then make efforts to get relations with China back on track. Thus, China's capabilities to influence other, mainly but not exclusively, Western, countries' behavior to conform to Beijing's wishes and make them refrain from showing public support for critics of China's human rights situation have proved limited, despite increases in Beijing's relative power and in circumstances where it has chosen to use its power in bullying ways.

However, while the impact is limited, it is not nonexistent and we can see areas where China's growing power is seen as responsible for "subtle changes" in Western human rights diplomacy. According to one author, U.S. Secretary of State Hillary Clinton's remarks in February 2009 that human rights should not stand in the way of cooperation on global issues,[26] and the way in which the relationship with China was repaired by Germany and France after Merkel's and Sarkozy's meetings with the Dalai Lama demonstrate the predicament of the West and allegedly ended in "embarrassment" for the governments in question. As Luo Yanhua put it: "It turns out that, when human rights conflict with economic interests, Chancellor Merkel and President Sarkozy eventually chose the latter."[27] While the "embarrassment" part of this interpretation can be challenged, it is a fact that Western governments have sought to mend their relationships with China as quickly as possible and have come out with public declarations in support of China's territorial integrity. And with respect to actual results for human rights in China, there have been no concessions by China on highly publicized cases such as Liu Xiaobo.

Other emerging powers

Economic globalization has accelerated and new constellations of states have formed, such as the G20, which has at least in part replaced the G7/8 and given emerging economies a seat at the table. Some of the emerging powers have come together under the acronym BRICS, a group of countries that loosely coordinate their positions on the international stage.[28] Although it is far from clear whether this group will really form into a viable bloc in international politics, it is important to note that these countries—with the exception of Russia—share the double identity of (future or potential) great power and developing country. China's position of defending sovereignty against outside interference (although, as mentioned previously, the principle has weakened and is handled on a case-by-case basis by Beijing itself) has been supported by these other emerging powers. India and Brazil, for example, despite being democracies and committed to universal human rights, have been advocating positions on sovereignty not unlike those of China.[29] A shared colonial past explains much of this, as does a commitment to defending the South against the North especially given the belief that it is the Western industrialized countries of the economic North that are in favor of intervening in countries of the global South (and not the other way round).

So far, however, the BRICS' countries have not developed fully coordinated positions, including on the issue of international human rights protection. China and Russia do seem to be in very close alignment on human rights questions, with South Africa not far behind; but Brazil and India disagree more often with these three states' positions. According to a 2012 study, during sessions of the UN Human Rights Council, China and Russia voted the same on 99 percent of occasions, followed by South Africa (96 percent), Brazil (83 percent) and India (78 percent).[30] Like China's own voting behavior in the Security Council, India, Brazil, and South Africa, which were members of this UN body in 2011, have made their decisions on a case-by-case basis. All the BRICS voted in favor of Resolution 1970 authorizing sanctions against Libya as a reaction to "the gross and systematic violation of human rights." South Africa voted in favor, while the other four countries abstained, on Resolution 1973 authorizing the enforcement of a no-fly zone over Libya in March 2011. When the Security Council voted on sanctioning Syria in October 2011, Russia and China used their veto power, and Brazil, India, and South Africa also voted against. Mainly, this was a reaction to what was perceived as an abuse of the international mandate in the Libya case: the implementation of a no-fly zone turned into a military intervention that ended in regime change. Yet, by February 2012, the BRICS no longer stood together: India and South Africa[31] voted in favor of a resolution that would have condemned "widespread gross violations of human rights" in Syria, while Russia and China decided to use their veto power again. Where they did regroup, however, was in the Indian as well as the South African response underlining the importance of preserving Syria's sovereignty and territorial integrity.[32]

The meetings among BRICS' leaders have produced some joint declarations, but due to the heterogeneity of the countries involved, BRICS countries are united more by what these countries are against than by a positive common agenda. China also often tries to "hide" itself in this group to be less exposed internationally. It is too early to say whether the increased influence of BRICS and other emerging powers like Indonesia, Mexico, Turkey, and Nigeria in international affairs will in the longer run have a weakening impact on the international human rights regime and norms. But at this point, we can argue that China's position on human rights has not received the benefits from a diffusion of power to these states in the way it might have expected.

Weakened credibility of the West

The terrorist attacks in the United States on September 11, 2001, were followed by the "global war on terror" and the UN-approved military intervention in Afghanistan, and later—without UN authorization—in 2003 in Iraq. Faced with the terrorist threat, many Western governments, and the United States in particular, reduced the level of protection of individual rights, like the assumption of innocence and the right to have adequate legal representation. Even the human rights norm forbidding torture, a practice that is nonderogable, came under serious attack. The threat of terrorism changed the atmosphere world-wide. When security was pitted against individual rights, security received the higher priority. The treatment of prisoners in Guantanamo and in secret prisons of the CIA (Central Intelligence Agency) around the world ("black sites"), atrocities during the war in Iraq, and the partial suspension of individual rights of foreigners and even U.S. citizens in the United States weakened the human rights position of the Western countries vis-à-vis China in general.[33] From the Chinese (and many other countries') perspective, the West has once again lost much of its credibility and has demonstrated its willingness to apply double standards.

China has taken up the violations of human rights in and by the United States in an annual report published by China's Information Office of the State Council since 1999. It usually has addressed the situation within the United States (gender, children, and racial discrimination) and has included social issues such as the gap between rich and poor. Beginning with the second edition, the report included a section on U.S. human rights violations in other countries, mainly criticizing the methods and effects of U.S. military interventions abroad.[34] The reports also have pointed to the weak balance sheet of the United States when it comes to its signature of international human rights conventions.[35] However, since 2002 the language has taken on a harder edge, pointing to U.S. atrocities in Afghanistan and later also in Iraq as prime examples of U.S. double standards and a failure to address its own role in human rights abuse.[36]

While the decisions of the United States after September 11, 2001, and the war on terror did not necessarily change China's position on human rights, in Beijing's view they have weakened Western claims of moral superiority.

Empowerment of society in China: mobility, activism, and new media

While we might note a mixed influence on China's human rights diplomacy as a result of a gradual diffusion of power at the global level, developments within China itself have been more significant. A gradual diffusion of power has also taken place internally, since the process of economic transformation has been accompanied by a social one. Chinese urbanites now have better access to information about the rest of the world, and traveling to other Asian or Western countries has become popular among the affluent middle class.[37] Opinions within China have become more diversified and social engagement has become more widespread. Today, thousands of grassroots organizations on environmental and other issues are active all over the country[38]; there are groups of lawyers who defend the rights of migrant workers or minorities, and journalists and academics comment on developments inside and outside China in a critical way.

While the 1990s had already witnessed a strong surge in the use of the internet and mobile phones in China, the numbers have been going through the roof over the last decade.[39] Short messages on mobile phones and microblogging (the Chinese version of social networks) have become important means to connect people within China and spread news that the official media outlets cannot report owing to censorship. Of course, only a fraction of the communication via short messages or microblogs is about uncovering and denouncing corruption or human rights violations. However, it is important to note that what was still possible in the 1990s is not possible anymore: namely, to prevent information on incidents, accidents, scandals, and abuse of power spreading to an interested community in China almost in real time. Sometimes, this information also finds its way out of China. Moreover, some of these cases spark such a heated and widespread debate among the Chinese public that they cannot be ignored by the official media and, ultimately, by China's leaders. At the same time, people within China can follow events outside China on the internet, as reported in the case of the parliamentary and presidential elections in Taiwan in January 2012.[40] One can also find that comments on events outside China, like the tenth anniversary of September 11 or the 2012 elections in Taiwan, are used indirectly to criticize the situation in China.

Domestic criticism and public outrage over (human) rights violations have led to some positive change. For example, the extraction of confessions through torture was declared illegal and new guidelines promulgated in 2010 after a case had come to light where a farmer was sentenced for killing his wife and the presumed victim showed up alive years later.[41] A similar case with far-reaching effects was the death of Sun Zhigang, a young designer who was detained and beaten to death because he carried no identification. As a reaction to his death, the "Measures on Aid and Management for Urban Vagrants and Beggars" were reformed. [42]

However, better access to the outside world through media information, traveling, or studying abroad does not necessarily lead to a call for greater convergence with international norms. Instead, it can also reinforce one's own sense of identity and result in negative reactions to wounded pride. Examples of this reaction include popular boycotts of goods or stores from certain countries, as happened to France after the incidents during the Olympic torch relay in Paris. Such outpourings of patriotism or nationalism cannot be shrugged off as irrelevant. Public opinion and public pressure do play a bigger role in Chinese political decision making, as chapter 3 demonstrates.

In sum, the different dimensions of power diffusion addressed above have had mixed effects on the development of human rights in China. China's involvement in the international human rights regime has become normal and China has been pursuing a pragmatic approach at the UN level. While outside criticism of China's human rights situation has not died down, China's reaction to it has become more self-confident if not more self-righteous. On the other hand, the Chinese authorities have been more responsive to public outrage over local scandals and incidents in China itself. However, this responsiveness has its limitations, as shown in the next section.

STABILITY AS THE PRIORITY AND THE FEAR OF CONTAGION

In essence, one factor has remained constant and has been shaping China's human rights policies since the beginning of the reform era: whenever the regime perceives a threat to the stability of the political system and to its own hold on power, it feels more than justified to ignore the rights granted to Chinese citizens by the Constitution, domestic laws, and the international documents that China has signed. The rule of law no longer applies, and rule by law takes over. These are also the cases in which Western pressure is met with determined official resistance from China.

Perceived or real, such threats to stability can come from inside China, but also from the outside. One of the biggest challenges in this respect in the last decade was posed by an international mega-event that took place in China and was therefore directly at the interface between the outside and the inside. The Summer Olympics in 2008 provided an excellent opportunity for Western governments and NGOs to articulate their criticism and their expectations for improvement of the human rights situation in China. For China's leaders and authorities, however, this event justified exactly the opposite: in order to guarantee security before and during the

Olympic Games, any chance of instability needed to be addressed, if necessary by strengthening controls and limiting individual rights. Therefore, they felt justified to reject external criticism on the basis of security considerations.

The Olympic Games in Beijing: gateway into fortress China?

China's first bid for holding the Olympic Games in the year 2000 was not successful. In 1993, the International Olympic Committee (IOC) decided in favor of Sydney, and China lost in the end by two votes. Reportedly, China's human rights record—the memory of June 1989 was still fresh—was at least in part responsible for the negative outcome. In China, the decision was received with huge disappointment, indignation, and negative public sentiment.

China was awarded the Olympic Games for 2008 in the year 2001, which was also the year of accession to the WTO. The country seemed, from the perspective of Western governments, back on track to stronger integration into the international system, maybe even to future convergence with a Western-style liberal order. For China's leadership, playing host to this major international event was an opportunity to demonstrate to the world the success of China's modernization process, a symbol for its arrival on the global stage and for acceptance as a full-fledged member of the international community.[43]

Significantly for the topic of this chapter, from the moment in 2001 when China was awarded the Olympic Games, a connection was made to the issue of human rights, although not explicitly by the IOC itself. In its explanation for the final decision, human rights were not mentioned at all. Instead, the IOC argued that China had good prospects of finishing the infrastructure in time and in general of organizing the event successfully.[44]

However, Chinese officials themselves confirmed a linkage between human rights and the Olympic Games before the decision of the IOC was made: in February 2001 then deputy mayor of Beijing (and in charge of the Olympic Games) Liu Jinmin stated: "By applying for the Olympics, we want to promote not just the city's development, but the development of society, including democracy and human rights." And Wang Wei, Vice President of the Beijing Olympics Bid Committee, was quoted as having said one day before the decision : "We are confident that with the Games coming to China we are going to not only promote the economy, but also enhance all social sectors including education, medical care and human rights."[45] So the argument that holding the Olympics would have a positive effect on the human rights situation was obviously seen as being supportive of China's Olympic bid and therefore brought forward by China's representatives themselves. A concrete promise was also made by the Chinese side concerning full freedom of reporting for journalists during the Olympics.[46]

Despite these hopes of convergence, this did not entirely remove the controversy surrounding the award of the Games to Beijing. Some Western critics argued on human rights grounds against staging the Games in the PRC. The Beijing event was compared to the Olympics in Berlin in 1936: as before, holding the Games in Beijing would signal international support and provide legitimization, this time to an autocratic regime in China.[47] Proponents, on the other hand, were hopeful that holding the Olympics would have a positive effect on the human rights situation in China: Chinese leaders would boost democracy and liberalization as had been the case in South Korea at an earlier stage.[48] The minimum that human rights organizations could expect was an opportunity to bring the situation in China into the spotlight of international attention, or even get some leverage to put pressure on China's leaders for improvements.

Thus, while China saw the Olympics as an opportunity to showcase its modernization and integration into international society, human rights groups and Chinese dissidents abroad saw this as an excellent chance to express their criticism and draw attention to China's shortcomings in human rights protections. Consequently, most of these groups were not in favor of boycotting the Olympics, when the debate in Western countries started moving in this direction in 2007. While the *threat* of a boycott could be successfully used for additional pressure, an actual boycott decision would not only have eliminated this leverage but could, on the contrary, turn out to be counterproductive with respect to the human rights situation.

In the end, however, discussion in the media on the question of a boycott was sparked not by China's *domestic* human rights situation but by the official Chinese support for the regime in Sudan during the Darfur conflict.[49] The label "genocide Olympics" was coined in this context. While officially denouncing the linkage between the Olympic Games and Darfur,[50] China dispatched special envoy Zhai Jun to Sudan, used quiet diplomacy to convince Khartoum to agree to a UN peacekeeping mission in the country, and pledged to participate in the UN mission with an engineering unit. Whether this was a reaction to the threat of a boycott or had been in the pipeline anyway, remains unclear. However, Western media portrayed these steps as a result of external pressure on China and certainly the timing is suggestive.[51]

From the official Chinese perspective, instead of fulfilling the vision of "one world, one dream," preparation for the Olympics turned into a nightmare. Pressure from Western governments and human rights organizations never subsided during the months before the Games. It became virulent when the relay of the Olympic flame, which was carried through some European countries and the United States, attracted not only cheering crowds but also many protesters. Many Chinese living in and outside China responded to the wave of international criticism with indignation and anger. It was perceived as unfair and as a clear sign that the West was neither willing to acknowledge China's modernization success nor ready to accept the PRC as an equal member of the international community—psychologically, this popular reaction can be understood as a "rally-round-the-flag" effect. For the Chinese regime, it provided welcome backing for its rebuttal of Western criticism.

The Arab Spring and the not-to-be "Jasmine Revolution"

Threats to stability can also come from outside China in the form of social upheavals that might inspire similar developments in China, such as the so-called color revolutions in some states of the former Soviet Union. They have raised suspicion among Chinese authorities concerning the activities of international NGOs as well as domestic NGOs which are supported from abroad. Thus, the "Rose," "orange," and "Tulip" or "pink" revolutions in Georgia (2003–04), Ukraine (2004), and finally, directly at China's borders in Kyrgyzstan (2005) have triggered official general mistrust vis-à-vis international NGOs and foreign governments providing financial support to local groupings.[52]

When popular unrest and demonstrations against the governments spread in some North African and Arab countries (e.g., Tunisia, Egypt, Libya, and Syria) in spring of 2011, Chinese media at first refrained from broad coverage of the developments. The focus of reporting was on Chinese citizens living in these countries and China's efforts to get them safely out. Even more so than with the color revolutions, China's leaders seemed to fear that the developments in North Africa could inspire Chinese demands for political reform and democracy.

As others have pointed out, China's response to the events was "Janus-faced."[53] On the one hand, China voted in favor of or abstained on UNSC resolutions (1970 and 1973 on Libya) that explicitly referred to the responsibility to protect human rights.[54] In the case of the situation in Libya, several factors have been cited to explain China's vote, none of which was related to human rights concerns directly, but rather related to the protection of the 38,000 Chinese citizens in the country, and the appeal of the African Union and the Arab League to support steps against Libya.

On the other hand, the Chinese authorities were concerned about the possibility of similar developments inside China and reacted by taking strong preventive measures. When calls for staging a so-called Jasmine Revolution by holding demonstrations (by "strolling") in some Chinese cities appeared on a Chinese website administered from abroad, they resulted in a whole range of measures: the strong presence of security forces (uniformed and plainclothes) at the places designated for the protests; house arrests and disappearances of suspected activists; and harassment of some Western journalists—in sum, a crackdown that was intended to nip any form of protest in the bud.

This approach can be explained not only by the lesson learned from events in Cairo and elsewhere in the Arab world but also by the experience of 1989, when the students had not been dispersed from Tian'anmen square at an early stage of the demonstrations. This background explains the over-reaction to the faint chance that China could be affected by the events in the Arab world. Moreover, China in early 2011 had started preparations for a leadership change (taking place in autumn of 2012 and spring of 2013), and in such a period social and regime stability becomes the overriding priority.

Triggered by the Arab Spring, China has in the ensuing discussions in the UN Human Rights Council underlined the right and the duty of governments to take necessary measures to maintain social stability and public order. According to a 2012 study, this was the first time that China took the lead in such an initiative and rallied for support of other countries for such a joint statement.[55] Even if this does not mark the beginning of a more proactive Chinese role in the Council, it demonstrates the importance of this issue from a Chinese standpoint.

CONCLUSION

The patterns of interaction between the Chinese domestic and external levels on human rights issues that first formed during the 1990s have not fundamentally changed. Despite active involvement in international human rights mechanisms, China's government still tries to hold the middle ground between accepting human rights as a legitimate topic in international politics and defending its own (and sometimes other countries') sovereignty against external criticism, pressure, and interference. Similarly, the question of universality of human rights versus their relativity in terms of the stage of development of a country, or its historical and cultural background, remains unresolved.

What has changed over the last decade is that China's economic, political, and even military weight in the world has become relatively stronger, and it is therefore now more tempting for China to try to use its leverage to create unwelcome choices for other governments. However, external pressure stemming from international NGOs and Western media has not subsided, and China is confronted with stronger demands to act as a responsible power globally and domestically. This does not only hold true for human rights but also in such issue areas as climate change and the nonproliferation of nuclear weapons. Certainly, with China's growing power, the "developing country" argument has lost much of its former persuasiveness.[56] But more than this, the Chinese have found that increases in its relative state-to-state power do not translate easily into the outcomes that they prefer in policy areas where global processes and actors can play an intrusive role.

The greater openness and stronger integration of China into the international system, and better access of an interested Chinese public to outside information and to new media for communication have not led to full acceptance and diffusion of universal rights. The debate on human rights and rights of citizens in general has become more diversified and more "normal" within China, but the frame of reference is not necessarily the international normative system but concrete grievances and injustices at home. The array of arguments used by China in the international debate has over time become more elaborate and refined; at the same time the official (and sometimes popular) reaction to criticism and pressure has become more confrontational. China's leadership is directed by one priority, namely, the stability of China which is perceived as tantamount to stability of the regime and the power monopoly of the party. This means that human rights policies are approached through a domestic lens despite their prominence in China's global diplomacy.

NOTES

1. Regular human rights reports on China are published by Amnesty International, Human Rights Watch, and the U.S. Department of State. On special rights like media freedom, see the reports of Freedom House (http://www.freedomhouse.org) and Reporters without Borders (http://en.rsf.org)
2. "West" or "Western countries" is used here for the group in the United Nations "Western Europe and others," namely, Western European countries, Canada, Australia, New Zealand, and additionally the United States and Japan.

3. E.g. Frédéric Krumbein, "Die Auswirkungen der westlichen Menschenrechtspolitik auf die Menschenrechtslage in China" ["The impact of Western human rights policies on the human rights situation in China"], *China aktuell*, Vol. 36, No. 5 (2007), pp. 115–36; Katrin Kinzelbach, *The EU's Human Rights Dialogue With China: Quiet Diplomacy and Its Limits* (London: Routledge, 2012); Katrin Kinzebach and Hatla Thelle, "Taking human rights to China: An assessment of the EU's approach," *The China Quarterly*, 205 (March 2001), pp. 60–79; Yitan Li and A. Cooper Drury, "Threatening sanctions when engagement would be more effective: Attaining better human rights in China," *International Studies Perspectives*, No. 5 (2004), pp. 378–94.

4. Michael Ignatieff, "Is the human rights era ending?" *The New York Times*, February 5, 2002; Rosemary Foot, *Rights Beyond Borders. The Global Community and the Struggle over Human Rights in China*, (Oxford: Oxford University Press, 2000).

5. Cf. Chen Dingding, "China's participation in the international human rights regime: A state identity perspective," *Chinese Journal of International Politics*, Vol. 2, No. 3 (2009), pp. 399–419; Chen Dingding, "Explaining China's changing discourse on human rights, 1978–2004," *Asian Perspective*, Vol. 29 No. 3 (2005), pp. 155–82.

6. Foot, *Rights Beyond Borders*, esp. ch. 4; Merle Goldman, *From Comrade to Citizen: The Struggle for Political Rights in China* (Cambridge, MA: Harvard University Press, 2005).

7. China had voted in favor of earlier resolutions on Iraq in 1990 authorizing sanctions. See Axel Dreher, Jan-Egbert Sturm, and James R. Vreeland, "Development aid and international politics: Does membership on the UN Security Council influence World Bank decisions?," *Journal of Development Economics*, Vol. 88, No. 1 (2009), pp.1–18.

8. See, in particular, Ann Kent, *China, the United Nations and Human Rights* (Philadelphia: University of Pennsylvania Press, 1999).

9. See "Nipped in the bud: The suppression of the China Democracy Party," *Human Rights Watch*, Vol. 12, No. 5 (September 2000). Available: http://www.hrw.org/reports/2000/china/.

10. See Kerry Dumbaugh, *Chinese Embassy Bombing in Belgrade: Compensation Issues*, CRS Report for Congress, RS20547, updated April 12, 2000, p. CRS-3. Available: http://congressionalresearch.com/RS20547/document.php. The second report on the human rights situation in the United States which was published in 2000, for the first time included a section on U.S. human rights violations in other countries and explicitly refers to the military intervention in Yugoslavia and the bombing of the Chinese embassy in Belgrade. See Information Office of the State Council, *U.S. Human Rights Record in 1999*, (February 2000). Available: http://www.china-embassy.org/eng/zt/ppflg/t36620.htm.

11. Some of these arguments can be found for example in Luo Haicai, "Efforts to respect and to protect," *China Daily*, September 1, 2011; and in Li Junru, "Development of human rights in China," *China Daily*, September 23, 2011.

12. See "The debate over universal values," *The Economist*, September 30, 2010; "This Fourth, light a sparkler for China's future," *The Christian Science Monitor*, July 1, 2011. There has been a lively debate on *pushi jianzhi* in Chinese newspaper articles and academic publications. See, for example, "Xifang pushi jiazhi de xuwei he badao" ["Hypocrisy and tyranny of Western universal values"], no date given, http://news.21cn.com/zhuanti/domestic/psjz/index.shtml.

13. For example, Prime Minister Wen Jiabao in a press conference at the National People's Congress in 2007. See Willy Lam, "Premier Wen's 'southern tour': Ideological rifts in the CCP?" *China Brief*, Vol. 10 No. 8 (September 10, 2008). Available: http:// www.jamestown.org/single/?no_cache=1&tx_ttnews%5Btt_news%5D=36809.

14. For China, the conditions for the use of force as a last resort are authorization of the UN Security Council, the backing of regional organizations and consent of the host country. On China and the Responsibility to Protect see in more detail Sarah Teitt, *China and the Responsibility to Protect* (Brisbane, Australia: Asia-Pacific Center for the Responsibility to Protect, December 19, 2008). Available: http:// responsibilitytoprotect.org/files/China_and_R2P%5B1%5D.pdf; Liu Tiewa, "China and responsibility to protect: Maintenance and change of its policy for intervention," *The Pacific Review*, Vol. 25, No. 1 (March 2012), pp. 153–73.

15. Position Paper of the People's Republic of China at the 63rd Session of the United Nations General Assembly, September 16, 2008. Available: http://www.fmprc. gov.cn/eng/zxxx/t512751.htm.

16. See Chapter II, Article 33 of the *Constitution of the People's Republic of China*; full text after amendment on March 14, 2004 [Online]. Available: http://www.npc .gov.cn/englishnpc/Constitution/node_2825.htm.

17. White Papers on Human Rights were published by the Chinese government in the years 1991, 1992, 1995, 1997, 1998, 2000, 2001, 2002, 2004, 2005, and 2010. For a list of government documents on human rights and related topic like minority rights, religious freedom, and so on, see website of the China Society for Human Rights Studies [Online]. Available: http://www.humanrights.cn/whitepa- pers/menu_w.htm (list end 2006).

18. The Information Office of the State Council, *National Human Rights Action Plan of China (2009–2010)*, April 13, 2009. Available: http://www.dhnet.org.br/dados/ pp/nacionais/pndh_china_2009_2010_a.pdf.

19. The report is based on paragraph 15 (a) of resolution of HRC 5/1. See Human Rights Council, Working Group on the Universal Periodic Review, Fourth session, Geneva, February 2–13, 2009, National Report Submitted in Accordance with Paragraph 15 (A) of the Annex to Human Rights Council Resolution 5/1: China, A/HRC/WG.6/4/CHN/I, November 10, 2008. Available: http://daccess-dds-ny. un.org/doc/UNDOC/GEN/G08/171/00/PDF/G0817100.pdf?OpenElement. For a detailed study on China's participation in the Human Rights Council, see Sonya Sceats with Shaun Breslin, *China and the International Human Rights System*, (London: Chatham House, October 2012). Available: http://www.chathamhouse .org/sites/default/files/public/Research/International%20Law/r1012_sceats- breslin.pdf.

20. Some Western governments started to have doubts about the usefulness of these exercises, since they lack clearly defined benchmarks as well as any assessment of progress. Human rights organizations and media had criticized the closed-door meetings from the beginning because of their nontransparent character. Canada actually suspended the dialogue in 2006. See Wenran Jiang, "Sino-Canadian rela- tions: 'Strategic Partnership' II," thestar.com, July 23, 2011.

21. Full text in English: Charter 08, December 9, 2008 [Online]. Available: http:// hrichina.org/content/238.

22. BRIC or BRICs was originally "invented" in 2001 by Jim O'Neill of Goldman Sachs to describe the group of emerging economies: Brazil, Russia, India, and China. These countries have in the meantime started to meet on a regular basis, and in 2011, South Africa also became a member (hence now the acronym BRICS).

23. The countries besides China that initially declined the invitation were Pakistan, Iran, Sudan, Russia, Kazakhstan, Colombia, Tunisia, Saudi Arabia, Serbia, Iraq, Vietnam, Afghanistan, Venezuela, the Philippines, Egypt, Ukraine, Cuba, and Morocco. See Tania Branigan, "Eighteen more countries refuse to attend Nobel peace prize ceremony," *The Guardian*, December 7, 2010.

24. See [Statistics Norway] "Export and import from China: No Nobel effect yet," September 9, 2011. Available: http://www.ssb.no/english/magazine/art-2011 –09–09–01-en.html.

25. See "China postpones EU summit over Dalai Lama visit," *People's Daily Online*, December 10, 2008. Available: http://english.people.com.cn/96054/ 96056/6550817.html.

26. "Our pressing on those issues [i.e. human rights and Tibet] can't interfere on the global economic crisis, the global climate change crisis and the security crisis." See Richard Spencer, "Hillary Clinton: Chinese human rights secondary to economic survival," *The Telegraph*, February 20, 2009.

27. Luo Yanhua, "Embarrassment of Western human rights diplomacy towards China," *China Human Rights*, Vol. 9, No. 1 (January 2010). Full text available: http://www.chinahumanrights.org/CSHRS/Magazine/Text/t20100211_542564. htm.

28. The three democratic countries in BRICS have formed their own format called IBSA (India, Brazil, and South Africa). Which grouping will prove more robust remains to be seen.

29. On BRICS and the issue of sovereignty, see Zaki Laidi, *The BRICS Against the West?*, Paris Nov. 2011, CERI Strategy Papers, No. 11. Available: http://www .ceri-sciences-po.org/ressource/n11_112011.pdf, especially pp. 9–10. The author aptly concludes: "The BRICS share a sovereignist approach to avoid sharing sovereignty" (p. 12). On the lack of ability and values of the emerging powers, see Jorge G. Castaneda, "The Trouble With the BRICs." Available: foreignpolicy.com, March 14, 2011.

30. Sceats with Breslin, *China and the International Human Rights System*, table, p. 22.

31. Brazil was no longer a nonpermanent member of the UN Security Council in 2012.

32. On Resolution 1970 (Libya) see http://www.un.org/News/Press/docs/2011/ sc10187.doc.htm; on Resolution 1973 (no-fly zone), see http://www.un.org/ News/Press/docs/2011/sc10200.doc.htm. On the failed Syria resolution (October 2011), see http://www.un.org/News/Press/docs/2011/sc10403.doc.htm; and on the failed resolution in February 2012, see http://www.un.org/News/Press/ docs/2012/sc10536.doc.htm.

33. See the very detailed overview of relevant literature: *Human Rights and the War on Terror*, with an introduction by Jack Donnelly, *Human Rights & Human Welfare Research Digest*, 1st ed. 2005, 2nd ed. (2007). Full text of both editions available: http://www.du.edu/korbel/hrhw/researchdigest/terror/index.html.

34. See, for example, Information Office of the State Council, Human Rights Record of the United States in 2001, March 11, 2002. Available: http://www.fas.org/irp/ news/2002/03/xin031102.html.

35. Information Office of the State Council, US Human Rights Record in 2000, Feb. 27, 2001. Available: http://missions.itu.int/~china/humanrights/ usrec2000e.htm. Links to all reports available: http://en.wikipedia.org/wiki/ Human_Rights_Record_of_the_United_States.

36. The State Council Information Office, "The US Human Rights Record in 2002," April 3, 2003, full text available: http://www.fas.org/irp/news/2003/04/xin040303. html; Information Office of the State Council, Full text of Human Rights Record of the United States in 2003, March 1, 2004, full text available: http://english. people.com.cn/200403/01/eng20040301_136190.shtml.
37. In 2010, 56 million Chinese traveled abroad (2009 + 8.3 million). See "57 million Chinese tourists set to visit abroad in 2011," Jan. 13, 2011. Available: http://www.chinatraveltrends.com/2011/01/57-million-chinese-tourists-set-to-visit-abroad-in-2011/.
38. On grassroots organizations, NGOs, and civic engagement in China, see, for example, Amy E. Gadsden, *Chinese Nongovernmental Organizations. Politics by Other Means?* (Tocqueville on China, Washington, DC: American Enterprise Institute, July 2010); Kate Zhou, *China's Grassroots Movement Toward Greater Freedom* (Washington, DC: Center for International Private Enterprise, August 28, 2008). Available: www.cipe.org; Bonny Ling, Wing Lam, Elisabeth Wickeri, and Tina Tan, "China's civil society: Controls, limits and role in a 'harmonious society,'" *China Perspectives*, No. 3 (2007), pp. 118–25; Teh-chang Lin, "Environmental NGOs and the anti-dam movements in China: A social movement with Chinese characteristics," *Issues & Studies*, Vol. 43, No. 4 (December 2007), pp. 149–84. On the transnational links of domestic NGOs in China, see Chen Jie, "The NGO community in China," *China Perspectives*, No. 68 (November–December 2006), pp. 29–40.
39. Some figures can illustrate this revolution in communications: the number of mobile phones grew from 400 million in 2005 to 750 million in 2010; as for the internet, users grew from 100 million to 420 million in the same period. See statistics for mobile phone on the website of the Ministry for Industry and Information Technology at http://www.miit.gov.cn/; and for Internet usage on the CNNIC website http://www.cnnic.net.cn/ [latest report on internet development up to June 2011, available: http://www.cnnic.cn/research/bgxz/tjbg/201107/P020110721502208383670.pdf]. While Western social media services such as Twitter are not available in China, so-called microblogs have become a popular means of communication. In 2011, internet users in China had registered 195 million microblogs.
40. See, for example, Damian Grammaticas, "China eyes Taiwan election freedoms," BBC Mobile, January 17, 2012. Available: http://www.bbc.co.uk/news/world-asia-china-16599678.
41. See Andrew Jacobs, "China bans court evidence gained through torture," *The New York Times*, May 31, 2010.
42. See Yun Xiang, "Sun Zhigang's Death and Reform of Detention System," 2004. Available: http://www.humanrights.cn/zt/magazine/20040200482694708.htm.
43. See Jacques deLisle, "After the gold rush: The Beijing Olympics and China's evolving international roles," *Orbis*, Vol. 53, No. 2 (Spring 2009), pp. 179–204; here: p. 182; "Jubilation on the streets of Beijing," *Time*, July 14, 2001. Available: http://www.time.com/time/arts/article/0,8599,167496,00.html.
44. International Olympic Committee, *Report of the IOC Evaluation Commission for the Games of the XXIX Olympiad in 2008*, Lausanne, Switzerland, April 3, 2011. Available: http://www.olympic.org/Documents/Reports/EN/en_report_299.pdf. The Report states in the General Introduction: "As stated, the Commission has a defined technical evaluation role but it is impossible to ignore the public debate on political issues such as human rights which, in the present context, is imposed

on sport. The Commission will not deal with this issue other than to acknowledge the existence of the debate and its continuation." p. 5.

45. Both quotations can be found on the website of Human Rights Watch. Available: http://china.hrw.org/in_the_words_of_chinese_officials.

46. Such rights (e.g., the right to travel freely and to interview people without prior permission from officials) were granted to foreign journalists more than a year before the Games. See official website of the Olympic Games in Beijing "Regulations on Reporting Activities in China by Foreign Journalists During the Beijing Olympic Games and the Preparatory Period," December 1, 2006. Available: http://en.beijing2008.cn/23/37/article212063723.shtml. While these regulations were welcomed by Western journalists, it was immediately demanded that their Chinese colleagues were granted the same rights.

47. See, for example, "China lashes out at British press for comparing Beijing Olympics to 1936 Nazi Berlin Games," *Mail Online*, March 26, 2008. This article covers China's reaction to an op-ed of former UK Cabinet Minister Michael Portillo: "Tibet: the West can use the Olympics as a weapon against Beijing," *Sunday Times*, March 23, 2008.

48. For a comparative analysis of South Korea and China before the Olympics, see David Black and Shona Bezanson, "The Olympic Games, human rights and democratisation: Lessons from Seoul and implications for Beijing," *Third World Quarterly*, Vol. 25 No. 7 (2004), pp. 1245–61.

49. The American actress Mia Farrow attacked China for not resolving the Darfur conflict and warned movie director Steven Spielberg, who had signed up as artistic advisor for the Games, on his complicity. Spielberg reacted by sending a letter to Chinese president Hu Jintao. See Helene Cooper, "Darfur collides with Olympics, and China yields," *New York Times*, April 13, 2007.

50. See the undated statement on the website of the Chinese embassy in Kenya "Darfur: China is doing right things." Available: http://ke.china-embassy.org/eng/zt/MediaComment/t425636.htm; Jonathan Watts, "China defends Darfur stance against Olympic warning," *The Guardian*, May 10, 2007.

51. See, for example, Barbara Slavin, "Olympics seen as leverage for Darfur," *USA Today*, September 20, 2007. The example of Sudan and Darfur shows how criticism concerning human rights issues is not limited to China's policy at home anymore but has also been directed at its foreign policy and economic involvement in other parts of the world, including countries like Burma, or Zimbabwe. Two points are noteworthy in this context: first, China is usually singled out among the countries that maintain good relations with these states, while others like India or Malaysia are rarely mentioned for their economic engagement. Second, there seems now to be a widespread assumption that China is the key to resolving conflicts like the one in Darfur—if China would only drop support for these regimes, would put enough pressure on them, or would back sanctions against them in the UN. China, on the other hand, usually argues in favor of the quiet diplomacy approach that it also asks of other countries in their dealings with China (e.g., in the human rights dialogues).

52. See Titus C. Chen, "China's reaction to the Color Revolution: Adaptive authoritarianism in full swing," *Asian Perspectives*, Vol. 34, No. 2 (2010), pp. 5–51.

53. Jonas Parello-Plesner and Raffaello Pantucci, *China's Janus-faced Response to the Arab Revolutions*, June 2011 (European Council on Foreign Relations Policy Memo 34). Available: http://www.ecfr.eu/page/-/ECFR34_CHINA_ARAB_REVOLUTIONS_AW.pdf.

54. For full text of the resolutions, see websites noted at note 32.
55. See Sceats with Breslin, *China and the International Human Rights System*, pp. 27–32.
56. In terms of per capita income and other indicators, however, China still ranks well below the developed world and should be recognized as a middle-income country with gross domestic product (GDP) per capita of about US$5,400 in 2011.

CHAPTER 8

China's Environmental Diplomacy

Climate Change, Domestic Politics, and International Engagement

JOANNA I. LEWIS

China has historically been a reluctant player in global environmental forums, and particularly the international climate change negotiations. However, as China's role in contributing to global climate change—one of the great global environmental challenges of our time—has increased, so has its role in international environmental diplomacy. This chapter investigates those factors that have been most important in shaping China's international diplomacy on global climate change. It also demonstrates the complex interplay between the core goal of sustaining domestic development and the stances Beijing adopts at diplomatic negotiations designed to deal with the issue of climate protection. Like the other chapters in this section, it points up the porousness of the borders separating the domestic and global, and how levels of domestic resistance to external pressure depend crucially on the degree to which there is alignment between values and interests in these two policy realms.

China's contributions to climate change, namely, greenhouse gas emissions from fossil fuel combustion and industrial activity, are inherently linked to China's economic development strategy (see Figure 8.1.) Beijing's approach toward climate change therefore must be understood in the context of its overall energy development strategy, which is driven by its overall economic development goals. China's increase in energy-related

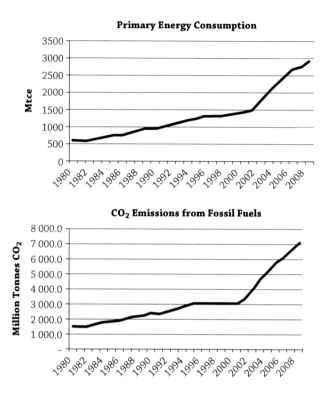

Figure 8.1
Trends in China's primary energy consumption and carbon dioxide emissions.
Source: National Bureau of Statistics (NBS). *China Energy Statistical Yearbook 2010.*Beijing: China Statistics Press, 2010; International Energy Agency. *CO_2 Emissions from Fuel Combustion 2010 Edition.* Paris: OECD/IEA, 2010.

emissions in recent years has been driven primarily by industrial energy use, fueled by an increased percentage of coal in the overall fuel mix. China relies on coal for more than two-thirds of its energy needs, including approximately 80 percent of its electricity needs. Currently more coal power plants are in operation in China than in the United States and India combined. China's coal power use is expected to more than double by 2030, representing an additional carbon commitment of about 86 billion tons.

While China still overwhelmingly relies on coal, and its carbon dioxide emissions are soaring (see Figure 8.2), its domestic policy actions are gradually making inroads on both. Low carbon development has come to be positioned at the core of China's overarching national economic plan, a concept that began taking hold in the last decade. As noted in China's November 2011 Climate Change White Paper, the Twelfth Five-Year Plan (FYP) for National Economic and Social Development has "established the

Coal Consumption per Capita

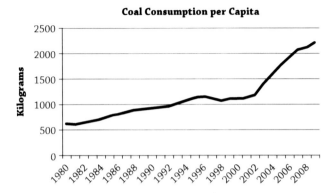

Carbon Dioxide Emissions by Source

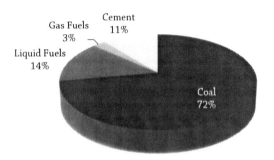

Figure 8.2
China's rising coal consumption per capita and contribution to its carbon emissions.
Source: National Bureau of Statistics (NBS). *China Energy Statistical Yearbook 2010*. Beijing: China Statistics Press, 2010. Carbon Dioxide Information Analysis Center (CDIAC). "Fossil Fuel CO2 Emissions," 2011.

policy orientation of promoting green and low-carbon development, and expressly set out the objectives and tasks of addressing climate change for the next five years."[1] The 11th FYP (2005–10) introduced a multipronged approach across the economy to decrease national energy intensity and to build up a set of strategic low-carbon industries. The 12th FYP (2011–15) has set the stage for China's first ever carbon intensity target and pilot cap and trade programs, representing a significant change in the country's approach to global climate change. These national targets are neither symbolic nor aspirational; there are many signs that China's low-carbon economy is becoming a reality. Now the largest deployer of wind power technology and the largest manufacturer of solar technology, China invested US$50 billion in renewable-energy development in 2010, far more than any other country in the world. China is also pursuing aggressive domestic expansion of more traditional low carbon sources of energy, including nuclear and hydropower.

This chapter demonstrates how China's energy challenges are shaping the way its leadership is approaching climate mitigation at the domestic level, which in turn shapes its positioning in international climate negotiations. Even as international pressure and attention shift to China as the largest global emitter, China's actions internationally are still predominantly shaped by domestic, rather than international, factors. As a result, changes in China's domestic energy policy agenda in the last decade have permitted a change in China's approach to global environmental diplomacy, particularly in the context of the international climate change negotiations. This began with the central government's emphasis on energy efficiency, followed by a dramatic push for low-carbon energy development, and the regulation of carbon emissions, all reviewed in this chapter. These domestic programs have been motivated by energy security concerns and industrial policy objectives that have potentially important implications for climate mitigation as well. In addition, an increase in the scientific and technical understanding of its own energy and emissions situation, bolstered by sustained investments in scientific capacity in this field, have permitted China's policy makers to legislate with more confidence domestically. While still a somewhat reluctant player in the international climate negotiations, this evolution in China's domestic policy environment has led to a dramatic shift in China's international negotiating position as well as in the way in which it interacts with the world on environmental issues.

UNDERSTANDING THE DRIVERS OF CHINA'S ENVIRONMENTAL DIPLOMACY

Global climate change presents a challenge to the international community that could be considered one of the greatest in our history. As the Introduction to this volume points out, it is one of those issues that demonstrates that we live in a shared space, even though climate change poses particular challenges to developing countries with limited scientific and technical capacity to address it. Global environmental regimes on climate change have served not only to attempt to address the climate change problem but to build capacity in these countries in recognition that such capacity will ultimately be important for their ability to understand and eventually solve the problem. Environmental regimes are often designed specifically to transmit new ideas and knowledge, in addition to providing finance and technology. This assistance, whether in the form of information, technology, or money, may ultimately change the behavioral norms of domestic actors.[2] In addition, the requirements of the regime itself may result in new domestic actors, institutional arrangements, or bureaucratic linkages being created, or introduce new actors from the scientific and expert communities into the policy-making process.

China was a latecomer to the international environmental negotiations that emerged in the late 1970s, but it has rapidly increased its interaction with the international community throughout the late 1980s and 1990s. This interaction has had a profound impact in several respects on China's participation in international environmental accords on issues such as ozone depletion, biodiversity, and climate change.[3] It likely has also substantially broadened the range of policy alternatives that China considers in response to these environmental problems, and it has provided China with access to new technologies and funds that will be crucial to any response that it might undertake.[4]

There are different paradigms that attempt to address the influence of international regimes on state policy making, from both the international relations[5] and comparative politics literatures.[6] As Elizabeth Economy and Miranda Schreurs have argued, "The state remains a powerful actor in international politics and continues to play a central role in the establishment and enforcement of domestic environmental laws and international environmental agreements," even as "a new class of environmental problems that are transnational, regional or even global in scale have emerged."[7] As a result, it is important to understand "both how the state is influenced by the emergence of new kinds of environmental problems...and how states are using the internationalization of environmental politics to forward their own policy priorities."[8]

While there is evidence that, at times, China has taken an approach in the international climate negotiations where its own actions are directly taken in response to the actions of other countries, the influence of the international community still remains sharply constrained when compared with the role of domestic interests.[9] For example, while China has often made its own climate policy announcements right after announcements from the United States,[10] China's plans were developed far in advance even if the timing of announcements had a strategic motive.[11] In addition, while China has long coordinated its position with the G-77,[12] and more recently with the BASIC (Brazil, South Africa, India, China) countries,[13] it has deviated from such coalitions when necessary to protect its own interests.

Scholars have long speculated about the extent to which Chinese domestic policies are shaped by international regimes, trying to reconcile international policy stances with China's domestic policy-making processes. According to Margaret Pearson, in her study of Beijing's role in multilateral economic institutions, multilateral participation may affect Chinese policy making via the transmission of new ideas, and new norms introduced by the multilateral economic institutions may provide leverage for domestic political actors.[14] These observations also hold for China in the climate change sphere. Many have pointed to China's use of environmental policy generally to help promote domestic policy priorities that have a superior status to environmental issues, including protecting Chinese sovereignty, acquiring foreign aid and technical assistance, and promoting economic development.[15] Others have argued that domestic reforms have led to more proactive engagement in international negotiations. For example, domestic institutional reforms that moved climate policy responsibility into the ministry responsible for energy policy making may have "eased China's integration into climate negotiations."[16] While domestic reforms have certainly facilitated China's engagement in the climate negotiations, the added technical capacity energy experts brought to the climate change challenge perhaps explains this more than the institutional shift itself.

Certainly countries act in their own self-interest, and many have pointed out that China has been rather successful at using international environmental processes to its advantage.[17] Environmental regimes often include external financial and technical assistance, and some regimes, including the United Nations Framework Convention on Climate Change (UNFCCC) and the Montreal Protocol, have included mechanisms to facilitate the transfer of environmentally friendly technologies and foreign investment.[18] China has attracted sizable climate mitigation funds through both the Global Environmental Facility (GEF) and the Clean Development Mechanism (CDM). Now the world leader in terms of CDM-induced greenhouse gas reduction credits, China has learned how to use the CDM to its advantage.[19] As of January 2012, 64 percent of total expected annual certified emission reductions registered globally were located in China.[20] The rules governing the CDM in China are viewed as "carefully crafted...to heavily favor Chinese interests and control, and to ensure Chinese 'resources' are protected," and have become a cause for complaint by many potential foreign investors—particularly the stipulation that only majority-owned Chinese enterprises may serve as project owners.[21] China's CDM dominance is certainly due in part to its sizable mitigation potential, but many other large developing countries have not been as successful at ensuring that CDM funds would be directed their way.

THE EVOLUTION OF CHINA'S CLIMATE CHANGE DIPLOMACY

China's positioning in the international climate negotiations has been consistently driven by domestic factors, namely, China's energy and industrial policy objectives. In addition, an increase in the scientific and technical understanding of its own energy and emissions situation has permitted China to legislate with more confidence domestically. This section chronicles China's evolving positioning in the international climate change negotiations, key developments in China's domestic low-carbon energy policy, and the relationship between the two.

China's historical positioning in global climate negotiations

China began its participation in global environmental processes as a somewhat adversarial actor. In June 1972, the United Nations Conference on the Human Environment met in Stockholm to discuss "the need for a common outlook and for common principles to inspire and guide the people of the world in the preservation and enhancement of the human environment."[22] The Stockholm Conference not only was the first UN-sponsored attempt to examine the impact that social and economic development have on the environment, but also the very first UN Conference on any topic attended by representatives of the People's Republic of China (PRC).[23] At this time China was in the midst of its Cultural Revolution, and closed off to much of the world. Yet China is on record as being actively involved in Stockholm, as well as outspoken in its criticism of the powerful countries of the time.[24] While the representative of China "stressed that the Chinese Government and people were actively in support of the Conference and that the delegation of China had made unremitting efforts to arrive at positive results," he also "emphasized that the draft Declaration had failed to point out the main reason for pollution of the environment: the policy of plunder, aggression and war carried out by imperialist, colonialist and neo-colonialist countries, especially by the super-Powers."[25] China's delegation did not sign onto the final agreement because they wanted it to contain strong socialist statements, and it did not.[26]

The Stockholm conference was followed by more international environmental meetings, but the modern era of international environmental diplomacy can really be said to have begun with the 1992 United Nations Conference on Environment and Development (UNCED) in Rio de Janeiro.[27] Chinese Premier Li Peng attended the Rio conference, where he emphasized that economic development should not be neglected in the pursuit of environmental protection, and that international cooperation should not interfere with national sovereignty,[28] thus setting the stage for China's subsequent environmental diplomacy. Rio also marked the start of the UNFCCC, signed initially by 154 states, and with the ultimate objective of stabilizing greenhouse gas concentrations in the atmosphere at a level that would prevent dangerous anthropogenic interference with the climate system.[29] As of mid-2012, 195 countries including China have ratified the UNFCCC.[30] At the time the UNFCCC was signed, China already was ranked third out of the parties to the Convention, behind the United States and Europe, in terms of emissions, but already ahead of Russia and with almost four times the emissions of the next largest developing country emitter, India.[31]

The first Conference of the Parties (COP) to the UNFCCC took place in Berlin in 1995, and China made a good showing, sending nineteen delegates—more than Russia or Brazil's nine, but slightly less than the number sent by Japan, the United States, and Australia.[32] The Kyoto Protocol followed in 1997. That year, China still lagged behind the United States and Western Europe as a leading greenhouse gas (GHG) emitter. This in combination with its non-OECD (Organization for Economic Co-operation and Development) status secured its position as a non-Annex I country.[33] A key obstacle to developing-country engagement in the international climate change negotiations is the firewall that has been placed between developed and developing countries. Institutionalized in the Kyoto Protocol (KP), this firewall emerged in the context of the negotiations initiated by the 1995 Berlin Mandate.[34] The Berlin Mandate allowed the international climate regime to advance by focusing only on developed country emissions, leaving developing country emissions not only off the table but also, by many interpretations, fully excluded from future discussion.[35] Removing this "firewall" has been a core goal of many developed countries ever since the beginnings of a two-track mandate to open new negotiations under both the UNFCCC and KP were initiated in 2005 at COP 11 (and "MOP 1:" the first Meeting of the Parties to the Kyoto Protocol) in Montreal.

Historically China's position in the international climate negotiations has rarely deviated from that of the rest of the developing world, as collectively articulated by the Group of 77 (G-77), a group of 132 (formerly 77) developing countries.[36] Developing countries have used their solidarity strategically to influence the climate change negotiations, despite the growing economic differentiation and often disparate climate policy interests within that bloc. Aware of their limited weight if acting in isolation, developing countries have attempted to build common positions in the coalition of the G-77, the largest intergovernmental organization of developing states in the United Nations. The G-77 has provided a means for these countries to articulate and promote their collective economic interests and enhance their joint negotiating capacity on all major issues within the UN system. On climate change, the grouping has consistently emphasized the historical responsibility that the industrialized world bears and the disparity between per capita emissions that persists between the developed and developing world, resisting any commitments to reduce the group's own GHG emissions.

China has been the largest developing country emitter of GHG for decades. As a major economy, China does not have the problem of limited weight if it acts alone, but it uses its membership in the G-77 to avoid being singled out as the largest emitter among developing countries. Yet its size also allows it to take a leadership role in formulating the positions of the G-77. China has a hand in crafting the group's positions while ensuring that a large contingent of countries will stand at its side when that position is presented before the world.

Throughout most of the 2000s China's alliance with the G-77 did not wane, though it did form new alliances. A subgroup of G-77 member countries, referred to as the "BASIC" negotiating block, emerged around the time of the 2009 Copenhagen negotiations. BASIC, the acronym given to the large, emerging economy emitters of Brazil, South Africa, India and China, has served primarily as a platform for mutual assurance, ensuring that no single one of these countries so crucial to the overall politics of the negotiations steps too far out of line with the negotiating positions of the others. Leading up to the 2007 climate negotiations in Bali, which had a large focus on the tropical forest nations due to the location in Indonesia, the members of the G-77 began to diverge somewhat in their positions. Some countries with tropical forests, including Brazil and a coalition of thirty-two rain forest countries such as Costa Rica and Papua New Guinea, stated a willingness to take on voluntary targets to reduce deforestation in return for compensation, even though the G-77 position historically had not included voluntary international targets of any form.[37] While the G-77 still constitutes a powerful negotiating block, signs of discord among members demonstrate a weakening alliance.

While there were signs of changes afoot in China's negotiating position in Bali in 2007, at this time China was in the midst of its 11th FYP period and only just beginning to see the results of its ambitious domestic energy efficiency programs. In addition, its national Renewable Energy Law had been launched the previous year and was only starting to incentivize large-scale renewable energy development. The evolution of these programs is described in more detail in the next section.

The emergence of China's domestic low-carbon energy strategy

The concept of a low-carbon economy began taking hold in the last decade. Some would trace the origins of China's low-carbon strategy to the emergence of what was called the "scientific viewpoint of development," developed in the Central Economic Work Conference in December 2004.[38] In the past, economic growth was based on high-volume consumption of energy and raw materials, causing heavy pollution, low output, and low efficiency.[39] This new growth mode would be based on conservation, science, and technology.[40]

Energy is directly tied to economic development, and the relationship between energy use and economic growth matters greatly in China. Although China quadrupled its gross domestic product (GDP) between 1980 and 2000, it did so while merely doubling the amount of energy it consumed during that period. This allowed China's *energy intensity* (ratio of energy consumption to GDP) and consequently the *emissions intensity* (ratio of carbon dioxide–equivalent emissions to GDP) of its economy to decline sharply, marking a dramatic achievement in energy-intensity gains not paralleled in any other country at a similar stage of industrialization. This achievement has important implications not just for China's economic growth trajectory but also for the quantity of China's energy-related emissions. Reducing the total quantity of energy consumed also contributes to the country's energy security. Without this reduction in the energy intensity of the economy, China would have used more than three times the energy than it actually expended during this period.

This shift was driven at least in part by increasing concerns among China's leadership about national energy security. China became a net importer of petroleum products in 1993 and is now the world's second-largest consumer of oil behind the United States. Concerns about energy security after embargoes from the United States and Soviet Union in the 1950s and 1960s initiated internal debates among the leadership. Discussions intensified during the early 2000s as domestic oil demand escalated.[41]

The beginning of the twenty-first century has brought new challenges to the relationships among energy consumption, emissions, and economic growth in China. Starting in 2002, China's declining energy intensity trend reversed, and energy growth surpassed economic growth for the first time in decades (see Figure 8.3). This trend continued until 2005. During that time, this reversal had dramatic implications for energy security and greenhouse gas emissions growth in China. In 2007, China's emissions were up 8 percent from the previous year, making China the largest national emitter in the world for the first time (surpassing U.S. emissions that year by 14 percent).[42] Looking ahead, recent projections put China's emissions in 2030 in the range of 400 to 600 percent above 1990 levels. Globally this translates to almost 50 percent of all new energy-related CO_2 emissions between now and 2030.[43] China's long-term energy security is dependent

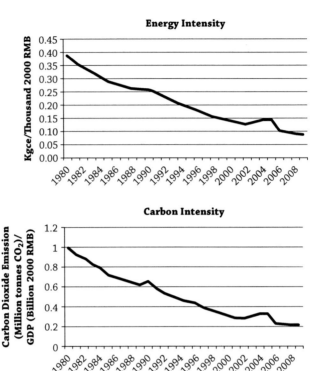

Figure 8.3
Trends in China's energy and carbon intensity.
Source: Calculated by author using data from National Bureau of Statistics (NBS). *China Energy Statistical Yearbook 2010*. Beijing: China Statistics Press, 2010; International Energy Agency. *CO₂ Emissions from Fuel Combustion* (2010 ed.). Paris: OECD/IEA, 2010; World Bank. *World Development Indicators (Population).*Washington, DC: World Bank, 2011.

not only on having sufficient supplies of energy to sustain its very high rate of economic growth but also on being able to manage the growth in energy demand without causing intolerable environmental damage.

China's increase in energy-related pollution in the past few years has been driven primarily by industrial energy use, fueled by an increased percentage of coal in the overall energy mix. Industry consumes about 70 percent of China's energy, and China's industrial base supplies much of the world. As a result, China's current environmental challenges are fueled in part by the global demand for its products. For example, China in 2010 produced about 44 percent of the world's steel and 66 percent of its aluminum.[44] These concerns about energy security, coupled with the reversal in national energy intensity trends from 2002–05, resulted in a new focus in energy savings and in low carbon development within the 11th FYP.

The 11th FYP (2006–10) began a multipronged approach across the economy to decrease national energy intensity and to build up a set of strategic low-carbon industries. The centerpiece of the plan was to promote the service industries—the so-called tertiary sector—because of their higher value-added to the economy and the energy and environmental benefits associated with a weaker reliance on heavy manufacturing. The goal was to move the economy away from heavy industry and toward the service-based industries. In so doing, energy use was expected to decline, and environmental quality expected to improve. The FYP included a major program to improve energy efficiency nationwide, including a goal of reducing energy intensity (energy consumption per unit of GDP) by 20 percent below 2005 levels by 2010. The government projected that meeting this target would reduce China's greenhouse gas emissions 10 percent below "business as usual"; researchers estimated that over 1.5 billion tons of carbon dioxide reductions would be achieved.[45] The energy-intensity target was part of a broader government goal of quadrupling economic growth while doubling energy consumption between 2000 and 2020.[46]

In 2006, the National Development and Reform Commission (NDRC) launched a major program to improve energy efficiency in China's 1,000 largest enterprises, which together consumed one-third of China's primary energy. The group included the largest energy users in the energy supply sectors (coal, electricity, oil) and in the largest energy-using industrial subsectors (including iron and steel). Under the program, each enterprise agreed to an energy efficiency improvement plan and to have its energy use monitored.[47]

The NDRC announced in early 2007 that it would close many inefficient industrial plants manufacturing a range of products including cement, aluminum, ferro-alloy, coking, calcium carbide, cement, and steel. All cement plants with annual capacity of less than 200,000 tons were to be closed by the end of 2008, with 250 million tons of outdated cement capacity to be eliminated by 2010. Shutdowns also extended to small, inefficient power plants, with 50 gigawatts (GW), targeted for shutdowns before 2010. The closure of inefficient power and industrial facilities also helped contribute to the decline in energy intensity during the 11th FYP period, with a reported 72.1 GW of thermal capacity closed—equivalent to 16 percent of the size of the capacity added over the period. An additional 8 GW of coal plants were reportedly shut down in 2011 alone, with further closures planned over the next years.

The NDRC has reported that the 11th FYP energy-intensity target was essentially met, claiming a 19.1 rather than a 20 percent reduction (see Figure 8.3), and there is no doubt that much was learned through efforts to improve efficiency nationwide. In addition, many changes were made to enhance levels of enforcement at the local level, including the incorporation of compliance with energy-intensity targets into the evaluation for local officials.

One key element of China's energy strategy, as well as its low-carbon development strategy, is the promotion of renewable energy technologies. This effort was kick-started with the passage of the Renewable Energy Law of the PRC, which became effective on January 1, 2006.[48] The law created a framework for regulating renewable energy and was hailed at the time as a breakthrough in the development of renewable energy in China. It established a national renewable-energy target, a mandatory connection and purchase policy, a feed-in tariff system, and a cost-sharing mechanism, including a special fund for renewable-energy development. The government has also set a target of producing 15 percent of its primary energy from nonfossil sources by 2020, which includes renewable energy and nuclear power. Power companies have mandatory renewable-energy targets for both their generation portfolios and annual electricity production that they must meet. In December 2009 amendments to the Renewable Energy Law were passed, further strengthening the process through which renewable-electricity projects are connected to the grid and dispatched efficiently.[49]

Policies to promote renewable energy also include mandates and incentives to support the development of domestic technologies and industries—for instance, by requiring the use of domestically manufactured components. China invested US$50 billion in 2010 in renewable-energy development, far more than any other country in the world.[50]

It is evident from the timeline above that China's positioning in the international climate negotiations lagged behind its domestic energy and climate action. It was not until the lead-up to the Copenhagen climate negotiations in the fall of 2009 that China's domestic climate and energy undertakings began to make their way into the international climate negotiation process. Taking many observers by surprise, the Chinese government came forward with its first ever carbon target, pledging a 40–45 percent reduction in national carbon intensity from 2005 levels by 2020. This carbon-intensity target built on the 11th FYP's energy intensity target, and foreshadowed China's 12th FYP.

BUILDING INSTITUTIONAL, SCIENTIFIC, AND TECHNICAL CAPACITY ON ENERGY AND CLIMATE

The 2000s were a crucial time for building institutional, scientific, and technical capacity on energy and climate change within China. At the time of the first international negotiations on climate change, the Chinese had only a very limited research effort under way. The research of the past decade, both on climate science as well as on the country's energy system, has laid the groundwork for both China's future domestic policy developments and its international positioning.

New domestic institutional arrangements

In the 1990s, the role of advising the government on policy options in international negotiations surrounding the UNFCCC shifted the responsibility from the State Meteorological Administration to the more powerful State Development and Planning Commission, which has since evolved into the National Development and Reform Commission. The move indicated a shift in the relative weight given to the issue, as well as perhaps a change in perspective, where climate change was seen not only as a scientific issue but also increasingly as an issue of economic development. The NDRC also serves as the primary energy policy decision-making authority in China, and this move may have reflected the clear need for climate priorities to be coordinated better with energy decisions.

The NDRC was also home to the former National Coordination Committee on Climate Change (NCCCC), which oversaw climate activities across the NDRC, the Ministry of Foreign Affairs (MFA), the Ministry of Science and Technology (MOST), and the former State Environmental Protection Administration (SEPA). The National Leading Committee on Climate Change replaced the former NCCCC in 2007, and it now includes representatives from twenty government agencies.

NDRC and MFA are currently responsible for formulating China's international negotiation positions, although the Chinese delegation at the UN climate negotiations includes representatives from many other agencies and organizations, including MOST, the Ministry of Finance, and the Ministry of Environmental Protection, as well as representatives from the forestry, transportation, meteorological, and agriculture agencies. The delegation also frequently includes academic experts from the Chinese Academy of Sciences and the Chinese Academy of Social Sciences, as well as Tsinghua University and Renmin University, and the Energy Research Institute (ERI). Leading Chinese research organizations that often provide analytical input to shape government policy decisions have significantly scaled up their work in this area over the past decade, and they are increasingly conducting research and analysis that is being used to directly shape policy decisions.[51] For example, ERI has been leading national energy modeling efforts to examine different scenarios for China's energy future and the implications of different energy-intensity and, more recently, carbon-intensity targets.

Representatives of the international scientific community were involved in initial efforts to build up China's technical capacity. For example, many of China's emerging energy specialists were brought to the United States for training in the 1990s.[52] The United States has also played a role in establishing leading clean energy research organizations in China. For example, The Beijing Energy Efficiency Center (BECon) was founded in 1993 with support from the Pacific Northwest Laboratory and Lawrence Berkeley Laboratory of the United States, along with the World Wildlife Fund for Nature. BECon is administratively part of the NDRC's Energy Research Institute but operates as a nonprofit, independent nongovernmental energy conservation and promotion organization. ERI has led much of the analysis on energy efficiency that has contributed to NDRC's energy efficiency policies of the past decade. It is also leading much of the work on collecting national energy data and estimating levels of Chinese CO_2 emissions.

Establishing a national scientific basis for climate change

In 1988, through a joint effort of the World Meteorological Organization (WMO) and the United Nations Environment Program (UNEP), the Intergovernmental Panel on Climate Change (IPCC) was created as an effort by the United Nations to provide the governments of the world with a clear scientific view of what is happening to the world's climate. According to the document on the protection of global climate for present and future generations, released by the General Assembly of the United Nations in December 1988, the goal of the IPCC is "to provide internationally coordinated scientific assessments of the magnitude, timing and potential environmental and socio-economic impact of climate change and realistic response strategies."[53] In 1990, the IPCC released its First Assessment Report (FAR), the scientific evidence of which "unveiled the importance of climate change as a topic deserving a political platform among countries to tackle its consequences."[54] The FAR "confirmed the scientific evidence for climate change and enabled governments to base their policy decisions on the most up-to-date information available," and therefore played a decisive role leading to the formation of the UNFCCC.[55]

China is a member of the IPCC and has been involved in the research as well as the leadership of the organization. In 2002, Qin Dahe of China was elected a member of the new IPCC Bureau as well as co-chair of Working

Group I on the physical science of climate change, and Zhou Lingxi serves on the Bureau of the Task Force on National Greenhouse Gas Inventories.[56] The IPCC's Fourth Assessment Report (AR4) was comprised of 460 lead authors world-wide, 28 of whom were selected from China.[57]

The Chinese government released its first "National Assessment Report on Climate Change" in late 2006, conducted as a collaborative effort among more than twenty government departments and taking four years to complete.[58] In late 2011, the 710-page Second National Assessment Report on Climate Change was released. Structured similarly to the IPCC reports, the Chinese assessment consists of three parts: climate change history and trends, impacts and adaptation, and mitigation and socioeconomic evaluation. It does not set policy but offers a basis of evidence and forecasts that will shape policy. The writing of the report is supervised by government officials, but it is written by teams of some of China's foremost climate scientists.[59]

Developing metrics for accountability

China historically has been consistent in its position that, as a developing country, it will not take on any binding international commitments to reduce its GHG emissions. Some of China's hesitancy to make international commitments stems from reasonable concerns about energy data quality and transparency.

In recent years, China's emissions have soared. It is estimated that around the year 2007 it became the world's largest annual emitter of greenhouse gases, surpassing the United States. As recently as 2004, experts were projecting that China's CO_2 emissions would not surpass those of the United States until after 2030.[60] In 2006 this date was revised to 2013,[61] but estimates released in 2007 demonstrated that China had already reached the number-one spot.[62] This caught many (including the Chinese government) off guard.

Now that China is in the number-one position among national greenhouse gas emitters, its leaders have recognized their need to get a much better handle on China's own emissions inventory and its projected emissions trajectory. In developing countries, where resource constraints result in limited data quality, inventories of national greenhouse gas emissions are notoriously inexact.[63] The uncertainty associated with national inventories makes it very difficult to implement greenhouse gas reduction commitments that rely on baseline inventories and estimated annual improvements at the national level, particularly in developing countries. Having in place a national emissions inventory system will likely be a crucial step in enabling the adoption and enforcement of any binding emissions reduction policies, whether enacted nationally or internationally.

At COP 16 in December 2010 in Cancun, developing countries agreed to increase the frequency of their national communications to at least every four years, and of national emissions inventories to every two years, as well as agreeing to the international measurement, reporting, and verification of both inventories and mitigation actions.[64] China has not publicly released any official carbon dioxide emissions inventories that date past 1994, although an updated inventory is expected to be part of its next national communication.[65]

A NEW ERA OF DOMESTIC ACTION AND INTERNATIONAL ENGAGEMENT

At the beginning of the 12th FYP period in early 2011, China was in a very different position than it had been in just a few years before. The results of the 11th FYP were now evident, and the leadership was increasingly confident that the 20 percent energy-intensity target had been essentially achieved. Also under way was a shift in the national statistical system used to measure energy consumption and energy efficiency, and the development of a more robust system to measure and estimate greenhouse gas emissions. As a result, provisions for the regulation of carbon explicitly appeared in China's core national economic plan for the first time. In addition, China, also for the first time, signaled in the international climate negotiations that it would be willing to take on a binding international commitment. Not only were China's international proclamations now being more directly linked to domestic policies, but the previous decade's achievements in energy efficiency and renewable energy, and the scientific basis for both action and assessment, had put China in a far more confident position as it entered the international climate negotiations at COP 17 in Durban.

The 12th Five-Year Plan

In China's 12th Five-Year Plan (2011–15) the government more explicitly identified a new set of high-value strategic industries as essential to the future of the Chinese economy,[66] with many low-carbon energy industries (including the nuclear, solar, wind and biomass energy technology industries, as well as hybrid and electric vehicles, and energy savings and environmental protection technology industries) mentioned.[67] These "strategic and emerging" industries are being promoted to replace the "old" strategic industries such as coal and telecom (often referred to as China's pillar industries), which are heavily state-owned enterprises (SOEs) and have long benefited from government support. Over 70 percent of SOE assets and profits are concentrated in the "old" strategic industries. This move to rebrand China's strategic industries likely signals the start of a new wave of industrial policy support for the new strategic industries which may include access to dedicated state industrial funds, increased access to private capital, or industrial policy support through access to preferential loans or research and development (R&D) funds. Other targets encourage increased innovative activity, including a target for R&D expenditure to account for 2.2 percent of GDP, and for 3.3 patents per 10,000 people. During the 11th FYP period, an estimated 15.3 percent of government stimulus funding was directed toward innovation, energy conservation, ecological improvements, and industrial restructuring.[68]

Adopted by the Chinese government in March 2011, the 12th FYP also set the stage for China's first ever carbon-intensity target and pilot cap and trade programs, representing a monumental change in the country's approach to global climate change. It also established a new set of targets and policies for the 2011–15 time frame.[69]

The 12th FYP establishes the goal of gradually establishing a national carbon trading market, and a handful of provinces have announced the beginnings of pilot carbon-trading schemes. An October 2011 NDRC notice included the announcement of the provinces and municipalities selected to pilot a cap and trade program for carbon dioxide: Guangdong, Hubei, Beijing, Tianjin, Shanghai, Chongqing, and Shenzhen.[70] The Tianjin Climate Exchange (TCX), a joint venture of China National Petroleum Corporation Assets Management Co. Ltd. (CNPCAM), the Chicago Climate Exchange (CCX), and the city of Tianjin, is positioning itself to be the clearinghouse for any future carbon-trading program, although there are several other exchanges that have been established around the country. Implementing a carbon trading scheme in China, even on a small-scale or pilot basis, will not be without significant challenges. Concerns have already been raised from both domestic and foreign-owned enterprises operating in China about how the regulation could affect their bottom-line profitability. But the key challenge is likely technical, resulting from the minimal capacity currently in place to measure and monitor carbon emissions in China. As a result, also promised in the 12th FYP is an improved system for monitoring GHG emissions, which will be needed to assess compliance with the carbon-intensity target, and to prepare the national GHG inventories that, under the Cancun Agreements, are to be reported more frequently to the UNFCCC and undergo international assessment.

The 12th FYP builds directly on the 11th FYP energy-intensity target and its associated programs, setting a new target to reduce energy intensity by an additional 16 percent by 2015. This may seem less ambitious than the 20 percent reduction targeted in the 11th FYP, but it probably represents a much more substantial challenge because the largest and least efficient enterprises have already undertaken efficiency improvements, leaving smaller, more efficient plants to be targeted in this second round. Under preparation is a new "Top 10,000" program, which is modeled after the Top 1,000 Program but adds an order of magnitude of companies to the mix. But as the number of plants grows, so do the challenges of collecting accurate data and enforcing targets.

The 12th FYP also includes a target to increase nonfossil energy sources (including hydro, nuclear, and renewable energy) to 11.4 percent of total energy use (up from 8.3 percent in 2010).[71] While not formally enshrined in the 12th FYP, another recent notable announcement is a cap on total energy consumption of 4 billion tons of coal equivalent (tce) in 2015.[72] To meet the cap on energy consumption, annual energy growth would need to slow to an average of 4.24 percent per year, from 5.9 percent between 2009 and 2010. The government is also trying to slow GDP growth rates, targeting 7 percent per year—far below recent growth rates. Lower GDP growth rates make it even more challenging for China to meet energy- and carbon-intensity targets, since energy and carbon need to grow more slowly than GDP for the country to achieve declining energy and carbon intensity.

The 2011 Durban climate negotiations

The 2011 climate negotiations in Durban, South Africa, saw two potentially significant changes to long-held elements of China's negotiating position. The first was a potential shift in China's willingness to adopt legally binding commitments as part of a future climate change agreement, rather than just voluntary commitments. This was reflected in China's support of the Durban Platform in which UNFCCC parties agreed "to launch a process to develop a protocol, another legal instrument or an agreed outcome with legal force under the Convention applicable to all Parties."[73] The second was a new openness toward discussing absolute GHG emissions targets, rather than just intensity targets. These changes are very likely a result of the programs that have been implemented domestically in the wake of China's carbon-intensity target and since the Copenhagen negotiations to both measure and monitor domestic emissions and to implement domestic carbon-trading programs. Since early 2011, China's National Energy Administration (NEA) has discussed implementing a cap on total domestic energy consumption by the year 2015, which could certainly pave the way for an absolute emissions target as well.[74]

Another notable change in China's approach to the international climate negotiations that was on display at the Durban climate talks was a new level of openness, displayed through a series of public events hosted by the Chinese delegation and featuring Chinese negotiators, researchers, and NGOs that far outnumbered those convened by China in previous negotiations. The Chinese delegation rarely spoke about their domestic energy and climate change initiatives at the UNFCCC meetings until 2007; and the first official UNFCCC side event hosted by a Chinese NGO only took place as recently as 2009. This shift toward more proactive engagement, both with other country delegations and with the civil society community, points to an increased willingness on the part of China to both explain its domestic climate and energy challenges and to articulate its accomplishments.

CONCLUSIONS

This chapter demonstrates how China's energy challenges are shaping the way its leadership is approaching climate mitigation at the domestic level, which in turn is shaping its positioning in international climate negotiations. For many years, China's climate change negotiating position favored inaction over action. At the beginning of the 12th FYP period in early 2011, however, China was in a very different position than a few years before. Provisions for the regulation of carbon explicitly appeared in China's core national economic plan for the first time. In addition, China also for the first time signaled in the international climate negotiations in Durban that it may be willing to take on a binding international commitment. An increase in the scientific and technical understanding of the energy and emissions situation within the country, accompanied by increased engagement with the international scientific community on climate change, has permitted China to legislate with more confidence domestically. Low carbon development has come to be positioned at the core of China's overarching national economic plan, which has now established a domestic policy framework to implement carbon management programs alongside a low-carbon development strategy.

China's domestic climate policy actions have in many respects been more vigorous than the international pledges the country's leadership is willing to make in the same policy area. However, this is unlikely to persist, with China's global environmental commitments eventually coming closer into line with those made at the domestic level. Not only are China's international proclamations now more directly being linked to domestic policies, but the previous decade's achievements in energy efficiency and renewable energy, and the scientific basis for both action and assessment, has put China in a far more confident position in the international climate negotiations.

NOTES

1. Information Office of the State Council, People's Republic of China, *"Zhongguo yingdui qihou bianhua de zhengce yu xingdong 2011 bai pi shu"* *["China's Policies and Actions for Addressing Climate Change"]*, White Paper (Beijing: State Council, November 2011).

2. Elizabeth Economy, "The Impact of International Regimes on China's Foreign Policy-Making: Broadening Perspectives and Policies but Only to a Point," in *The Making of Chinese Foreign and Security Policy in the Era of Reform 1978–2000*, edited by David Lampton (Stanford, CA: Stanford University Press, 2001), pp. 230–56.

3. Elizabeth Economy, "Chinese Policy-Making and Global Climate Change: Two-Front Diplomacy and the International Community," in *The Internationalization of Environmental Protection*, edited by Elizabeth Economy and Miranda A. Schreurs (Cambridge: Cambridge University Press, 1997), pp. 19–41.

4. Economy, "Chinese Policy-Making and Global Climate Change: Two-Front Diplomacy and the International Community."

5. See Oran Young, *Natural Resources and the State* (Berkeley: University of California Press, 1981); David A. Kay and Harold K. Jacobson, *Environmental Protection: The International Dimension* (Totowa, NJ: Allenheld, Osmun and Co., 1983); Stephen D. Krasner, *International Regimes* (Ithaca, NY: Cornell University Press, 1983); Robert O. Keohane and Joseph S. Nye, *Power and Interdependence: World Politics in Transition* (Boston: Little, Brown and Co., 1977); David A. Baldwin, *Neorealism and Neoliberalism: The Contemporary Debate* (New York: Columbia University Press, 1993); Robert O. Keohane, *After Hegemony: Cooperation and Discord in the World Economy* (Princeton, NJ: Princeton University Press, 1984).

6. See David Vogel, "The Comparative Study of Environmental Policy: A Review of the Literature," in *Comparative Policy Research: Learning from Experience*, edited by Meinolf Dierkes, Hans N. Weiler, and Ariane Berthoin Antal (Hants, UK: Gower Publishing Co., 1987), pp. 99–170; Cynthia Enloe, *The Politics of Pollution in a Comparative Perspective: Ecology and Power in Four Nations* (New York: David McKay Co., Inc., 1975).

7. Elizabeth Economy and Miranda A. Schreurs, "Domestic and International Linkages in Environmental Politics," in *The Internationalization of Environmental Protection*, edited by Elizabeth Economy and Miranda A. Schreurs (Cambridge: Cambridge University Press, 1997), pp. 1–18.

8. Economy and Schreurs, "Domestic and International Linkages in Environmental Politics."

9. Economy, "Chinese Policy-Making and Global Climate Change: Two-Front Diplomacy and the International Community." While Economy pointed this out in 1997, this remains perhaps even truer in 2012.

10. White House Press Office, "President to Attend Copenhagen Climate Talks: Administration Announces US Emission Target for Copenhagen" (White House Press Office, November 25, 2009); State Council, *"Guowuyuan Changwuhui Yanjiu Jueding Woguo Kongzhi Wenshiqiti Paifang Mubiao"* ["Standing Committee of China State Council to Study the Decision to Control Greenhouse Gas Emissions Targets"], November 26, 2009. Available: www.gov.cn/ldhd/2009–11/26/content_1474016.htm.

11. Paul Eckert and Claudia Parsons, "China's Hu Vows to Cut Carbon Output Per GDP by 2020," *Reuters UK*, September 22, 2009. Available: http://uk.reuters.com/article/2009/09/22/us-climate-china-idUKTRE58L4XE20090922; Emma Graham-Harrison, "Hu's Carbon Commitment Marks New Era for China," *Reuters*, September 24, 2009. Available: http://www.reuters.com/article/2009/09/24/us-china-climate-analysis-idUSTRE58N15W20090924.

12. Joanna I. Lewis, "China's strategic priorities in international climate negotiations," *The Washington Quarterly*, Vol. 31, No. 1 (2007), pp. 155–74.

13. Karl Hallding, Marie Olsson, et al., *Together Alone? Brazil, South Africa, India, China (BASIC) and the Climate Change Conundrum*, Policy Brief (Stockholm Environment Institute, 2010). Available: www.sei-international.org/…/Climate/sei-basic-preview-jun2011.pdf.

14. Margaret M. Pearson, "The Major Multilateral Economic Institutions Engage China," in *Engaging China: The Management of an Emerging Power*, edited by Alastair Iain Johnston and Robert S. Ross (New York: Routledge, 1999), pp. 207–34. See also Rosemary Foot and Andrew Walter, *China, the United States, and Global Order*, (Cambridge: Cambridge University Press, 2011).

15. Elizabeth Economy, "China's Environmental Diplomacy," in *China and the World: Chinese Foreign Policy Faces the New Millennium*, edited by Samuel S. Kim (Boulder, CO: Westview Press, 1998), pp. 264–65.

16. Kentaro Tamura and Eric Zusman, *The Politics of Climate Policy in China: Interests, Institutions and Ideas* (IGES: Japan, November 2011).

17. Yuka Kobayashi, "China: Luxury vs. Survival Emissions," in *Global Warming and East Asia: The Domestic and International Politics of Climate Change*, edited by Paul G. Harris (London: Routledge, 2003), pp. 86–108.

18. Zhihong Zhang, "Forces Behind China's Climate Change Policy: Interests, Sovereignty, and Prestige," in *Global Warming and East Asia: The Domestic and International Politics of Climate Change*, edited by Paul G. Harris (London: Routledge, 2003), pp. 66–85.

19. Lewis, "China's Strategic Priorities in International Climate Negotiations"; Gorild Heggelund, "China's climate change policy: Domestic and international developments," *Asian Perspectives*, Vol. 31, No. 2 (2007), pp. 155–91; Joanna I. Lewis, "The evolving role of carbon finance in promoting renewable energy development in China," *Energy Policy*, Vol. 38, No. 6 (June 2010), pp. 2875–886.

20. UNFCCC, "CDM: Registration," *UNFCCC*, January 20, 2012. Available: http://cdm.unfccc.int/Statistics/Registration/AmountOfReductRegisteredProjPieChart.html.

21. Tauna Szymanski, "China's take on climate change," *Sustainable Development, Ecosystems and Climate Change Committee Newsletter of the American Bar Association*, Vol. 9, No. 1, pp. 2–8, (May 2006).

22. United Nations Environment Programme, *Declaration of the United Nations Conference on the Human Environment* (Stockholm, June 16, 1972). Available: http://www.unep.org/Documents.Multilingual/Default.asp?documentid=97&articleid=1503.

23. Shouqiu Cai and Mark Voigts, "The development of China's environmental diplomacy," *Pacific Rim Law and Policy Journal*, No. 3 (1993), pp. 18–42.

24. United Nations Environment Programme, *Working Group on the Declaration on the Human Environment* (Stockholm: UNEP, 1972). Available: http://www.unep.org/Documents.Multilingual/default.asp?DocumentID=97&ArticleID=1529&l=en.

25. Ibid.

26. Cai and Voigts, "The development of China's environmental diplomacy."

27. Ibid.

28. Ibid.

29. UNFCCC, "UNFCCC, Article 2: Objective," 1992. Available: http://unfccc.int/essential_background/convention/background/items/1353.php.

30. UNFCCC, "Background on the UNFCCC: The International Response to Climate Change," 2012. Available: http://unfccc.int/essential_background/items/6031.php.

31. Western European emissions exceeded those of China, which represents a subset of the European Union. The Former Soviet Union and Eastern Europe combined exceeded China's emissions in 1992, but not by 1997. Energy Information Administration, "International Energy Annual 2003" (U.S. Department of Energy (DOE), July 11, 2005).

32. UNFCCC, "Directory of Participants, UNFCCC Conference of the Parties, First Session, Berlin (FCCC/1995/Inf.5/Rev.2)" (UNFCCC, April 6, 1995). Available: http://unfccc.int/cop4/resource/docs/cop1/inf05r02.pdf.

33. The Convention divides countries into three main groups according to differing commitments. Annex I Parties include the industrialized countries that were members of the OECD in 1992, plus countries with economies in transition (EIT). Annex II Parties consist of the OECD members of Annex I, but not the EIT Parties. They are required to provide financial resources to enable developing countries to undertake emissions reduction activities under the Convention and to help them adapt to adverse effects of climate change. Non-Annex I Parties are mostly developing countries. Certain groups of developing countries are recognized by the Convention as being especially vulnerable to the adverse impacts of climate change, including countries with low-lying coastal areas and those prone to desertification and drought. UNFCCC, "Parties & Observers," 2012. Available: http://unfccc.int/parties_and_observers/items/2704.php.

34. United Nations Framework Convention on Climate Change (UNFCCC), *Decision 1/CP.1 The Berlin Mandate: Review of the Adequacy of Article 4, Paragraph 2(a) and (b), of the Convention, Including Proposals Related to a Protocol and Decisions on Follow-up* (UNFCCC, 1995).

35. Daniel Bodansky, "Preliminary thoughts on the Copenhagen Accord," *The Ethiopian Review*, December 21, 2009. Available: http://www.ethiopianreview.com/index/17713.

36. The Group of 77 at the United Nations, "About the Group of 77," 2012. Available: http://www.g77.org/doc/.

37. Coalition of Rainforest Nations, "Reducing Emissions From Deforestation in Developing Countries: Approaches to Stimulate Action" (submission of views of

seventeen parties to the 11th COP to the UNFCC, January 30, 2007). Available: http://unfccc.int/files/methods_and_science/lulucf/application/ pdf/bolivia.pdf.

38. Dongsheng Zang, "Green from above: Climate change, new developmental strategy, and regulatory choice in China," *Texas International Law Journal*, Vol. 45 (2009), pp. 201–32.

39. "China sets energy, resources saving as one of key economic targets," *People's Daily Online*, December 6, 2004. Available: http://english.peopledaily.com.cn/200412/06/eng20041206_166239.html.

40. Editorial, "Put into effect scientific viewpoint of development in an all-round way," *People's Daily Online*, December 15, 2004. Available: http://english.people-daily.com.cn/200412/14/eng20041214_167332.html.

41. Erica S. Downs, "The Chinese energy security debate," *The China Quarterly*, No. 177 (2004), pp. 21–41; Shu Guang Zhang, *Economic Cold War: America's Embargo against China and the Sino-Soviet alliance, 1949–1963* (Washington, DC: Stanford, CA: Woodrow Wilson Center Press; Stanford University Press, 2001).

42. Netherlands Environmental Assessment Agency, "China Now No. 1 in CO_2 Emissions; USA in Second Position," 2007. Available: http://www.pbl.nl/en/dossiers/Climatechange/moreinfo/Chinanowno1inCO$_2$emissionsUSAinsecondposition.html.

43. The 2011 International Energy Outlook's reference case estimates China's CO_2 emissions in 2030 will be 463 percent above 1990 levels, while the high oil price case and low oil price case estimate 567 percent and 396 percent above 1990 levels, respectively. See *International Energy Outlook* (Washington, DC: U.S. Energy Information Administration, 2011).

44. World Steel Association, "World Steel Association Statistics Archive," 2012. Available: http://www.worldsteel.org/statistics/statistics-archive.html; International Aluminum Institute, "International Aluminum Institute Current and Historical Statistics," 2012, Available: http://www.world-aluminium.org/Statistics/Current+statistics; Energy Information Administration, US Department of Energy, *International Energy Outlook; Trevor Houser, China's Energy Consumption and Opportunities for US-China Cooperation to Address the Effects of China's Energy Use* (Washington, DC, 2007), Available: www.uscc.gov/hearings/2007hearings/written_testimonies/07_06_14_15wrts/07_06_14_houser_statement.php.

45. Jiang Lin, Nan Zhou, Mark Levine, and David Fridley, *Taking Out One Billion Tons of CO2: The Magic of China's 11th Five Year Plan?* (Berkeley, CA: Lawrence Berkeley National Laboratory, 2007); Catherine Brahic, "China to promise cuts in greenhouse gases," *New Scientist*, February 14, 2007. Available: http://www.newscientist.com/article/dn11184-china-to-promise-cuts-in-greenhouse-gases.html.

46. Development Research Center of the State Council, *China's National Energy Strategy and Policy 2000–2020*, 2003. Available: http://www.efchina.org/documents/Draft_Natl_E_Plan0311.pdf.

47. NDRC, Environment and Resources Division, "Notice on the Issuance of the Top 1000 Enterprises Energy Conservation Implementation Actions (No. 571)," 2006. Available:http://hzs.ndrc.gov.cn/newzwxx/t20060414_66220.htm; International Energy Agency (IEA), *China's Quest for Energy Efficiency: Its Top 1000 Enterprises Programme* (International Energy Agency/OECD, June 2006), Available: www.iea.org/work/2006/gb/papers/ChinaQuest.pdf.

48. State Council of the PRC, "Zhonghua Renmin Gongheguo Kezaisheng Nengyuan Fa" ["Renewable Energy Law of the People's Republic of China"], February 2005.

49. National People's Congress Standing Committee, "China Renewable Energy Law Decision," 2009. Available: http://www.npc.gov.cn/huiyi/cwh/1112/2009–12/26/content_1533217.htm.
50. RenewableEnergyWorld.com Editors, "2010 clean energy investment hits a new record," *Renewable Energy World*, January 11, 2011. Available: http://www.renewableenergyworld.com/rea/news/article/2011/01/2010-clean-energy-investment-hits-a-new-record.
51. Xinhua, "CAS outlines strategic plan for China's energy development over next 40 years," *Beijing Review*, September 24, 2007. Available: http://www.bjreview.com.cn/science/txt/2007–09/25/content_77642.htm.
52. Economy, "Chinese Policy-Making and Global Climate Change: Two-Front Diplomacy and the International Community."
53. United Nations General Assembly, "A/RES/43/53. Protection of Global Climate for Present and Future Generations of Mankind," December 6, 1988. Available: http://www.un.org/documents/ga/res/43/a43r053.htm.
54. Intergovernmental Panel on Climate Change, "History," 2012. Available: http://www.ipcc.ch/organization/organization_history.shtml#.T8kPqr8hdGc.
55. Information Unit for Conventions (IUC), United Nations Environment Programme, *The International Response to Climate Change: A History*, Climate Change Information Sheet 17, July 18, 2000. Available: http://unfccc.int/cop3/fccc/climate/fact17.htm.
56. IPCC China Office, "Chinese Climate Change Network," 2012. Available: http://www.ipcc.cma.gov.cn/Website/index.php?WCHID=33.
57. Ibid.
58. China Ministry of Science and Technology, "National Assessment Report on Climate Change Released," *Ministry of Science and Technology Press Release*, December 31, 2006. Available: http://www.most.gov.cn/eng/pressroom/200612/t20061231_39425.htm.
59. Chris Buckley, "China report spells out grim climate change risks," *Reuters*, January 17, 2012. Available: http://www.reuters.com/article/2012/01/18/us-china-climate-idUSTRE80H06J20120118.
60. Energy Information Administration, U.S. Department of Energy, *International Energy Outlook* (Washington, DC, 2004).
61. Energy Information Administration, U.S. Department of Energy, *International Energy Outlook* (Washington, DC, 2006).
62. Netherlands Environmental Assessment Agency, "China Now No. 1 in CO2 Emissions; USA in Second Position"; *BP Statistical Review of World Energy* (London: BP, 2007).
63. GAO, *Selected Nations' Reports on Greenhouse Gas Emissions Varied in Their Adherence to Standards* (U.S. General Accounting Office, December 2003). Available: http://www.gao.gov/new.items/d0498.pdf.
64. UNFCCC, "Outcome of the Work of the Ad Hoc Working Group on Long-term Cooperative Action Under the Convention, Draft Decision -/CP.16 (advance Unedited Version)" (UNFCCC, December 2010).
65. China's initial national communication received by the UNFCCC in November 2004 reported national emissions data through 1994—emissions estimates that at that point were ten years old and therefore revealed little about China's current emissions situation and likely future trajectory.
66. Government of the People's Republic of China, "12th Five-Year Plan for National Economic and Social Development of the People's Republic of China

(Chinese Version)," March 16, 2011. Available: http://news.xinhuanet.com/politics/2011–03/16/c_121193916.htm.

67. Government of the People's Republic of China, "Decision on Speeding up the Cultivation and Development of Emerging Strategic Industries (in Chinese)," September 8, 2010. Available: http://www.gov.cn/ldhd/2010–09/08/content_1698604.htm.

68. HSBC, "China's Next 5-year Plan: What It Means for Equity Markets" (HSBC, October 2010).

69. Government of the People's Republic of China, "12th Five-Year Plan for National Economic and Social Development of the People's Republic of China (Chinese Version)"; Joanna Lewis, "Energy and Climate Goals in China's 12th Five-Year Plan" (Pew Center on Global Climate Change, March 2011). Available: http://www.pewclimate.org/docUploads/energy-climate-goals-china-twelfth-five-year-plan.pdf.

70. National Development and Reform Commission, "Guojiafazhangaigewei Bangongting Guanyu Kaizhan Tan Paifangquan Jiaoyi Shi Dian Gongzuo De Tongzhi" ["NDRC Notice on Pilot Trading Programs for the Development of Carbon Emissions Rights"], Notice 2601, October 2011. Available: http://www.ndrc.gov.cn/zcfb/zcfbtz/2011tz/t20120113_456506.htm.

71. Government of the People's Republic of China, "China Announces 16 Pct Cut in Energy Consumption Per Unit of GDP by 2015," March 5, 2011. Available: http://www.gov.cn/english/2011–03/05/content_1816947.htm; People.com.cn, "Zhang Guobao: 'Twelfth Five' Push to Non-fossil Energy to Account for 11.4 Percent Share of Primary Energy (in Chinese)," January 6, 2011. Available: http://energy.people.com.cn/GB/13670716.html.

72. Joshua Fellman, "China to hold primary energy use to 4.2 billion tons in 2015, Xinhua says," *Bloomberg*, October 20, 2010. Available: http://www.bloomberg.com/news/2010–10–30/china-to-hold-primary-energy-use-to-4–2-billion-tons-in-2015-xinhua-says.html.

73. UNFCCC, "Establishment of an Ad Hoc Working Group on the Durban Platform for Enhanced Action Draft Decision (CP.17)," December 2011.

74. Xinhua, "China to cap energy use at 4 bln tonnes of coal equivalent by 2015," *China Radio International (CRI)*, March 4, 2011. Available: http://english.cri.cn/6909/2011/03/04/1461s624079.htm.

INDEX

Lightning Source UK Ltd.
Milton Keynes UK
UKOW01f0740090916

282600UK00003B/77/P